Edward Frederic Benson

Charlotte Brontë : A biography

© 2025, Edward Frederic Benson (domaine public)
Édition : BoD · Books on Demand, 31 avenue Saint-Rémy, 57600 Forbach, bod@bod.fr
Impression : Libri Plureos GmbH, Friedensallee 273, 22763 Hamburg (Allemagne)
ISBN : 978-2-3225-7222-9
Dépôt légal : Avril 2025

CHAPTER I

When the Reverend Patrick Brontë arranged with Mrs. Gaskell that she should undertake to write the life of his daughter Charlotte he supplied her, by letters and interviews, with information about her subject, and included therein some slight history of his own early life. He was the eldest of the ten children of Hugh Brontë, a small farmer in County Down, Ireland.

There was some family tradition, [she tells us] that humble as Hugh Brontë's circumstances were, he was the descendant of an ancient family. But about this neither he nor his descendants have cared to enquire.... He opened a public school at the early age of sixteen, and this mode of living he continued to follow for five or six years.

That makes a picturesque prelude: we feel interested at once in this remarkable boy who was to be the father of such illustrious children. But it was as well, for the sake of romantic origins, that further inquiries were not made in the parish of Drumballyroney, County Down, where, on March 17, 1777, Patrick Brontë was born, for it would have been found that his father was a stranger to the noble surname which his eldest son subsequently assumed, and had been always known as Hugh Brunty, peasant farmer. His family was numerous—ten sons and daughters had been born to him. All these had been entered in the register as Brunty or Bruntee, and it was Patrick who abandoned the ancient patronymic of his family and adopted the more modern Brontë. Nelson, it may be remarked, had been created Duke of Brontë in 1799, and the new name had a distinction. But it seems to have been of the ancient Brontës of County

Down (hitherto unknown) that Mr. Brontë spoke to Mrs. Gaskell, and probably she was unaware of the existence of the humbler patronymic, or, knowing, she loyally concealed the family secret. As for Patrick Brunty, as he then was, having opened a public school at the age of sixteen, the fact was that he was an assistant master at the village school. These trifles, otherwise quite unimportant, have a certain significance, as being the earliest of those embroideries which have since disfigured rather than decorated the household images of the hearth at Haworth.

Patrick Brontë's early history is really more remarkable when stripped of the august details which he gave to Mrs. Gaskell. He taught at the village school for some five or six years, and then for three or four more was tutor to the family of Mr. Tighe, parson of the parish. From that remote occupation he was transported, as on a magic carpet, to the gate of St. John's College, Cambridge, where he was admitted as an elderly under-graduate at the age of twenty-five in the year 1802. Boys then used to go up to the University at the ages of sixteen or seventeen, and he must have been older than many of the Fellows of the College. How he managed it, who paid the fees and the expenses of his year-long board and lodging and clothing (for he never went back to Ireland) is quite unknown. His father, Hugh Brunty, small peasant farmer, with ten children to rear, can hardly have done so, and it is improbable that he could have saved enough himself. The most reasonable conjecture is that Parson Tighe helped him. Patrick was a tall, extremely handsome young man; he was full of intelligence, vitality, and ambition, and the guess (for it is no more) that this benevolent clergyman saw that money could not be better spent than in giving his children's tutor a chance is probably true.

It is worth noting how these instincts for self-education and for teaching, and this grit in triumphing over difficulties were transmitted by this young Irishman to his family, and in especial to Charlotte. From their earliest years learning was a passion with them all, and those who outlived childhood, Charlotte and Emily and Anne, were all governesses before they were out of their teens, and Branwell, a little later, a tutor. The idea of setting up a school (though not a public school) was one of the long-cherished dreams of Haworth, and to fit herself and her sisters for it Charlotte carried through a scheme for the further education of herself and Emily at Brussels, which was scarcely less improbable of accomplishment, when she conceived it, as that young Patrick Brontë should, forty years before, have succeeded in going up to Cambridge from Drumballyroney, County Down, and getting a University education. Indomitable will, the power to make and then grasp opportunities, teaching, authorship, were fruitful in the blood; while, in minor detail, even as Patrick Brunty, when he went incredibly forth to make his way in the world, assumed a more prepossessing surname, so his daughters, when their destiny declared itself, went forth to the world as Currer, Ellis, and Acton Bell for fear that an avowal of feminine authorship might prove a handicap to success.

So Patrick Brunty on his magic carpet went up to Cambridge, and took his new name and his degree. A volunteer movement, anticipating the larger and later organisation, was being developed all over the country as a defence against possible invasion by the French, and Lord Palmerston, who came up to St. John's College the year after Patrick Brontë, was a member of the same corps as he: Mr. Brontë told Mrs. Gaskell that they drilled together. He was ordained in 1806, and appointed to a curacy in the parish of Wethersfield, Essex, where he became engaged to a girl named Mary Burder. There was some opposition on the part of the girl's uncle to the match, but the end of the matter was that Mr. Brontë broke the engagement. He did not apparently mention this episode to Mrs. Gaskell, nor the sequel to it which will appear later. He then moved to Yorkshire, where he was curate first at Dewsbury, and then at Hartshead. While there he published, in 1811 and 1813, two volumes of poems: these are *Cottage Poems* and *The Rural Minstrel*. Many of them are definitely religious, and all have a moral. It is difficult to quote from them: some rather discouraging verses sent *To a Lady on her Birthday* may be taken as typical of his muse:

In thoughtful mood your parents dear,

Whilst joy shines through the starting tear,

Give approbation due,

As each drinks deep in mirthful wine

Your rosy health, and looks benign

Are sent to heaven for you.

But let me whisper, lovely fair,

That joy may soon give place to care,

And sorrow cloud this day;

Full soon your eyes of startling blue,

And velvet lips of scarlet hue

Discoloured, may decay.

As bloody drops on virgin snows,

So vies the lily with the rose

Full on your dimpled cheek,

But ah! the worm in lazy coil

May soon prey on this putrid spoil,

Or leap in loathsome freak.

Fond wooers come with flattering tale,

And load with sighs the passing gale,

And love-distracted rave;

But hark, fair maid! whate'er they say,

You're but a breathing mass of clay,

Fast ripening for the grave.

These volumes cannot have fallen flatter than the poems published by his daughters thirty-three years later, of which only two copies were sold, and of them but one line survives, because it is identical with that heart's-cry of Jane Eyre's, which was singled out by Mr. Swinburne as the supreme utterance of Charlotte's genius. This was taken verbatim from one of Mr. Brontë's poems, and thus he is responsible for: 'To the finest fibre of my nature, sir.'

At Hartshead Mr. Brontë met Miss Maria Branwell, third daughter of a Methodist merchant in Penzance. Her father and mother were both dead, and she was on a visit—visits in those days were affairs that lasted for many weeks—to an aunt who had married a Methodist preacher, Mr. John Fennel, who was Governor of the Wesleyan Academy at Wood House Grove, near Bradford. Mr. Brontë, after a brief acquaintance, proposed to her and was accepted. He kept some letters of hers written to him during their engagement, gave them in after years to Charlotte, and they were published for the first time in their entirety by Mr. Clement Shorter. They convey a wholly delightful impression of the writer; there is about them, as Charlotte felt when first she saw them thirty years after her mother's death, a wonderful sweet charm and fineness, a sincere affection and piety. They are like egg-shell china for transparent delicacy; they are fresh and virginal as a primrose growing on some be-smoked Yorkshire moor.

I will frankly confess [she writes in the earliest of these] that your behaviour and what I have seen and heard of your character has excited my warmest esteem and regard, and be assured that you shall never have cause to repent of any confidence you may think proper to place in me, and that it will always be my endeavour to deserve the good opinion which you have formed, although human weakness may in some instances cause me to fall short. I do not depend upon my own strength, but I look to Him who has been my unerring guide through life and in whose continued protection and assistance I confidently trust.

Then, so we gather, Mr. Brontë made some lover-like demand that she should protest her affection for him, and very properly she proceeds:

The *politeness of others* can never make me forget your kind attentions, neither can *I walk our accustomed rounds* without thinking on you, and, why should I be ashamed to add, wishing for your presence. If you knew what were my feelings while writing this, you would pity me. I wish to write the truth and give you satisfaction yet fear to go too far, and exceed the bounds of propriety.

She takes a walk she had taken with him,

not wholly without a wish that I had your arm to assist me and your conversation to shorten the walk. Indeed, all our walks have now an insipidity in them which I never thought they would have possessed....

Or she hears Mr. Watman preach a very excellent sermon.

He displayed the character of our Saviour in a most affecting and amiable light. I scarcely ever felt more charmed with his excellencies, more grateful for his condescension, or more abased at my own unworthiness: but I lament that my heart is so little retentive of those pleasing and profitable impressions....

Again and again, without exceeding the bounds of propriety (though once she addresses him as 'dear saucy Pat,' which was rather daring for those days), she assures him of her unalterable affection.

With the sincerest pleasure do I retire from company to converse with him whom I love beyond all others. Could my beloved friend see my heart he would then be convinced that the affection I bear him is not at all inferior to that which he feels for me—indeed I sometimes think that in truth and constancy it excels.

The final letter announces that they are busy at her uncle's house with making the cakes for the wedding, and that she has already learned by heart 'the pretty little hymn' he sent her, 'but cannot promise to sing it scientifically, though I will endeavour to gain a little more assurance.' Throughout this delicious little series of letters, extending over four months, there runs the note of love and piety crystal-clear in naïve sincerity and sparkling with humorous touches of demure merriment and chaff of her saucy Pat. Had Mrs. Brontë lived to bring up the family, which soon arrived with such speed and regularity, who knows what kindlier quality, what more indulgent attitude towards the failings and imperfections of others might not have softened the judgments of one of her daughters, have redeemed her only son from a sordid and premature doom, and even have given to the genius of the family some solvent for that steely remoteness with which she surrounded herself? True, we cannot imagine Emily saying her prayers at her mother's knee and yet remaining Emily, nor, if she would thereby have lost anything of her wild pagan mysticism, could we wish her capable of her mother's pieties; but it is impossible not to wonder what would have happened if so lonely and supreme a soul could have had the opportunity of confiding something of its secret raptures and despairs to one whose essential tenderness and sympathy could not have failed to understand something of them.

The marriage of Maria Branwell and Patrick Brontë took place at Guiseley near Hartshead in December 1812, and never again did she return from the moors and mists of the austere north to the prim home of her brother, ex-Mayor of Penzance, where the grates were so beautifully cleaned, and palm trees grew in those gardens to which the snows of the Yorkshire moors and the long savage winters of the uplands were strangers. She was wedded to her dear saucy Pat, and the bearing of his children was business enough.

At Hartshead were born, in 1813 and 1815, her two eldest children, Maria and Elizabeth. In 1815 Mr. Brontë published at Halifax a romance in prose, called *The Cottage in the Wood: or, The Art of Becoming Rich and Happy*, and in the same year he was appointed curate of Thornton in the parish of Bradford, and was minister at a chapel of ease called the Bell Chapel. Here they were on the most intimate social terms with Mr. John Frith of Kipping House and his motherless daughter, Elizabeth. Elizabeth kept a diary, and it is a catalogue of tea-drinkings with the Brontës, and of the Brontës drinking tea or dining at Kipping House. Here there were born to him four more children, the story of whose lives, short as they were in the measure of years, forms the tragic and imperishable history of the Brontës. The eldest of these children was Charlotte, born on April 21, 1816; the second was the only boy, Patrick Branwell—thereafter known as Branwell—born on June 26, 1817; the third Emily Jane, born on July 30, 1818; and the fourth Anne, born on January 17, 1820.

At Thornton Mr. Brontë wrote the second of his prose romances, called *The Maid of Killarney, or Albion and Flora. The Maid of Killarney* contains some warnings against the carnal tendencies fostered by dancing, and, like the rest of Mr. Brontë's works, derives its sole interest from the fact that the author was the father of his children. Mrs. Brontë, as well as her husband, had literary aspirations, and it was at Thornton that she wrote an essay entitled *The Advantage of Poverty in Religious Concerns*. It was intended for some religious periodical, but was never published till Mr. Clement Shorter unearthed it. There is a Calvinistic touch about it, for though the true Christian can be blithe, as she certainly was, in poverty, finding it a state which, taken rightly, is attended with innumerable blessings, it is not necessarily a sign of the Divine favour, and she concludes:

But O, what words can express the great misery of those who suffer all the evils of poverty here, and that, too, by their bad conduct and have no hope of happiness hereafter, but rather have cause to fear the end of this miserable life will be the beginning of another, infinitely more miserable, never, never to have an end!

Then came the final ecclesiastical 'step' for Mr. Brontë, and on that step he remained without further promotion for forty-one years. On February 25, 1820, he was licensed to the chapelry of Haworth, ten miles from Bradford and in the parish of that town. Though, strictly speaking, it was only a perpetual curacy, the incumbent to all intents and purposes was vicar. He did not at once go there, for we find that Anne, the youngest of the family, was baptized at Thornton a month later. But some time during the spring the move was made, and from thenceforth, with one exceedingly important exception, the setting of the Brontë-drama, was laid at the Parsonage there. Standing at the top of the steep hill up which the village climbs, it faces, across a small oblong of walled-in garden, the west door of the Church of St. Michael. It is girt about with the graveyard; the public-house, the 'Black Bull,' is neighbourly; a 'short lone lane' leads to the moors. These four, parsonage and church, public-house and moors, are the main furnishing of the scene. Of them the church is the least significant and the moors the most, for from the moors came *Wuthering Heights*.

CHAPTER II

The house was small for this family of eight persons. On the ground floor to right and left of the flagged passage from the front door were two parlours: that on the left was the dining-room and family sitting-room; to the right was Mr. Brontë's study where, in later years, he took his midday dinner alone, being vexed with digestive troubles and preferring solitude. At the back was a kitchen, and a store-room big enough to be converted later into a studio for Branwell, when he took to painting and meant to make it his career. Upstairs were four bedrooms, and over the flagged passage of entrance a further slip of a room without a fireplace. We may dismiss therefore as apocryphal the lurid tale which has crept into the Brontë-Saga, with a view to heightening the picturesque horror of the early years of the sisters, that all five of them slept together in this closet, since there is no apparent reason why some or all of them should not sleep in the other bedrooms.

Hitherto we have traced little more than the bare events in the life of Mr. Brontë up to the time of his appointment to Haworth, but in the first edition of Mrs. Gaskell's work, which presently brought the hornets about her, she launches into details of the most lurid sort about his manners and his habits. She acquired her facts, she tells us, from a 'good old woman in Haworth,' who had been Mrs. Brontë's nurse in her last illness. Mrs. Brontë died in 1821, and thus it was thirty-four years after the time to which it refers, when Mrs. Gaskell, collecting materials for the *Life of Charlotte Brontë*, obtained the information on which she founded the following account:

She told me that one day when the children had been out on the moors and rain had come on, she thought their feet would be wet, and accordingly she rummaged out some coloured boots which had been given them by a friend.... These little pairs she ranged round the kitchen fire to warm, but, when the children came back, the boots were no where to be found, only a very strong odour of burned leather was perceived. Mr. Brontë had come in and seen them: they were too gay and luxurious for his children, and would foster the love of dress; so he had put them into the fire. He spared nothing that offended his antique simplicity. Long before this someone had given Mrs. Brontë a silk gown; either the make or the colour or the material was not according to his notions of consistent propriety, and Mrs. Brontë in consequence never wore it. But for all that she kept it treasured up in her drawers, which were generally locked. One day, however, while in the kitchen, she remembered that she had left the key in her drawer, and hearing Mr. Brontë upstairs, she augured some ill to her dress, and, running upstairs, she found it cut into shreds.... He did not speak when he was annoyed or displeased, but worked off his volcanic wrath by firing pistols out of the back door in rapid succession. Mrs. Brontë, lying in bed upstairs, would hear the quick explosions, and know that something had gone wrong: but her sweet nature thought invariably of the bright side, and she would say, 'Ought I not to be thankful that he never gave me an angry word?' Now and then his anger took a different form but still was speechless. Once he got the hearth-rug and stuffing it up the grate, deliberately set it on fire, and remained in the room, in spite of the stench, until it had smouldered and shrivelled away into uselessness. Another time he took some chairs, and sawed away at the backs till they were reduced to the condition of stools. I have named these instances of eccentricity in the father because I hold the knowledge of them to be necessary for a right understanding of a life of his daughter.

This is a lurid picture, and even if Mrs. Gaskell would have gone bail for the memory and the accuracy of her aged informant, and really believed that the knowledge of these facts was necessary for the right understanding of the life of the daughter of so violent a lunatic, it was exceedingly rash of her to have picked up from an old woman in Haworth these unconfirmed stories of the man at whose request she was writing his daughter's biography, and to have published them in his lifetime was scarcely decent. He was an old man and ailing, already close on his eightieth birthday; perhaps Mrs. Gaskell thought he would be dead before the book came out. Again he could no longer read much, and she may have thought that he would never ascertain what, on the authority of the good old woman, she had written about him. But justice and retribution decreed that he should still be alive, and that his son-in-law Mr. Nicholls, Charlotte's widower, should read aloud to him these delirious paragraphs about himself. A milder man than he would have been annoyed, and Mr. Brontë was furious. He stated to Mr. William Dearden, who had been a friend of his son Branwell, that these stories were wholly untrue.

'I did not know,' he said, with a certain grim irony, 'that I had an enemy in the world who would traduce me before my death till Mrs. Gaskell's Life of Charlotte appeared. Everything in that book which relates to my conduct to my family is either false or distorted. I never did commit such acts as are there ascribed to me.'

Then he must have got hold of the source of these libels, for in a subsequent interview he told Mr. Dearden that Mrs. Gaskell had listened to village scandal and got her information from some discarded servant. That was precisely what had happened, for the good old woman who had been Mrs. Brontë's nurse had been dismissed from his service. No doubt when Mr. Brontë said that some of these stories were 'distorted,' he alluded to his alleged habit of firing pistols out of the back door in rapid succession as a speechless method of expressing annoyance. That was founded on the fact that in the early days of his incumbency he was on the side of the law against the Luddites, and, as Mrs. Gaskell herself says, was unpopular among the mill-workers. He used, therefore, to carry a loaded pistol up to bed with him and discharge it next morning out of the window.

We can test the general accuracy of the good old woman's memory by the story she told Mrs. Gaskell of the six Brontë children often walking out hand in hand towards the moors, at the time when she was nursing their mother. When Mrs. Brontë died, Anne the youngest was only twenty months old, having been born in January 1820, and precocious as they all were, it is impossible to credit such early athleticism. The same informant, in a speech Mrs. Gaskell quotes verbatim, told her that the children were never given flesh-food of any sort; potatoes were their entire dinner. Also that with only young servants in the house there was, in the absence of a mistress's supervision, much waste going on with regard to food. More retribution followed on these garrulities, for there were still living in Haworth, when Mrs. Gaskell's book came out, two sisters, Nancy and Sarah Garrs, one of whom had come with the Brontës from Thornton, while the other had entered Mr. Brontë's service at Haworth. He now gave them, as a counterblast to these accusations, a written testimonial that they had not been wasteful but had been admirable servants in all respects, and Nancy, the cook-general, deposed that the children's dinner every day consisted of beef or mutton followed by milk pudding. Not exciting, but not potatoes. In turn she gave a testimonial to her old master, and said that 'there was never a more affectionate father, never a kinder master.... He was not of a violent temper at all, quite the reverse!'

Mr. Brontë then wrote to Mrs. Gaskell, saying that her whole narrative concerning him and his habits and his relations to his family were false, and requested her to cancel it in the next edition of her book. 'To this,' he said, 'I received no other answer than that Mrs. Gaskell was unwell and not able to write.' She was, as will appear, being threatened at the time by two libel actions arising out of other contents of her book, and no doubt was busy. Two editions of it had already appeared, but from the third edition onwards, these sensational and unfounded stories were omitted.

Now the trouble arose from Mrs. Gaskell's forgetfulness that she was now writing a biography and not a romance. There is every reason to suppose that Mr. Brontë had a high, even a violent, temper, but she had obtained her instances of it from a tainted source, and they seem to have been unfounded. She did what she could, by withdrawing them, to repair the needless pain they had given, and having done that she had made such amends as were in her power for having published them at all. But the mischief did not end there, and these stories are believed by many Brontë students to this day, for regardless of the fact that she cancelled them, as being untrue, biographers who have followed her have had no hesitation in disinterring such discredited stuff from her unexpurgated editions and giving it renewed currency with comments. Sir T. Wemyss Reid, for instance, who, chronologically, is the next successor to Mrs. Gaskell, repeats the legend of the pistol firing, exuberantly adding fresh details. The villagers, he tells us, were quite accustomed to the sound of pistol shots 'at any hour of the day' from their pastor's house: Mr. Brontë not only deliberately cut to bits his wife's pretty dress but 'presented her with the tattered fragments.' He tells us that it was Mrs. Brontë's lot to 'submit to persistent coldness and neglect,' and that she lived 'in perpetual dread of her lordly master.' This is falsification, for since he got these stories of violence from Mrs. Gaskell's book, he must have found there also her record that Mrs. Brontë used to say, 'Ought I not to be thankful that he never gave me an angry word?' Unkindness to his wife was thus incorporated into the Brontë-Saga, and a monstrous disregard of the proper diet for young children has been deduced from the apocryphal story that they had only potatoes for dinner. My only object in referring to what Mrs. Gaskell withdrew is that, though it was withdrawn, it has been served up again by others.

Mrs. Brontë lived only eighteen months after the family came to Haworth, and died of internal cancer in September 1821. It is curious that Charlotte, whose childish memories were so extraordinarily vivid, and who was five and a half years old when she died, could remember practically nothing of her mother. She could recall only the picture of her playing with Branwell, then aged four, in the parlour. Towards the end, when too weak to move, Mrs. Brontë used to ask her nurse to raise her in bed, so that she might see the grate being cleaned, for the servant cleaned it in the way it was done in Cornwall. She was buried at Haworth, and practically the whole of what we know of her is derived from those letters she wrote to Mr. Brontë when she was engaged to him.

He was now left with six children, the youngest of whom, Anne, was still little more than eighteen months old, and in the course of the next year there came to live at Haworth, in order to look after them, Miss Elizabeth Branwell, Mrs. Brontë's eldest sister, and the Parsonage was her home until her death. She lived much in her bedroom, where she taught her nieces to sew, and where there were grouped round her a spinster's household gods—an Indian workbox, a workbox with a china top, and a 'Japan' dressing-box: she took snuff out of a small gold box. After the warmth and sunny climate of Penzance, where snow and frost were as unknown as in the valley of Avilion, she hated this bleak and wintry upland, and habitually wore pattens in the house for fear of the chill of the stone stairs stabbing through her shoes. The Branwell family in Penzance mixed much in social circles, but here there were no circles of any sort: it was a dismal change, and we must credit her with having been a woman with a strong sense of moral obligation to have given up all that constituted life's amenities at the call of duty. She had an income of her own, derived from investments, of £50 a year, out of which she contributed to household expenses, and shortly before her death she showed that she was a woman of generous impulses. Her favourite among the children was Branwell, and he of them all was the only one who ever wrote of her with affection, and, after her death, with regret. She seems to have been lacking in lightness and geniality. We can find, at any rate, no hint of the gentle gaiety and tenderness of her sister, and in the absence of such evidence she has been fashioned into a grim, forbidding personage. Commentators, with the passion for identifying all the characters in Charlotte's novels with people whom she had known, have pounced on this poor lady as being the 'original' of Mrs. Reed in *Jane Eyre*, and have suggested that in the bedroom where she taught her nieces to sew, she kept a switch with which she used 'to lace the quivering palm or shrinking neck' for misdeeds they had never committed. The evidence rests entirely on the fact that Charlotte and her sisters used to sew in Miss Branwell's bedroom, and Jane Eyre used to be whipped in Mrs. Reed's bedroom.

Mr. Brontë, after his sister-in-law's advent, made two attempts to marry again. Miss Elizabeth Firth, who had been friends with the family at Thornton, was his first choice, but the lady was already engaged to the Rev. James Franks, Vicar of Huddersfield. Then he harked back to the days of his curacy at Wethersfield, and wrote a quite amazing letter to Miss Mary Burder, to whom he had once been engaged, but whom he had subsequently thrown over, informing her how he had improved in the last fifteen years, how popular he was in his parish (the Vicar of Dewsbury would bear him out), and how eager to make up to her for the disappointment he had caused her. She replied with singular clarity, piously thanking God that He had already preserved her from the fate of being his wife, but she wished him nothing but well. A second appeal produced no sign of softening, and he resigned himself to celibacy.

CHAPTER III

For a little while yet as regards the early history of Mr. Brontë's children, we have, before we get to firmer ground, to continue to get our information from what he told Mrs. Gaskell. They were studious and highly intelligent children: Branwell, perhaps, was the most promising of them all, but at the age of ten Maria used to study the Parliamentary debates in the newspapers, and could discuss with her father the leading topics of the day, with the grasp and perception of an adult. He suspected that all of them thought more deeply than appeared on the surface, and knowing that they were very shy, he adopted the strangest device that ever entered a father's head to encourage fluency and frankness in the mouths of these babes and sucklings. He found a mask in his study; he set his children in a row, and bade them each assume it in turn, so that they might speak boldly under cover of it, and answer the cosmic questions he put to them. This unique plan, instead of terrifying them, produced the most gratifying results. He began with the youngest, and question and answer ran as follows:

MR. BRONTË. Anne, what does a child like you most want?

ANNE (aged four). Age and experience.

MR. BRONTË. Emily, what had I best do with your brother Branwell, when he is a naughty boy?

EMILY (aged five). Reason with him, and when he won't listen to reason, whip him.

MR. BRONTË. Branwell, what is the best way of knowing the difference between the intellects of man and woman?

BRANWELL (aged six). By considering the difference between them as to their bodies.

MR. BRONTË. Charlotte, what is the best book in the world?

CHARLOTTE (aged seven or eight). The Bible.

MR. BRONTË. And what is the next best, Charlotte?

CHARLOTTE. The Book of Nature.

MR. BRONTË. Elizabeth, what is the best mode of education for a woman?

ELIZABETH (aged eight or nine). That which would make her rule her house well.

MR. BRONTË. Maria, what is the best mode of spending time?

MARIA (aged ten or eleven). By laying it out in preparation for a happy eternity.

Now Mr. Brontë vouched for the substantial exactness of these answers to his questions; they made (and no wonder) 'a deep and lasting impression' on his memory, and the story must therefore be treated with the utmost respect. But we cannot help wondering whether his memory of the manner of the questions was as exact as that of the answers. We admit that they were very remarkable children. We know, on indisputable evidence, that at a very early age Charlotte and Branwell wrote prodigious quantities of poems, tales, articles, dramas, magazines and novels, but we find difficulty here in accepting the literal truth of Mr. Brontë's account. Take Anne. Anne, we have already seen, is recorded to have walked on the moors with her brother and sisters when she was only twenty months old. A baby who did that was almost *capable de tout*; but could even she, at the age of four, when asked what a child like her most wanted, answer straight off 'Age and experience'? There was surely a little prompting, something like this:

MR. BRONTË. Now, Anne, take the mask and remember you are only four years old. Other people are much older. What do you lack?

ANNE. Age.

MR. BRONTË. Excellent. And you have seen little of the world yet, nothing much has happened to you. What else do you lack?

ANNE. Experience.

Our craving for probabilities demands something of this sort. Mozart, it is true, composed fugues at the age of four, but then Mozart fulfilled the promise of his extraordinary precocity, while Anne, gentle and pious, gave birth to nothing worthy of her spontaneous insight at the age of four. The replies of the other children are hardly less amazing, Branwell's in particular, though it is difficult to see exactly what he meant. Maria's reply is infinitely pathetic, for her preparation for eternity was nearly accomplished.... With this episode Mr. Brontë makes his last contribution to the chronicles of his family.

II

There had been established in the year 1823 at Cowan Bridge in the West Riding of Yorkshire a boarding-school for the education of the daughters of indigent clergymen. The fees charged were £14 a year, with certain small supplements, and the girls wore a uniform which was provided for them: £3 was charged for this. So small a sum for board and education did not cover the running expenses of the place, and the Reverend William Carus Wilson, who was mainly responsible for its establishment, had got together a body of annual subscribers, and their contributions paid for the salaries of the mistresses and other outgoings. Mr. Brontë no doubt had heard well of the school, and in July 1824, a year after it had been opened, he entered his two eldest daughters as pupils. Maria and Elizabeth had lately suffered from measles and whooping-cough, and it was doubtful whether they were well enough to go.

Mr. Brontë took them there himself: he stayed at the school, he ate his meals with the children, and he was shown over the whole establishment. He must presumably have been satisfied that the pupils were well looked after and cared for, for he returned there again in August, bringing with him Charlotte, aged eight, and again in November, bringing Emily, aged six. His four eldest daughters were thus all at Cowan Bridge together. Of them individually during their schooldays we know little. Maria was constantly in disgrace, owing to habits common to children who have not sufficient physical control, and was often punished by a junior mistress called Miss Andrews in a harsh and excessive manner. Elizabeth had some accident in which she cut her head, and Miss Evans, the senior mistress, looked after her with the greatest care, taking her to sleep in her own room. Charlotte was described as a bright, clever little child; the youngest, Emily, was the pet of the school. During the ensuing spring of 1825 there broke out some epidemic spoken of as 'low fever,' and probably allied to influenza. Mr. Carus Wilson did everything possible for the girls sick of this 'low fever' in the way of diet and medical attendance, and evidently the epidemic was not of any severe or malignant type, for only one girl died, and that from after-effects. None of the four Brontë girls caught it, but in February 1825, while it was prevalent, Maria became seriously ill, and Mr. Brontë, who had not known that she was ailing, was sent for, and he took her back to Haworth, where she died of consumption on May 6. He certainly did not attribute her illness to ill-treatment or neglect, for the other three girls remained at Cowan Bridge. Then, at the end of May, Elizabeth was seen to be suffering from the same symptoms as Maria, and was taken back to Haworth, and Charlotte and Emily went home a week afterwards. Elizabeth died, also of consumption, on June 15.

The school continued to prosper, and was subsequently moved from Cowan Bridge to Casterton, where in 1848 it was doing excellent work, providing the pupils with places as governesses and starting them on their careers. During these intervening years Charlotte, in her very voluminous and intimate correspondence, never alluded to her own schooldays at Cowan Bridge, nor to those of her sisters. But she was pondering certain things in her heart, keeping them close, as in a forcing-glass, and letting none of the heat and the bitterness in which she grew them escape in trivial utterance. Then, in 1846, she took up the forcing-glass of her silence and her concentration, and, in *Jane Eyre* (published the next year), branded with infamy the school which she had left at the age of nine. Nowadays we know to some extent what the psychological effect of such suppression is. Painful impressions made on a child's mind grow to monstrous proportions, and the adult mind fully believes in the actuality of its own distortions.

There is no need to go, with any detail, into those chapters in *Jane Eyre* which deal with the Orphan Asylum at Lowood. It suffices to say that Charlotte Brontë avowed that they were drawn accurately and faithfully from life. 'Lowood' was Cowan Bridge; 'Helen Burns' was her sister Maria; the black marble clergyman, 'Naomi Brocklehurst,' was Mr. Carus Wilson; the epidemic was typhus, and it caused many girls to die at their homes when they were removed there, others to die at school. But by no possibility can the 'low fever' which broke out at Cowan Bridge, when she was at school there, have been typhus; for typhus is an exceedingly deadly fever, a plague of the Middle Ages, and the rate of mortality among its victims is, in spite of the most skilled attendance and nursing, about twenty-five per cent. Here, however, out of forty cases there was, as a matter of fact, only one death, and that from after-effects, and these in typhus are unknown. When once the crisis is past, if the patient lives through it, convalescence is swift and uninterrupted. Jane Eyre describes the infection as having been due to damp air coming into the open windows of the school and the dormitories.

Charlotte expressed regret that Cowan Bridge was instantly identified, on the publication of *Jane Eyre*, as being Lowood, but if a very vivid and gifted writer uses the utmost of her skill to render unmistakable the features of the place she describes, she has no business to be surprised if recognition follows, and her regret must be suspect. Indeed, it is clear that so far from regretting it she was pleased with the identification, for she wrote to her friend, Mr. Williams, saying:

I saw an elderly clergyman reading it (*Jane Eyre*) the other day, and had the satisfaction of hearing him exclaim, 'Why they have got —— School, and Mr. —— here, I declare, and Miss ——' (naming the originals of Lowood, Mr. Brocklehurst and Miss Temple). He had known them all. I wondered whether he would recognise the portraits, and was gratified to find that he did, and that, moreover, he pronounced them faithful and just. He said too, that Mr. —— (Brocklehurst) deserved the chastisement he had got!

Since the age of nine she had nursed her bitterness of heart at the death of her sisters till it became an obsession to her, for not only in *Jane Eyre*, under the more licensed imagination of fiction, but in a private letter to her old friend and mistress, Miss Wooler, who had asked her for her opinion on Cowan Bridge, she made the following indictment:

Typhus fever decimated the school periodically and consumption and scrofula in every variety of form, which bad air and water, and bad, insufficient diet, can generate preyed on the ill fated pupils.

It is impossible to accept such a statement; it bears on the face of it its own refutation, for no school periodically decimated by typhus can possibly continue to exist. Years of bitter brooding had caused Charlotte to imagine a state of affairs that was wildly exaggerated.

On the other hand, the awful moral precepts, the threats of hell and damnation, which she put into the mouth of Mr. Brocklehurst, the 'black marble clergyman' and effigy of Mr. Carus Wilson, were founded on fact. He published, for instance, in 1828, an appalling little volume called *Youthful Memoirs*, and edited and contributed poems to a magazine called the *Children's Friend*, which teems with just such sentiments as she attributed to him. A verse from one of these runs:

It's dangerous to provoke a God

Whose power and vengeance none can tell;

One stroke of His almighty rod

Can send young sinners quick to hell.

These volumes were, of course, accessible to Charlotte long before she wrote *Jane Eyre*, but, whether she saw them or not, the man who wrote them was certainly capable of the harangues of Mr. Brocklehurst.

Then came Mrs. Gaskell with the first edition of her *Life*, and her definite disclosure that Lowood in *Jane Eyre* was an accurate picture of Cowan Bridge: it was no wonder that the hornets came about her. The porridge for breakfast was often burned and had offensive foreign fragments in it, the beef was high, the house morning, noon, and night reeked of rancid fat, the water in which the rice was boiled was rain water, drained from the roof into a wooden tub and thence drawn off for the kitchen, the little Brontës, craving for food, could often eat nothing whatever, and when Mr. Carus Wilson heard complaints about such inedible diet he replied that the children were to be trained up to regard higher things than dainty pampering of the appetite, and lectured them on the sinfulness of their carnal propensities. The epidemic of typhus is duly recorded, and its cause definitely assigned to the state of semi-starvation in which the pupils were kept. Mrs. Gaskell did not, she expressly tells us in a later edition of her book, get her information from Charlotte Brontë, who never spoke to her about Mr. Carus Wilson at all, and only once alluded to Cowan Bridge and the careless way in which the food was prepared, but she based her narrative on *Jane Eyre*, collecting also stories that suited her picture without verifying them or finding out whether there was rebutting evidence. She was threatened with a libel action, she was bombarded with letters from old pupils at Cowan Bridge, expressing the highest regard and affection for Mr. Carus Wilson, and their appreciation of the admirable way in which the school was conducted. As for the revolting diet, all that could be substantiated was that there had once been a careless cook who spoiled the porridge and was dismissed.

So Mrs. Gaskell made the needful omissions and additions in her account, confessing that it had been one-sided; but here, again, her successors in the Brontë-Saga have adopted her original and discarded version, adding appropriate embroideries of their own. From one we learn that 'during the whole time of their sojourn there the young Brontës scarcely ever knew what it was to be free from the pangs of hunger'; another called it 'the counterpart for girls of Mr. Squeers's Academy for Young Gentlemen'; another announced that Mr. Carus Wilson 'seems to have pushed his campaign against the flesh a bit too far, and was surprised at his own success when one after another the extremely perishable bodies of these children were laid low by typhus.' Whatever is the truth about Cowan Bridge, and the sadist cruelties related in *Jane Eyre*, we must remember that Mr. Brontë was satisfied with the management of the school, and that Mrs. Gaskell acknowledged that she had not, in her *Life of Charlotte Brontë*, stated her case against it fairly. After the publication of her book a highly acrimonious correspondence on the subject came out in the *Halifax Guardian*.

III

By midsummer 1825 the family, now consisting of the three sisters and Branwell, were back at Haworth, and there they remained for five years. They saw little or nothing of their neighbours. They made no friendships with children of their own age; for recreation they had walks on the moors, which already were beginning to work their spell in the heart of one of them, and they read omnivorously. The girls helped in the housework; they did their sewing with their aunt, their father's library was open to them, and while he taught his son, Charlotte taught her sisters. And as in the darkness of the hive the unseen and furious industry of the bees generates the curtains of wax on which are built the honey cells, so in the dining-room of the sequestered parsonage and round the kitchen fire the weaving of dreams and the exercise of imagination were their passionate preoccupations, and in the case of Charlotte and Branwell took shape in ceaseless and profuse experiment in all forms of the written word. All that they came across in their father's books and in the tales in *Blackwood's Magazine* was material for this honey-gathering; the news in the daily papers contributed to it; the public characters of the nation were their pets and their heroes. The Duke of Wellington and his family generally were the property of Charlotte, Branwell was the patron of Napoleon; even the wooden soldiers his father bought for him were christened Field-Marshals. The Corn Laws, the Catholic question, Mr. Peel's speech, Mr. Christopher North, editor of *Blackwood's Magazine*, James Hogg, were all grist for their mills: never were four small children more personally and vividly concerned in the movements of the world from which they were so sundered. Nor was it only from the affairs of the world and from their lessons that they drew the substance of their dreams, for in the kitchen Tabby had begun her reign of thirty years over their dinners and their hearts, and Tabby had stories of fairies in the glen and moonlit folk of the moorland, and then it was Emily, now taller than the rest, and the prettiest of her plain sisters, whose dark eyes kindled. Tabby was far more than servant, and from the time she came to Haworth she held a peculiar place in the hearts of them all. She slipped on a film of ice one day going down the steep street of Haworth, and, falling, broke her leg. In the interval the girls did all the housework, but when she was recovered, Aunt Branwell and Mr. Brontë decided that she was not up to her work, and must go. Upon which all the children went on hunger-strike, and Tabby stayed. Later her lameness caused her to give up her post, and she lived with her sister in the village for four years. But the Brontës could not get on without her, and she returned and died at the age of over ninety, still in service at the Parsonage, a few weeks only before the last of her children followed her.

Day-dreams and the Duke of Wellington, fairies by the beck, and riots at the mills, all went into one common vat, from which were brewed poems and dramas and magazines, and romances and essays. The children 'established plays,' to use Charlotte's words; some were secret plays, and they were the best. Of these some seem to have been verbal romances; they constructed them only in talk, making up adventures; others were written down, and of such was a play called *The Islanders*. Each of them, as they chattered together by the fire, chose an island and peopled it with celebrated folk. Charlotte's island was the Isle of Wight, and, needless to say, the Duke of Wellington and his two sons and Christopher North were the principal inhabitants. Out of such developed whole sagas of joint imagination. Two groups were formed. Charlotte and Branwell collaborated over a state called Angria, somewhere in the West of Africa, near the delta of the Niger. The Angrians were ruled by King Zamorna, and the affairs of the Angrians were celebrated in poems and chronicles. Emily and Anne had another kingdom of their own devising called Angora, a hyperborean and mountainous land inhabited by a folk called Gondals, and ruled by the Emperor Julius; it was the scene of Royalist and Republican wars. Originally, as we may guess from the similarity of the names, Angria and Angora were one, but Charlotte and Branwell preferred the tropics, Emily and Anne the Arctic regions, and the joint-play separated into two, and these in turn became secret plays not common to them all. The Angrian cycle was the less long-lived; Branwell wrote *The Rising of the Angrians* when he was nineteen and Charlotte twenty, and with that the Angrian-Saga was finished; but Emily and Anne continued secretly to play at Gondals with unabated enthusiasm up till the last years of their lives. Emily was very busy over Gondal poems at the time when that wondrous genius of hers was fashioning *Wuthering Heights*.

The surviving fragments of prose and poetry that Charlotte and Branwell produced as children are of no striking merit. They are such as might have been written by any clever children with vivid imaginations. But such a sentence as this, written by Charlotte at the age of thirteen, not as a literary composition, but as a mere domestic chronicle, might give pause to anyone trained, when he reads, to listen for the sound of an individual voice.

One evening, about the time when the cold sleet and stormy fogs of November are succeeded by the snow storms and high piercing winds of confirmed winter, we were all sitting round the warm blazing kitchen fire having just concluded a quarrel with Tabby concerning the propriety of lighting a candle, from which she came off victorious, no candle having been produced....

There is something there, a management of words, an economy in their use, so that they convey as simply as possible, yet very vividly, the complete scene, which can hardly fail to strike the connoisseur of style. Charlotte's virtues are foreshadowed there, just as in an effusion about the Genii, who

in their impudence assert that by their magic they can reduce the world to a desert, the purest water to streams of livid poison, and the clearest lakes to stagnant waters, the pestilential vapours of which will slay all living creatures except the bloodthirsty beasts of the forest, and the ravenous bird of the rock,

she as clearly foreshadows some of the delirious imagery in *Jane Eyre* and *Shirley*.

But we cannot accept Mrs. Gaskell's account of the prodigious quantity of these early compositions. She describes how she had been given a packet of Charlotte's early manuscripts, a page of which, the opening of a story called *The Secret*, she reproduced in lithographic facsimile. It is in a script so minute as to be almost indecipherable. In this packet we learn was a paper in Charlotte's handwriting headed as follows: 'Catalogue of my books with the period of their completion up to August 3rd, 1830.' This catalogue gives the titles and short descriptions of the poems, stories, essays, dramas, magazines, and articles she had written up to date, and at the end of them there is the entry:

Making in the whole twenty-two volumes.

C. BRONTË. Aug. 3, 1830.

Mrs. Gaskell then proceeds:

As each volume contains from sixty to a hundred pages, and the size of the page lithographed is rather less than the average, the amount of the whole seems very great if we remember it was all written in about fifteen months. So much for the quantity....

The amount, indeed, is very great; in fact, it is so incredible that there must be some mistake. For the lithographed page which Mrs. Gaskell reproduces for us contains not less than 1280 words. Each volume, so we are told, contained sixty to a hundred pages, so, if we take eighty pages as the average length of each volume, we find that each volume contains 102,400 words. There are twenty-two of these volumes, written within a period of fifteen months. In fifteen months, therefore, Charlotte produced literary compositions containing 2,252,800 words, or an amount equivalent to twenty-two substantial novels. There is a mistake somewhere. These volumes, which were small, paper-bound notebooks, could not have contained so many pages of closely written script as the page Mrs. Gaskell reproduced. Still, the literary activities of these five years were truly enormous. It may be noticed that they did not entirely meet with Mr. Brontë's approval, for when, a few years later, Southey counselled Charlotte in answer to a letter of hers not to neglect her household duties for the sake of writing, she replied that her father had always held the same view.

But even when we have eliminated the impossible and qualified the improbable, we are left with a picture of those five years which succeeded the deaths of the two eldest daughters and the return of Charlotte and Emily from Cowan Bridge, of unique and extraordinary interest. There was Mr. Brontë busy with his parochial work, taking his dinner by himself in his study, going long walks alone, being called in sometimes to settle disputes as to the respective genius in generalship of Hannibal and Napoleon, or tearing open the paper to read to his excited family a speech of the Duke of Wellington's, but not having any part in the essential literary passions of his children; there was Aunt Elizabeth Branwell clattering about the house in pattens for fear of catching cold, and living chiefly in her bedroom among her work-boxes; there was Tabby making scones in the kitchen, with her stories of the fairies in the glens of the moor, and refusing to let the children have a candle; and there were the four children caring nothing for the games and ordinary pursuits of childhood, and seeing nobody but the inhabitants of the house. In the catalogue of their early compositions, Charlotte and Branwell alone seem to have written at this time, and all the interests of life, all the products of their imagination, were turned, as by some process of spontaneous transubstantiation, into poems and plays and tales of adventure. Whether Emily and Anne wrote anything during those years we do not know; no signed and dated manuscripts of theirs exist, but the theory that Charlotte after their deaths destroyed most of their manuscripts does not prove that there were any of this date. Perhaps at this time they conducted the affairs of Gondaland only by the spoken word, though in later years they both wrote poems about them, signing them by Gondal names, such as Julius Angora, A. G. Alsaida, Alexandrina Zenobia, and others of that turbulent and mysterious people. But Emily already was distilling drop by drop from the moor and from Tabby's tales of fairies that finest ichor of all, feeding on a honey-dew unknown to the others.

This completely sequestered life during the formative years of childhood had inevitable reactions upon them all; once only, till Charlotte went to school again, do any of the children appear to have left the Parsonage, when all together they paid a visit to their aunt, Mrs. Fennell, and employed their time in drawing. At the Parsonage itself they saw nobody but each other. This isolation, teeming though it was with inner interests, must have fostered, even if it did not produce, Charlotte's abnormal shyness when she was among strangers, which was the curse of her maturer years. She was also the eldest of the four and, with Aunt Branwell immured in her bedroom and her father in his study, she naturally took the lead; she managed, she set the tune for them, and assumed that habit of controlling their destinies, which she continued to exercise to the end. Then there was Branwell, brilliant and unstable, Charlotte's particular friend and confidant, and his aunt's favourite. Quite unlike his sisters he was gregariously disposed, whereas they all fled from the face of a stranger. He liked the company of others, easily winning flattery, and more easily swallowing it, by the wit and intelligence of his tongue. He ought, of course, to have been sent to school, but Mr. Brontë preferred to conduct his mental education himself, and leave his morals free to develop in the direction of least resistance. Then there was Emily, essentially solitary and silent, whose shyness was such that she would steal from the kitchen on the knock of the butcher or the baker. On her Haworth and the open void of the moor cast such a spell that all her life she pined with home-sickness, whenever she was away from the bleak home. Then there was Anne, as unlike her two sisters as Branwell was unlike them all. Her bent was for gentleness and piety.

CHAPTER IV

An end came for the present to Charlotte's colossal literary activities, when in January 1831 she went to school again. For that period of eighteen months she seems to have written nothing, though Branwell at home kept the sacred fire burning by composing The *History of the Young Men,* and six volumes (notebooks) of *Letters from an Englishman.* This new school was an establishment kept by Miss Margaret Wooler at Roe Head, not twenty miles from Haworth, and there Charlotte formed the three most lasting friendships of her life—one with the excellent Miss Wooler herself, the others with two of the pupils. Mary Taylor was one of these, and it is with the aid of her exceedingly vivid pen, in a letter to Mrs. Gaskell, that we get the first impression of how Charlotte struck others outside the family circle at the Parsonage. It was a forlorn little figure that got out of the cart with a hood to it that had brought her from Haworth, and she was dressed in the outlandish fashion thought suitable by Aunt Branwell for little girls of fourteen. It was a snowy day, and when she had seen Miss Wooler she came into the schoolroom, where seven or eight girls were playing, and stood looking out of the window, quietly crying. She was very small; so too, even in proportion to her diminutive stature, were her hands and feet. Her nose was enormous for that little face, her mouth was large and crooked, her eyes and hair were brown. She was desperately shy, and when she spoke it was with an Irish brogue. Then one of the girls stopped her play and came and spoke to her: she was to be the third and closest of her lifelong friends, Ellen Nussey, though at first Charlotte did not like her. Charlotte was abnormally short-sighted, the books which she was always reading must be held so close to her face that her eyes nearly touched them. For games she had no use at all, for there had been no game played in the parlour at Haworth; besides, her short sight entirely prevented her from seeing the ball when it came to her, and when games were in progress she stood under the trees and looked at the view.

The self-education system at Haworth had resulted in strange lacunæ in certain branches of knowledge. In spite of her literary compositions, Charlotte knew nothing technically about grammar, and in spite of the Angrian kingdom in the West of Africa, she knew nothing about geography. Miss Wooler, therefore, decided to place her in the second class among the junior girls of the school, but Charlotte's tears of humiliation caused her to relent and put her in the first class, telling her she must work hard and catch up with the rest. There was never any question about Charlotte working hard, but it was soon evident that however hard the others worked they would never catch her up in those other branches of knowledge which had been part of the self-imposed curriculum at Haworth. If the first class was set to learn by heart some stanzas from an admired English poet suitable for young ladies, it was found that Charlotte knew them by heart already, and could proceed to spout the next page or two. If a political discussion arose about the Reform Bill and the young ladies were a little vague about the names of Ministers, Charlotte could repeat for them the complete list of the last two ministries. That naturally led on to the Duke of Wellington, and she told them the names of all his victories in the Peninsular War. Then she drew: it was a delight to her to get hold of some small print, and burying her face in it, copy it line by line and touch by touch, with minute accuracy. She was a marvellous story-teller of gruesome tales, and realised the highest ambition of the blood-curdling specialist when one night she frightened one of her listeners into hysterics. Weekly she wrote to some member of the family at Haworth, and oftenest to Branwell, for she found she had more to say to him than to the others, and though during her year and a half at Roe Head she embarked on neither original romance nor magazine, nor poetical work, she was keeping her hand in with English composition. The following extract, written to her brother, has a cramped air about it, suggesting, perhaps, that Miss Wooler, in the approved style, looked over the girls' letters home before they were sent.

I am extremely glad that Aunt has consented to take in *Fraser's Magazine*, for though I know from your description of its general contents, it will be rather uninteresting when compared with *Blackwood*, still it will be better than remaining the whole year without being able to obtain a sight of any periodical whatever: and such would assuredly be our case, as, in the little moorland village where we reside, there would be no possibility of borrowing a work of that description from a circulating library. I hope with you that the present delightful weather may contribute to the perfect restoration of our dear papa's health and that it may give Aunt pleasant reminiscences of the salubrious climate of her native place.

After that we feel Miss Wooler would have been quite safe not to censor any more of Charlotte's letters home.

II

Here we must leave for a space the actual chronicle of events, and detach from it an emotional thread that for years was of vividest colour in Charlotte's life, and continued, more soberly hued, to the end of it. This was her passionate affection for Ellen Nussey, whom she first saw when she arrived at Miss Wooler's school, and whom at first she did not take to. But that indifference soon passed and gave place to one of those violent homosexual attachments which, so common are they among adolescents of either sex, must be considered normal rather than abnormal. They are full of yearnings and sentiment and aspirations, of blind devotion that tortures itself with enchanting fires, and presently burns out into cinders of indifference as often as it survives in the glow of friendship. But at the age of sixteen, Charlotte writes to her friend saying that she believes 'our friendship is destined to form an exception to the general rule regarding school-friendships,' and the sequel proved how right she was: this was not quite an ordinary *schwärm*. After she left Miss Wooler's, a monthly correspondence was instituted, of which many of Charlotte's letters remain, but she did not keep Ellen's contributions, and our knowledge of the affair is unfortunately one-sided, though to some extent we can construct the complement.

At first Charlotte is evidently the predominant partner: she exhorts, she encourages, she approves, she educates, and the lover has something of the governess about her. She discusses literary topics and assures Ellen that 'your natural abilities are excellent, and under the direction of a judicious and able friend, you might acquire a decided taste for elegant literature and even poetry.' Then there was some alarm about Ellen's health, and Charlotte, in that laboured style that both she and Branwell considered literary, hoped that

your medical adviser is mistaken in supposing that you have any tendency towards a pulmonary affection. Dear Ellen, that would indeed be a calamity.... Guard against the gloomy impression that such a state of mind naturally produces.

That alarm passed off, and when Charlotte was eighteen Ellen went on a visit to London, and Charlotte's letters unconsciously show not only what the friendship was becoming to her, but give us, intimately and inevitably, something of the ripening characteristics of her mind. At first she was afraid that the distractions and gaiety of 'modern Babylon' would prove too potent a diversion to Ellen, and take her mind away from her adorer, but she found this was not so. Ellen remained not only her friend, but her 'true friend.' Then in this letter follows a passage in which devotion is strangely mingled with the approbation of a governess who is satisfied with her pupil.

I am really grateful [she writes] for your mindfulness of so obscure a person as myself, and I hope the pleasure is not purely selfish, I trust it is partly derived from the consciousness that my friend's character is of a higher and more steadfast order than I was once perfectly aware of. Few girls would have done as you have done—would have beheld the glare and glitter and dazzling display of London with dispositions so unchanged, hearts so uncontaminated. I see no affectation in your letter, no trifling, no frivolous contempt of pain, and weak admiration of showy persons and things.... Continue to spare a corner of your warm affectionate heart for your true and grateful friend.

But Ellen's mind, her intellectual advancement must still be seen to, and when she wrote to Charlotte asking her for a list of books to read, the instructress and moralist is altogether in the ascendant, and 'the judicious and able friend' recommends 'Milton, Shakespeare, Thomson, Goldsmith, Scott, Byron, Campbell, Wordsworth and Southey.'

Now don't be startled [she writes] at the names of Shakespeare and Byron. Both these were great men, and their works are like them. You know how to choose the good and avoid the evil; the finest passages are always the purest, and the bad are invariably revolting. Omit the comedies of Shakespeare, and the *Don Juan*, perhaps the *Cain* of Byron ... read the rest fearlessly: that must indeed be a depraved mind which can gather evil from *Henry VIII*, *Richard III*, from *Macbeth*, and *Hamlet*, and *Julius Caesar*. In fiction read Scott alone: all novels after his are worthless. For biography, read Johnson's *Lives of the Poets*, Boswell's *Life of Johnson*, Southey's *Life of Nelson*, etc., etc. For divinity your brother Henry will advise you.

This list is interesting, as showing how large a province in Charlotte's mind was occupied by poetry; poetry to her taste, though she was a most indifferent muse when she turned her hand to it herself, was the highest form of literary expression, to an appreciation of which, if judiciously guided, Ellen might attain. The list appears to have been enough to last her friend for her lifetime, for literature is hardly mentioned again in these letters. For a brief space before the Parliamentary election of 1835 Charlotte tried to kindle Ellen's interest in politics with dithyrambic outbursts.

The Election! The Election! [she writes] that cry has rung even amongst our lonely hills like the blast of a trumpet. How has it roused the populous neighbourhood of Birstall? Under what banner have your brothers ranged themselves? The Blue or the Yellow? Use your influence with them, entreat them, if it be necessary, on your knees to stand by their *country* and religion in this day of danger.

But that passes too, and the personal relation, ripening into passion, dethrones all other topics. So far from the schoolgirl *schwärm* cooling down into the mere warmth of friendship or the chill of indifference, it begins to flame, reducing the governess and the politician to ashes, and the growing human adoration feeds itself with the fuel of religious aspirations.

I am at this moment [wrote Charlotte, now in her twenty-first year] trembling all over with excitement after reading your note: it is what I never received before—it is the unrestrained pouring out of a warm, gentle, generous heart, it contains sentiments unrestrained by human motives, prompted by the pure God himself, it expresses a noble sympathy which I *do* not, *cannot* describe. Ellen, Religion has indeed elevated your character. I *do* wish to be better than I am, I pray fervently to be made so. I have stings of conscience—visitings of remorse—glimpses of Holy, inexpressible things, which formerly I used to be a stranger to.... This very night I will pray as you wish me. May the Almighty hear me compassionately! and I humbly trust He will—for you will strengthen my polluted petition with your own pure requests.... If you love me, *do, do* come on Friday. I shall watch and wait for you, and if you disappoint me, I shall weep....

Again she writes:

At such times in such moods as these, Ellen, it is my nature to seek repose in some calm, tranquil idea, and I have now summoned up your image to give me rest. There you sit, upright and still in your black dress and white scarf, your pale marble-like face, looking so serene and kind—just like reality. I wish you would speak to me. It is from religion you derive your chief charm, and may its influence always preserve you as pure, as unassuming, and as benevolent in thought and deed as you are now. What am I compared to you? I feel my own utter worthlessness as I make the comparison. I am a very coarse, commonplace wretch, Ellen.... Give my love to both your sisters. The bonnet is too handsome for me. I dare write no more.

The flame of this furnace compounded of human passion and the religious ecstasies and questionings which it kindled, mounts higher and licks the skies. She writes:

My Darling, if I were like you, I should have to face Zionward, though prejudice and error might occasionally fling a mist over the glorious vision before me ... but *I am not like you*. If you knew my thoughts, the dreams that absorb me, the fiery imagination that at times eats me up, and makes me feel society as it is, wretchedly insipid, you would pity and I daresay despise me. But I know the treasures of the Bible, and love and adore them. I can see the Well of Life in all its clearness and brightness, but when I stoop down to drink of the pure waters they fly from my lips as if I were Tantalus....

Again she writes:

Ellen, I wish I could live with you always. I begin to cling to you more fondly than ever I did. If we had but a cottage and a competency of our own, I do think we might live and love on till *Death* without being dependent on any third person for happiness....

Then there was a fear of Ellen leaving the neighbourhood of the school where Charlotte was now a teacher, and, crying out against this inscrutable fatality, she asks:

Why are we to be divided? Surely, Ellen, it must be because we are in danger of loving each other too well, of losing sight of the *Creator* in idolatry of the *creature*. At first I could not say 'Thy Will be done.' I felt rebellious, but I knew it was wrong to feel so. Being left a moment alone this morning, I prayed fervently to be enabled to resign myself to *every* decree of God's Will, though it should be dealt forth with a far severer hand than the present disappointment.

This love of the creature obscuring the Creator is in Charlotte's novels her strongest expression of human love. Jane Eyre, for instance, speaks of Rochester in precisely these terms: 'I could not in these days see God for his creature of whom I had made an idol.' In *Villete*, Lucy Snowe speaks of her love for Dr. John in the same way. Then this temporary obstacle passes, there is a plan of Ellen's coming to stay at Haworth, and Charlotte writes:

If I could always live with you, if your lips and mine could at the same time drink the same draught at the same fountain of mercy, I hope, I trust, I might one day become better, far better than my evil wandering thoughts, my corrupt heart, cold to the spirit and warm to the flesh, will now permit me to be.

Her heart was a 'hot-bed for sinful thoughts,' but Ellen's notes were 'meat and drink' to her. But she was not good enough for Ellen. Ellen must be kept 'from the contamination of too intimate society.'

Now much comment has been expended on this fervency of religious emotionalism, which has been represented as a morbid but temporary hysterical affection: biographers, Mrs. Gaskell among them, slightly bewildered at it, have preferred largely to suppress it as being a disturbing and inharmonious feature in their preconceived portrait of Charlotte. Certainly nothing can be more unlike any subsequent aspect of her religious views than this Maenad mood; glaring, indeed, is the contrast between this fervour of religion and the piety, almost prim and proper (though heart-felt and sincere) and void of all spark of excitement, which is so abundantly in evidence in her other letters, while here she is dancing like David before the Ark in girded ecstasy, instead of worshipping God in a Sunday bonnet. But it does not seem impossible to find a reconcilement between the two, and the key to it, I think, is this. Never again did she give her heart to anyone, man or woman, in joy and exaltation, and it was her human adoration for Ellen that kindled in her this religious emotionalism. Ellen was at the bottom of it. It was her desire to make herself worthy of her friend that caused Charlotte to lament her own deficiencies in a manner otherwise alien to her, and pray that they should pass away from her; it was human love that inspired those spiritual aspirations, and lit them with its own passion for the perfect. They were in no sense whatever trumped-up or insincere, they flowed out as spontaneously as did the water when Moses struck the rock; but the source of them and their inspiration was Ellen. Charlotte is even consciously aware of this, for in a later letter she practically admits it, and puts her two passions in their relatively correct places:

In writing at this moment, [she says] I feel an intense disgust at the idea of using a single phrase that sounds like religious cant. I abhor myself, I despise myself, if the doctrine of Calvin be true, I am already an outcast. You cannot imagine how hard, rebellious and intractable all my feelings are. When I begin to study on the subject, I almost grow blasphemous and atheistical in my sentiments. Don't desert me, don't be horrified at me, you know what I am. I wish I could see you, my darling; I have lavished the very warmest affection of a very hot tenacious heart upon you—if you grow cold, it is over.

In the light of such passages as these, it is impossible to doubt the source of her outbreaks of religious fervour. It was not primarily the Throne of Grace before which she made her adoration but before Ellen—Ellen was her Rock of Ages. Never again did she attain to such soaring in her relations with any human being, for the strong and most unhappy attachment to M. Héger, as we shall see, so far from giving her that expansion of wing, rendered her merely abject, and she besought him of his clemency just to write her a few words, crumbs from his table on which she could feed. Nor was there such emotional fervour in her marriage, happy though its briefness was, bringing her the content which she had missed all her life, and drying up that well-spring of bitterness in her temperament which had long caused her to be incapable of enjoyment. Sexless though this passion for Ellen was, it was inspired by the authentic ecstasy of love.

For four years this intense attachment continued to blaze, but in 1838, when Charlotte was twenty-two, there comes just a hint of covert reproach, usual with the more domineering and more dominant lover who finds the adorable one too little responsive; for Ellen, though devoted to Charlotte, kept her head, was calm and sensible, and did not indulge in rhapsodies. Charlotte at that time had gone back to Miss Wooler's school, pupil no longer but a mistress. She became thoroughly unhappy, left rather suddenly, and wrote from

Haworth to tell her friend why:

> I stayed as long as I was able, and at length I neither could nor dared stay any longer. My health and spirits had utterly failed me, and the medical man whom I consulted enjoined me, if I valued my life, to go home.... A calm and even mind like yours, Ellen, cannot conceive the feelings of the shattered wretch who is now writing to you, when after weeks of mental and bodily anguish, not to be described, something like rest and tranquillity began to dawn again.... I fear from what you say that I cannot rationally entertain hopes of seeing you before winter. For your own sake I am glad of it.

Next year, when Charlotte was close on twenty-three, a surprising development occurred, and one quite unforeshadowed in her correspondence. Henry Nussey, Ellen's brother, an amiable and blameless young clergyman, wrote her a letter proposing marriage. She refused him, and wrote to tell Ellen, who was certainly privy to her brother's intention, what she had done. 'There were,' she said, 'in this proposal some things which might have proved a strong temptation. I thought if I were to marry Henry Nussey, his sister could live with me, and how happy I should be.' Propinquity to a sister-in-law seems rather an unusual consideration in favour of matrimony, and has probably never before, or since, been so frankly acknowledged.

For more than seven years this eager devotion to her friend, though expressed in less exuberant language, continued without abatement, and Charlotte was unable to see any speck in her perfection, except that of her comparative irresponsiveness. Then, coincident with and possibly in consequence of her wretched experience at Brussels, where she fell in love with M. Héger, the flame of it expired, and though to the end of her life the friendship remained deep and stable, there was no more excitement, religious or otherwise, in it, and she wrote to Ellen, 'In the name of Common Sense, no more lovers' quarrels!' She began to see flaws in the peerless crystal; the governess rose ascendant over the lover, and Charlotte warned her of the 'danger of continued prosperity, which might develop too much a certain germ of ambition latent in your character. I saw this little germ putting out green shoots when I was staying with you at Hathersage.' She warned her also against vanity and the perishable nature of personal attractiveness, when Ellen was pleased with a new white dress which set off her comeliness. Then Miss Ringrose became a fellow-worshipper at Ellen's shrine, and wrote to Charlotte with enthusiastic admiration of their mutual friend. Upon which Charlotte again felt it laid upon her to be good for Ellen, and in her most emphatic governess style told her that Miss Ringrose's feelings for her were 'half truth, half illusion. No human being could altogether be what she supposes you to be.' She also said that the notion of her being jealous of the new friend was altogether too ludicrous.

The splendours had faded, no longer did the bugle blow a royal salute, she could dissect with a calm hand what had dazzled her. 'Ellen,' she wrote, 'is a calm, steady girl, not brilliant, but good and true. She suits me and has always suited me well.' But now her defects had hardened into qualities, and there was no longer the slightest chance of Ellen's acquiring a taste for poetry, 'for she is without romance. If she attempts to read poetry or poetic prose aloud, I am irritated and deprive her of the book. If she talks of it, I stop my ears: but she is good, she is true, she is faithful, and I love her.'

The long-continued ardour of this attachment which, when it cooled down, subsided into a firm and deep friendship, is of great importance in arriving at any true view of Charlotte's inner nature, especially when we consider her often-expressed dislike of men as a sex. She thought them coarse, selfish, and conceited. Charles Lamb's devotion to his sister, for example, she pronounced to be 'an instance of abnegation of self, scarcely, I think, to be paralleled in the annals of the coarser sex.' Women, she believed, were infinitely finer, and it was a woman's portion to be married 'to a mate who generically is inferior to herself in their [sic] aim in making themselves agreeable.' She warned Ellen against falling in love, and counselled her thus about marriage:

After that ceremony is over and after you have had some months to settle down and to get accustomed to the creature you have taken for your worse half, you will probably make a most affectionate and happy wife.

She was all for a woman leading her own life, violently protesting against the idea that she was always on the look out for a husband.

I know [she wrote] that if women wish to escape the stigma of husband-seeking, they must act and look like marble or clay—cold, expressionless, bloodless, for every appearance of feeling, of joy, sorrow, friendliness, antipathy, admiration, disgust are all alike construed by the world into the attempt to hook a husband. Never mind! Well-meaning women have their own conscience to comfort them after all. Do not therefore be too much afraid of showing yourself as you are, affectionate, and good-hearted: do not too harshly repress sentiment and feelings excellent in themselves, because you fear that some puppy may fancy that you are letting them come out to fascinate him: do not condemn yourself to live only by halves, because if you showed too much animation some pragmatical thing in breeches might take it into his pate to imagine that you designed to dedicate your life to his inanity.

There is a very robust contempt for men in general in this spirited passage, and similar volleys of disdain are exceedingly common in her letters. Psycho-analytical commentators have interpreted this to mean that Charlotte was the victim of sex-obsession, that she was longing to get a husband, and, being unable to do so, vented her spite against the sex in these diatribes. But, while it is perfectly true that when she did marry she found the happiness that she had missed all her life, such a conclusion is altogether at variance with the facts. For three other men, Henry Nussey being the first, wanted to marry her and she refused them. It is more reasonable, in view of this passionate affection of hers for Ellen Nussey, to conclude that for a considerable period of her life her emotional reactions were towards women rather than men.

CHAPTER V

Charlotte left Miss Wooler's when she was sixteen and returned to Haworth, where she remained for the next three years. She undertook the education of her two sisters, and with her brother Branwell continued to pour out that torrent of prose works with occasional poems, which had been interrupted during her schooldays. But now, as if the waters had been accumulating in a reservoir, they flowed in absolutely unparalleled volume. She wrote most of them under pseudonyms, and we see that the Duke of Wellington was still her demigod, for their authorship is chiefly attributed to Lord Charles Albert Florian Wellesley, and that gifted creature in 1833 alone wrote: *Arthuriana: or Odds and Ends: Being a Miscellaneous Collection of Pieces in Prose and Verse*; *The Secret and Lily Hart* (two tales); *Visits in Verdopolis* (two volumes); *The Green Dwarf: A Tale of the Perfect Tense*; and in 1834, *My Angria and the Angrians*; *A Leaf from an Unopened Volume*; *Corner Dishes: Being a Small Collection of Trifles in Prose and Verse*; *High Life in Verdopolis*; and *The Spell, an Extravaganza*. In addition to these there is *The Foundling: A Tale of our Own Times,* by Captain Tree (1833); *Richard Cœur de Lion and Blondel*, by Charlotte Brontë (1833); and *The Scrap Book: A Mingling of Many Things*, by Charlotte Brontë, and compiled by Lord C. A. F. Wellesley.

Of this library of manuscript *The Spell* has been lately published by the Oxford University Press. It is the first tale in a very curious volume of Charlotte's manuscripts in the British Museum, and with it are bound up *High Life in Verdopolis*, mentioned above, and *The Scrap Book*. The binding is French, the title on the cover is *Manuscrits de Miss Charlotte Brontë* (*Currer Bell*), and the book was purchased in the year 1892 in a second-hand bookshop in Brussels. What the previous history of it was is quite unknown. The suggestion has been made that Charlotte, when at the *pensionnat* in Brussels, gave these manuscripts to M. Héger, or left them behind when she went back to England, and that he, when she became famous, had them bound. There is no evidence to support the theory, but it is certainly a reasonable one.

The Spell, therefore, is now accessible to readers, and we have in it a solid sample of the Angrian-Saga and of Charlotte's style in this year 1834, when she was eighteen. The story is highly sensational, the plot utterly mystifying, and the writing of the purplest. It was worth printing as a curiosity, but solely because it was Charlotte Brontë who wrote it. Intrinsic merit cannot be claimed for it, nor is there in it any foreshadowing of that supreme talent which was so soon to develop in her. What is interesting is the devouring rage for literary expression that consumed her, and the enormous quantity of narrative which poured from her rather than its quality.

Branwell in the same period, chiefly under the pseudonym of Captain John Flower, M.P., or the Right Honourable John Baron Flower, produced *Real Life in Verdopolis*; *The Politics of Verdopolis*; *The Pirate*; *Thermopylæ* (a poem); *And the Weary are at Rest*; *The Wool is Rising*, an Angrian adventure; *Ode to the Pole Star*, and other poems; and *The Life of Field-Marshal the Right Honourable Alexander Percy, Earl of Northangerland* (two volumes).

The brain reels with the thought of Charlotte's activities during these years. She was giving lessons to her younger sisters, she was teaching in the Sunday school, she was entertaining district visitors to tea, she was pouring out those oceans of literary work, she was sewing for hours every day under the eye of Aunt Branwell. When everything sewable for the use of the Parsonage and its inmates had been sewed, the industry of her nieces was devoted to sewings for the needy of the parish, and from after the midday dinner at half-past one till tea-time all needles were busy. Sewing, according to that admirable letter-writer, Miss Mary Taylor, who came to stay at Haworth during those years, was, in Aunt Branwell's opinion, good for the sewers as well as the sewed for; it was an essential part of woman's work in the world, and she presided at these gatherings in her large mob cap of the period with auburn curls attached to it, and took her snuff, and anticipating the refinements of America she would not allow the word 'spit' to be used in her presence. When tea came in, sewing was finished for the day, and after Mr. Brontë had read prayers to the household at eight, she went up to her bedroom in her pattens and was seen no more till breakfast-time next morning. An hour later Mr. Brontë retired for the night, winding the clock on the stairs as he passed, and called out, 'Don't sit up late, girls!' And then the real day, the living exciting part of the day began, and Lord Charles Albert Florian Wellesley was free, for till then there had not been a moment's leisure, and he wrote like mad.

Somehow or other there was squeezed in the time for drawing lessons, and the time for sketching and painting between the visits of Mr. William Robinson of Leeds, a pupil of Sir Thomas Lawrence and of the delirious Swiss artist Fuseli, who painted nightmares with so sure a hand. The whole family had lessons at the inclusive fee of two guineas a visit, and it is legitimate to trace, in the account of the pictures which Jane Eyre showed Mr. Rochester, some influence of the pupil of Fuseli. These, it may be remembered, comprised one of a cormorant sitting on the mast of a ship sunk in a rough sea and holding a bracelet in its beak, which it had taken from the arm of a drowned corpse that was visible through the water. But Mr. William Robinson's morals, whatever his skill as an artist, were not all they should be. Mrs. Gaskell alludes with such discretion to some indiscretion on Mr. Robinson's part which caused Mr. Brontë to decide that he should teach his daughters no longer, that even the hardiest biographers have not ventured to tell us what it was.

As the result of this tuition and the artistic promise shown by Branwell at the age of eighteen, it was decided that he should adopt art as his career, and go up to London in order to study at the Art Schools of the Royal Academy. There is no evidence to show that he ever went, though he wrote to the Secretary asking particulars about admission, and it is probable that the idea was abandoned. He then tried to turn to account his literary gifts, and wrote some truly amazing letters to the editor of *Blackwood's Magazine,* and, somewhat in the style of Mr. Micawber, told him that he was ready to write for him, and positively challenged him to take him as a regular contributor either in prose or verse, enclosing a specimen poem and promising to send prose if desired, on any subject that Mr. Robert Blackwood might select. He enjoined him not to condemn him unheard; he cautioned him not to behave like a commonplace person and miss such an opportunity; he reminded him that 'you have lost an able writer in James Hogg, and God grant you may get one in Patrick Branwell Brontë.' But Mr. Blackwood preferred to be commonplace, though Branwell gave him four opportunities of showing a finer quality. Somewhere about this time he painted a portrait group of his three sisters, which Mrs. Gaskell saw when she stayed with Charlotte at Haworth: Emily and Anne were linked together; Charlotte stood apart on the right side of a column which nearly bisects the picture. Mrs. Gaskell's verdict on it was that though it possessed little artistic merit, the portrait of Charlotte was strikingly like her, and that it was reasonable to suppose that those of the other two sisters were equally faithful. Her description of this picture answers so closely to the picture by Branwell now in the National Gallery, that it is difficult to suppose that it was not this which she saw. On the other hand, Mr. Shorter tells us that after Mr. Brontë's death in 1861, Mr. Nicholls took this picture to Ireland with him, and destroyed it, keeping only the figure of Emily, which he considered to be like her. This also is now in the National Portrait Gallery, but there is a question whether it does not represent Anne. The only explanation of the confusion seems to be that Branwell painted two portrait groups of his sisters, of which Mr. Nicholls destroyed one.

In these three years between Charlotte's leaving Miss Wooler's school and returning there again as teacher, we still lack any glimpse beyond the most misty of Emily. In person she was taller than the others, she had beauty of feature, and Ellen Nussey, on her visits to the Parsonage, was evidently very much struck with her. But she describes her in a way that does not much help us to realise her, for though she was keenly aware that 'there was depth and power in her nature,' that 'one of her rare expressive looks was something to remember through life,' such observations however appreciative are mere generalities, and we still have to imagine Emily for ourselves, and clearly what impressed Ellen most was Emily's impenetrable reserve. But it is something to be told that when she was out on the moors she was a different person, brimful of glee and the joy of life, absorbed in the affairs of tadpoles in a pool; that she could poke fun at Charlotte, who was terrified of cows, by luring her into a field where those fierce animals were grazing. Ellen also tells us that Anne was her inseparable companion, and that her piano-playing was really remarkable. Instructive too is the story that one day when Charlotte was unwell, Emily was sent out a walk with Ellen. This was a hazardous experiment, for Emily was capable of remaining completely silent for indefinite periods, and so on their return Charlotte naturally asked how her sister had behaved. This casual question has been taken up, like a challenge, by one accomplished Emily-ite, who triumphantly assures us that Emily had behaved well; 'she had shown her true self, her noble energetic truthful soul.' But Charlotte only wanted to know if Emily had spoken at all during the walk, and whether she had is not recorded. Anne finally remains mysterious, not because she was enigmatical, but because her only characteristics were gentleness and piety, and from the dim, cool shade of these excellences she never really emerges.

It is now that a side of Charlotte, ever afterwards characteristic of her, definitely shows itself, and she begins to take command of the family ship and its destinies, to set its sails and to direct its course. Mr. Brontë's income was £200 a year, Aunt Branwell had £50 a year, and it was evident to Charlotte's intensely practical mind that she and her sisters must do something to earn money. Branwell, in this year 1835, according to plan, was to become a pupil at the Academy Art Schools in London, and would be an additional drain on the family finances, and she must make her living, or, at any rate, not be an expense. Teaching offered the best if not the only opening, and for the next nine years she devoted her energies towards making a career for herself and her sisters in this direction, with the idea of eventually setting up a school for girls. Experience was the first thing needed, and now at the age of nineteen she became a teacher at Miss Wooler's school where, three years before, she had been a pupil. She had already received two offers for a post as private governess in a family, but she naturally preferred to go to Miss Wooler, who was already a friend; besides, Mary Taylor and Ellen Nussey, with whom the passionate friendship was now at its height, both lived within a few miles of Roe Head. Then there were Emily and Anne to be thought of, for she was acting for them too, and with a view to fitting Emily for the same profession as herself, she arranged that she should accompany her to Roe Head as a pupil and complete her education. Anne at present was only fifteen, and she would continue her studies at home; her turn would come later.

Charlotte looked forward to the adventure. 'My lines,' she wrote to her friend, 'are fallen in pleasant places,' and it was a consolation to her and Emily that they would be together. So in July the two sisters, teacher and pupil, went to Miss Wooler's, but Anne's turn came sooner than anyone had expected. Emily, unconsoled, pined for Haworth and the moors; she became ill from homesickness, and Charlotte believed that her life was in danger. In a memoir she wrote after Emily's death, for a selection of her poems, she says:

I felt in my heart she would die, if she did not go home, and with this conviction obtained her recall. She had only been three months at school, and it was some years before the experiment of sending her from home was again ventured on.

This memoir contains several curious errors in actual fact. Charlotte states in it that Emily was in her sixteenth year when she went to Roe Head: she was really in her eighteenth year. Odder is the inaccuracy that Emily, so acute was her nostalgia, causing great emaciation and even danger to life, never left Haworth again for some years: the experiment was too risky. For, as a matter of fact, within a year from the time that Charlotte 'obtained her recall,' Emily, with no kind Miss Wooler in charge and no sister to remind her of home, was a teacher in Miss Patchett's school at Law Hill, Southorran, near Halifax. Emily's life there, Charlotte told Ellen, was an intolerable slavery—she was at work from six in the morning till eleven at night; and yet in the memoir quoted above, Charlotte seems to have forgotten that Emily had left Haworth again till after some years had passed, or, in other words, till she took her to Brussels, as the same memoir states. Directly on Emily's recall from Roe Head, Anne was sent for to take her place as pupil in Miss Wooler's school, and there she remained, completing her education, for two years.

The scheme of sending Branwell to study at the Art Schools of the Royal Academy in London had been given up, and though getting on for twenty years old, he was still at home, keen, apparently, on his painting and a good scholar in Latin, but with no settled occupation of any sort. Mrs. Gaskell tells us that, at this time, 'the young man seemed to have his fate in his own hands. He was full of noble impulses as well as extraordinary gifts.' As an instance of his literary ability, she speaks of a fragment of his prose which she had seen.

'The actors in it are drawn with much of the grace of characteristic portrait-painting in perfectly pure and simple language which distinguishes so many of Addison's papers in the *Spectator*.' This is high praise as coming from one of so delicate a literary judgment, and must be received with all respect. He had charm, it would appear, ability and ambition, but he was without ballast and lacked the discipline through which alone ambition can be fulfilled. He was still considered the genius of the family—he had wit, a brilliant tongue and the vanity to demand an audience; and it is hardly to be wondered at that on long winter evenings, with Aunt Branwell immured in her bedroom, and his father in his study, with Charlotte and Anne away, with Emily silent as the grave, he sought the more congenial atmosphere of the bar at the 'Black Bull,' where he would find talk and laughter and an atmosphere of good fellowship. Sometimes a commercial traveller or such would be putting up there for the night, and the landlord told him of this brilliant young fellow at the Parsonage near by, who would certainly come down and have a chat with him over a glass or two of whisky-toddy to pass the hour before bedtime. So Branwell appeared, and perhaps he exhibited for the general astonishment a remarkable faculty he had of writing simultaneously with his right hand and his left two different letters. At other times there would be farmers from the country round dropping in on market-day before they set off again across the hills to scattered homesteads, and there was just such talk and companionship as must have been Branwell's father's before he left County Down for Cambridge.

Then, again, the 'Black Bull' was the headquarters of a village club, 'The Lodge of the Three Graces,' faintly masonic in title, of which John Brown, the sexton of the church, at whose house in later days lodged more than one curate of Haworth, was Master, and Branwell was Secretary. What the official proceedings were or what sort of entries the Secretary made in the book of minutes, we have no idea, but, as we shall find excellent reason to believe, the proceedings were punctuated with bawdy talk and whisky-toddy. Considering what the mode of life was at the Parsonage, it is really little wonder that a young man, eminently 'clubbable,' fond of talk and talking with extreme brilliance, should have frequented the 'Black Bull.'

In the holidays they were again all together, and though teaching was the destiny that Charlotte was weaving for herself and her sisters, literary ambitions, now taking second place, were not entirely extinguished. Poetry was ascendant over prose, and in the Christmas holidays of 1836-1837 she wrote, in that microscopic hand, twenty-six pages of verse. She finished one of these poems, *We Wove a Web in Childhood*, on December 19, and then conceived the daring project of writing to Robert Southey, the Poet Laureate, enclosing a specimen of her own verse (probably this), and asking him for his opinion on it. We may guess that this was a concerted plan between her and

Branwell to interest the eminent in their compositions, for Branwell gave the editor of *Blackwood's Magazine* another chance, telling him that he had written a very lengthy and remarkable composition in prose which he was ready to bring up to Edinburgh to show him. He rated him for his silence, asking if it were prejudice which actuated it, and bidding him be a man, sir! He wrote also to William Wordsworth, who succeeded Southey in the Laureateship, enclosing, like Charlotte, a poem of his, which he described as the

Prefatory Scene of a much longer subject, in which I have striven to develop strong passions and weak principles struggling with a high imagination and acute feelings, till, as youth hardens towards age, evil deeds and short enjoyments end in mental misery and bodily ruin....

This is interesting, for the poor wretch was even now playing in his own person the prefatory scene of just such a tragic career.

Wordsworth appears not to have answered this letter, though he kept it, but eventually there came to Charlotte, long after she had gone back to Miss Wooler's after the Christmas holidays, a reply from the Laureate. It was a kind, a long and a careful letter, but it was very far from being encouraging. He told her she had the faculty of verse, but reminded her that this was no rare gift: he felt bound when any young aspirant asked him for his advice about adopting literature as a profession, to caution him 'against taking so perilous a course.' Then came passages which surely laid an icy finger on her enthusiasm.

The day-dreams in which you habitually indulge are likely to induce a distempered state of mind.... Literature cannot be the business for a woman's life, and it ought not to be. The more she is engaged in her proper duties, the less leisure she will have for it, even as an accomplishment and a recreation.... However ill what has been said may accord with your present views and temper, the longer you live the more reasonable it will appear to you....

This letter was, in fact, quite as discouraging as Wordsworth's silence to Branwell, and its discouragement was, for the present, effective. Charlotte wrote back saying, 'I trust I shall never more feel ambitious to see my name in print: if the wish should rise, I'll look at Southey's letter and suppress it.' She put away all literary ambition, and devoted her energies to the task of gaining such experience in teaching for herself and her sisters as should qualify them for the educational career which she had chosen for them all.

Southey lived long enough to see *Jane Eyre* take the world by storm and to know (if such information ever reached him) that the author of that book and of *Shirley* was the young lady to whom he had written that literature neither could nor ought to be the business of a woman's life. But it must be remembered that Charlotte had sent to him (as had Branwell to Wordsworth) a specimen of her poetry, and, from what we know of it, he was as certainly right to discourage her muse as was Wordsworth in finding nothing to say to Branwell, for neither of them had any real gift for poetry at all. But it was perhaps odd that neither he nor Wordsworth perceived of what admirable prose (though that was not submitted to their judgment) their correspondents were capable. Both of them, when they were not being literary, wrote fine and apt English, rhythmical and dignified, with that indefinable verbal inevitability which is the hall-mark of the writer. Here, for instance, is a paragraph from Branwell's letter to Wordsworth:

Do pardon me, sir, that I have ventured to come before one whose work I have most loved in our literature, and who most has been with me a divinity of the mind, laying before him one of my writings, and asking of him a judgment of its contents. I must come before someone from whose sentence there is no appeal, and such a one is he who has developed the theory of poetry as well as its practice, and both in such a way as to claim a place in the memory of a thousand years to come.

Any boy who at the age of nineteen could write that, had already a good command of his material; equally excellent, though by no means superior, and with a curious resemblance in rhythm and construction is the following from Charlotte's letter to Southey. Her grip on words was already firm, and, when she was not trying to be literary or to write poetry, she had nothing to learn.

At the first perusal of your letter I felt only shame and regret that I had ever ventured to trouble you with my crude rhapsody: I felt a painful heat rise to my face when I thought of the quires of paper I had covered with what once gave me so much delight, but which now was only a source of confusion; but after I had thought a little and read it again and again the prospect seemed to clear.

But the oracle had spoken, and in obedience to it she entirely dismissed her dreams of Parnassus, and continued at Dewsbury Moor, where Miss Wooler had moved her school from Roe Head. Emily had spent six months as a teacher in Miss Patchett's school near Halifax, pursuing the same object, but her health had broken down and she had returned to Haworth and its moors and its liberties, away from which she seemed to lose all health and happiness. Anne was still with Charlotte as a pupil at Miss Wooler's, but just before the Christmas holidays of 1837 she began to suffer from coughs and pains which put Charlotte in mind of the illness of her two elder sisters at Cowan Bridge, and she thought these were symptoms of consumption. All allowance must be made for her, for she was overwrought and hysterical, and in a panic she went to Miss Wooler and, in what must have been a horrid scene, flew, as she confessed, 'into a regular passion,' which she considered perfectly justified, and told her that Anne was extremely ill and that Miss Wooler was quite indifferent to the danger. Miss Wooler was very much hurt at this monstrous accusation and wrote to Mr. Brontë, who, though he realised that Charlotte had been unreasonable, settled that they should both leave Dewsbury Moor and come home.

Miss Wooler, who had always shown the most motherly kindness and consideration to Charlotte, had a tearful scene of reconciliation with her before they went. Charlotte wrote to Ellen pouring scorn on the poor lady's tears, but allowing that 'in spite of her cold repulsive manners she had a considerable regard for me.' She seems not to have realised that before. She went back after the Christmas holidays for another term at Miss Wooler's, Anne and Emily and Branwell all remaining at home; but now she had a nervous breakdown, and returned in the early summer of 1838 to Haworth, where the whole family remained for a year. All her plans and ambitions for herself and her sisters had come to nothing as yet. Emily first, then Anne, and finally she herself had been obliged, for reasons of health, to give up the education and the experience in teaching which she had arranged with a view to their career: the oracles had been dumb or deeply discouraging when consulted about her poems and Branwell's, and there was nothing whatever ahead. Never throughout her life was she optimistic; she expected little, as she told Mrs. Gaskell in after years, and was always prepared for disappointment, but no amount of disappointment, however embittering, caused her to relax her efforts in securing anything on which she had set her heart and which she believed was within attainment.

In the spring of 1839 Branwell, in pursuance of Art, left Haworth and the conviviality of the 'Lodge of the Three Graces' and took a studio at Bradford. His departure is perhaps commemorated in Emily's poem *Absence*, dated April 19, 1839.

One is absent, and for one

Cheerless, chill is our hearthstone;

One is absent, and for him

Cheeks are pale and eyes are dim.

It is usually stated that this refers to Anne, who had just gone out as governess to Mrs. Ingham: the gender of the pronoun, however, is hard to explain. At Bradford he painted a few portraits, but seems to have spent most of his time in the society of local artists and at the bars of hotels, and after a few months his father stopped supplies, and recalled him to Haworth. Much has been made of this incident: vivid embroideries have been stitched over it, and we learn from the Brontë-Saga that 'he disappeared from Bradford heavily in debt and was lost to sight until, unnerved, a drunkard and an opium eater, he came back home.' This lurid picture, however, has no shadow of foundation in fact. He never disappeared at all, except for those hours in which he was travelling back from Bradford to Haworth, nor is there any reason for supposing that he was in debt or that he had yet taken to opium.

In March of the same spring Henry Nussey, as we have already seen, proposed to Charlotte. He was now a curate at Donnington in Sussex, and wrote her a very businesslike letter, saying that after Easter he intended to take pupils into his house, and intimated (as Charlotte told his sister)

that in due time he should want a wife to take care of his pupils, and frankly me to be that wife. Altogether the letter is written without cant or flattery, and in a common-sense style which does credit to his judgment.

Charlotte refused this proposal, though the prospect of having Ellen to live with her was a strong temptation to accept it, on the very sensible grounds that she did not love him, and her letter to him, giving 'a decided negative,' was equally free from cant and flattery and might have been written not by the girl he wanted to marry but by a sententious aunt.

In forming this decision [she told him] I trust I have listened to the dictates of conscience more than those of inclination. I have no personal repugnance to the idea of a union with you, but I feel convinced that mine is not the sort of disposition calculated to form the happiness of a man like you. It has always been my habit to study the character of those among whom I chance to be thrown, and I think I know yours and can imagine what description of woman would suit you for a wife. The character should not be too marked, ardent, and original, her temper should be mild, her piety undoubted, her spirits even and cheerful, and her *personal attractions* sufficient to please your eyes and gratify your just pride.

This letter irresistibly reminds us of Jane Austen at her very best, and it is indeed no wonder that Charlotte in later years was so entirely incapable of appreciating her art, when we find her writing in all seriousness passages that could be cited as admirable examples of Jane Austen's humour. Henry Nussey, we may guess, was no more in love with Charlotte than she with him, for little more than six months elapsed before he wrote to tell her that he had secured another young lady to look after the pupils at Donnington, and again she replied with just such edifying sentiments as Jane Austen gives to Mr. Collins when he retails the counsels of Lady Catherine de Bourgh on the subject of matrimony. In her letter of congratulation she said:

The step no doubt will by many of your friends be considered scarcely as a prudent one, *since* fortune is not amongst the number of the young lady's advantages. For my own part I must confess that I esteem you the more for not hunting after wealth, if there be strength of mind, firmness of principle and sweetness of temper to compensate for the absence of that usually all powerful attraction.... The bread earned by honourable toil is sweeter than the bread of idleness, and mutual love and domestic calm are treasures far preferable to the possessions rust can corrupt and moths consume away.

She continued to encourage and advise him, and wrote again to her ex-suitor shortly before his marriage:

From what you say of your future partner I doubt not she will be one who will help you to get cheerfully through the difficulties of this world and to obtain a permanent rest in the next; at least I hope such may be the case. You do right to conduct the matter with due deliberation, for on the step you are about to take depends the happiness of your whole lifetime.

Charlotte, when she thus refused matrimony as her destiny, had been three-quarters of a year at Haworth, and during this period she seems to have written nothing whatever: Southey's discouragement was evidently potent with her. But Emily all the time was at work, secretly and constantly, on her poems, and Charlotte knew nothing of them. Many of them were concerned with the Gondals, and possibly therefore Anne, but Anne alone, was privy to them. But Emily did not confide them to her elder sister, for when, six years later, Charlotte 'discovered them,' as she tells us in her memoir of her two sisters after their death, she says that she was aware, but no more, that Emily did write poetry, but up to that time she had seen none of it. Earlier, as she tells us, they used to talk to each other about what they were writing, but that habit must already have ceased, since the discovery of Emily's poems gave her her first sight of them. This is rather important, for it goes against the assertion, constantly made by Mrs. Gaskell, that there existed between Emily and Charlotte a deep and intense intimacy. There is no evidence for this. The evidence, in fact, which becomes cumulative, goes to show that Emily and Charlotte were never intimate in any real sense, and the first glimpse we get of that is that during this year at Haworth, while the sisters were together and Emily wrote a considerable number of poems, Charlotte knew nothing of them.

Anne meantime had regained such measure of strength as was ever hers, and in April 1839 she went forth from Haworth again, and for five out of the next six years was a governess. She went first to the family of Mrs. Ingham at Blake Hall where, as Charlotte wrote to Ellen, she was very kindly treated; she added, humorously no doubt, but rather acidly, that owing to Anne's habit of silence she 'seriously apprehends that Mrs. Ingham will sometime conclude that she has a natural impediment of speech.' A month or so later Charlotte obtained a similar situation herself and went as governess to the children of Mrs. John Benson Sidgwick at Stonegappe, a few miles out of Skipton.

Less fortunate than Anne, she appears from her letters to have fallen among fiends. The place, she wrote to Emily, was beautiful, and she tried hard to be happy, but her life was an intolerable slavery. The children were 'the most riotous, perverse, unmanageable cubs ever born,' and she refers to them as 'little devils incarnate.' Mrs. Sidgwick did not know her, and did not want to know her. Her manners were

fussily affable, she talks a great deal but little to the purpose.... She cares nothing in the world about me except to contrive how the greatest possible quantity of labour may be squeezed out of me, and to that end she overwhelms me with oceans of needlework.... I see now more clearly than I have ever done before that a private governess has no existence, is not considered as a living and rational being except as connected with the wearisome duties she has to fulfil.

Mr. Sidgwick was not such a brute as his wife, 'he has less bustling condescension but a far kinder heart.... He never asks me to wipe the children's smutty noses or tie their shoes or fetch their pinafores or get them a chair.' The only pleasant afternoon that she spent at Stonegappe was when he walked with his children and his dog, and Charlotte had orders to 'follow a little behind.' She tells Emily not to show this depiction of hell to her aunt or her father, or they would think 'I am never satisfied wherever I am.' This caution is significant.

After a few weeks the whole family went to stay at Swarcliffe, near Harrogate, a country house belonging to Mrs. Sidgwick's father, and, she writes to Ellen, life was more miserable than ever. Mr. Greenwood had filled his house with guests, who were gay and enjoyed themselves; there was a large family party, 'proud as peacocks and wealthy as jews,' and all the time, as Charlotte bitterly complains, she had a set of 'pampered, spoilt, and turbulent children' to look after. She was in agonies of shyness and in the depth of depression, and to crown all, Mrs. Sidgwick took her to task for her glum demeanour, and she broke down and cried. Then she pulled herself together and reflected that 'Adversity is a good school—the Poor are born to labour, and the Dependent to endure.' She recollected the fable of the Willow and the Oak, and bent to the storm. Mrs. Sidgwick, she allowed, was generally considered an agreeable woman, 'But, oh, Ellen, does this compensate for the absence of every fine feeling, of every gentle and delicate sentiment?'

Now it wrings the heart to picture the woe and the wretchedness of this extremely sensitive, self-conscious girl, whose shyness was such an obsession to her that throughout her life the presence of a stranger would plunge her into gulfs of silent misery, and it warms the heart to think of her indomitable courage in going forth not once only but again and again to take situations which necessarily threw her among strangers, for the sake of contributing to the family finances, and advancing the ambitions which she had determined to accomplish for herself and her sisters. This iron willpower scorned the miseries which were incidental to the working out of its purpose, and though she bitterly complained, and increasingly formed the most censorious conclusions about those who unwittingly incurred them, she never allowed her unhappiness to deter her. Further instances of these characteristic traits in her character, admirable and regrettable, emerge later. But together with her memories of Stonegappe and Swarcliffe she brought away some valuable material for the ruthless caricaturing in *Jane Eyre* of the guests, whose callous gaiety was etching itself in the mind of the silent little governess, and was to be reproduced with ridicule that was indeed ridiculous, in the figures of the smart party, 'Baroness Ingram of Ingram Hall' and the rest, who swept about Mr. Rochester's house, and told the footman 'to cease thy chatter, blockhead,' and took no notice of Jane Eyre.

This wretched experience lasted but for three months, and once more, exhausted and nerve-racked, she returned in July 1839 to Haworth. Here she recovered her spirits and her speech: she was not shy at home, she talked with ease among familiar faces, and within a week or two of her return she received her second proposal of marriage, again from a clerical admirer. There came to spend the day a former curate of Mr. Brontë's, now a vicar. With him Mr. Hodgson brought his own curate, Mr. Bryce, who had lately left Dublin University. Mr. Bryce, Charlotte wrote to Ellen, was a witty, lively young man, lacking in discretion and dignity, but though she saw his faults, she was amused at his originality, and laughed at his jests. Before the evening was over his 'Hibernian flattery' caused her to cool towards him, and off the visitors went having left a pleasant though no permanent impression. A few days afterwards, Charlotte, to her amazement and amusement, received a proposal of marriage from young Mr. Bryce, ardently professing his attachment. Another decided refusal followed. Six months later Mr. Bryce died suddenly, and Charlotte confesses that when she heard of it she felt both shocked and saddened; 'it was no shame to feel so, was it?'

Charlotte remained at Haworth, after leaving Mrs. Sidgwick's house of bondage, for nearly two years before she took another situation as governess, and her letters of the period, sometimes pungent and censorious, sometimes elderly and hortatory, sometimes childlike and brimming with eager enthusiasm and sly ironies, paint her own portrait with a vividness and a fidelity that no biographer can hope to rival, and one is tempted to believe that had she never written anything whatever except letters, she would have won through them a niche in English literature at least as permanent as Horace Walpole's. She infuses her subject, whatever it is, with the intense interest which it had for her, and at the same time enthralls us with a study of herself. We read, for instance, how she and Ellen had made a plan to go together to the seaside. Miss Branwell and Mr. Brontë had given 'a reluctant assent,' and Charlotte's box was packed. Then there was a difficulty about her conveyance, for Haworth's only gig was at Harrogate, and likely to remain there. Mr. Brontë objected to Charlotte's going by coach, and Miss Branwell changed her reluctant assent to the whole scheme for 'decided disapproval,' and the visit was abandoned. But then Ellen descended on Haworth with a carriage lent her for the occasion, and like Perseus, rescued Andromeda. Charlotte wept with emotion when, now for the first time, she saw the sea, and they had a marvellous holiday together. She left her spectacles behind, and on her return to Haworth could neither read, write, nor draw with any comfort, but hoped that the landlady of their lodgings would not refuse to give them up. Another pair of spectacles, apparently, was not to be thought of. Trivial as all this is, the intensity of the experience to her renders it enthralling, and it is because it is about a young lady of twenty-three who lived in a remote parsonage, and tells us with inimitable vividness about herself, and not in the least because that young lady a few years afterwards wrote *Jane Eyre*, that we are absorbed in what she has to say. Almost next day she wrote to Henry Nussey, in a letter already quoted, as if she was his guardian aunt, commending him for not seeking a wealthy wife; but we find these edifications, which show the serious side of her character, hardly more informative than the news that Tabby had become so lame that she left the Parsonage and had gone to live with her sister.

In the meantime Emily and I [she writes] are sufficiently busy as you may suppose: I manage the ironing and keep the rooms clean, Emily does the baking and attends to the kitchen. We are such odd animals that we prefer this mode of contrivance to having a new face amongst us.... Human feelings are queer things. I am much happier black-leading the stoves, making the beds, and sweeping the floor at home than I should be living like a fine lady anywhere else.

In leisure from housework she wrote, over the signature of Charles Townsend, a story in three books called *Caroline Vernon*, and another story, unnamed, with the same signature. Southey's discouragement of poetry apparently still was potent, but the instinct for composition of some sort was irresistible.

CHAPTER VI

In the familiar surroundings of home, with no strange faces to reduce her to silence and aloof discomfort, and no immediate prospect of going out again on educational exiles, Charlotte blossomed into a gaiety and sense of fun that never again revisited her, and we rapturously read in her letters the account of the loves of the Reverend William Weightman, Mr. Brontë's curate. Certainly there enters into it a very decent allowance of acidity and of ridicule, but it is mixed with kindliness and genuine laughter. It was not long before curates—the genus 'Curate'—became to her a target for peculiarly malicious arrows. She could see no good in them; 'they were a self-seeking, vain, empty race,' and in *Shirley* she made them the butt of immortal and libellous satire, designed to give pain. Later yet, by a providential irony of kindlier humour than hers, it was with one of Mr. Brontë's curates of whom she had hitherto entertained the gloomiest opinions, that she found, in marriage, the few months of real happiness which she had missed all her life.

At present the Rev. William Weightman concerns us. He was a graduate of Durham University, he was gay and handsome and an incorrigible flirt; his brief history must be detached from the main narrative. Charlotte's letters are full of him: she dubbed him, owing to an effeminacy of manner and appearance, Miss Celia Amelia, and all the young ladies of the neighbourhood were the objects of his passion and fell victims to his invincible charms. There was Sarah Sugden, there was Caroline Dury, and there was Agnes Walton, of whom Charlotte painted a portrait to remind him of this charmer. 'You would laugh to see,' she wrote to Ellen, 'how his eyes sparkle with delight when he looks at it, like a pretty child pleased with a new plaything.' She painted his portrait as well, and there were very many sittings required for this. Too many, thought Ellen, and she warned Charlotte that she was falling in love with Celia Amelia; in turn Charlotte warned Ellen that she was doing precisely the same, and she must not lose her heart to him, for he made eyes at every girl he saw. Even when he was performing his sacred ministries he could not take his mind off them, and he sat opposite Anne in church, 'sighing softly and looking out of the corner of his eyes to win her attention!' He introduced unusual gaieties to the Parsonage; he found that none of the three girls had ever received a Valentine, so he sent them each one with an accompaniment of amorous verses, walking ten miles to post them, so that Aunt Branwell should not suspect him of this light conduct. He gave a lecture on some classical subject at Keighley, and insisted that the three sisters should come to hear it: they did not get back to the Parsonage till midnight, and Aunt Branwell, who had prepared coffee for the girls only, found that more was required for Celia Amelia and his chaperoning friend, and lost her temper. This lecture was printed in a local paper, and Celia Amelia sent a copy of it to Ellen, with a couple of ducks. Badinage abounded, and again and again Charlotte counselled Ellen not to lose her heart to the all-conquering curate, who thought her a fine-looking girl, for he was fickle as the wind. He had an *inamorata* at Swansea, but he quarrelled with her and sent her back all her letters, while the more fortunate Caroline Dury received 'a most passionate copy of verses.' He went to Ripon to pass his examination for priest's orders, and enjoyed the balls there immensely and twice more fell desperately in love. There were games at the Parsonage now, drawing games, and Charlotte sent Ellen a sketch of a horse's head 'by the sacred fingers of his reverence William Weightman ... you should have seen the vanity with which he afterwards regarded his productions. One of them represented the flying figure of Fame inscribing his own name on the clouds.' Charlotte sometimes signs these sprightly letters to Ellen 'Charivari' or 'Caliban,' and addresses her as 'Mrs. Menelaus.'

Now all this exuberant chaff which pervaded Charlotte's letters to Ellen for a year and a half at the least was so unlike the picture which Mrs. Gaskell had formed of her and of her deep and invariable seriousness of character that, though she saw the letters, and quotes from them, she omits the whole of these frivolities. They were not suitable: they could not be recounted without spoiling the composition of that picture of Charlotte, always grave and tender and loving, which she so misleadingly painted. Out of these letters concerning Celia Amelia (though she does not even hint at this frivolous nickname by which Charlotte habitually speaks of him) all that she gives is the edifying information that he preached a most violent sermon against Dissenters in Haworth Church, that he was extremely kind to the poor, and picks out a few sentences in which Charlotte, evidently in answer to badinage, assures Ellen that she was not on very amiable terms with him. 'We are distant, cold and reserved. We seldom speak, and when we do, it is only to exchange the most trivial and commonplace remarks.' But, as a matter of fact, throughout this period Charlotte's letters are effervescent with fun at the kindly expense of Celia Amelia. Such a strain of gaiety is certainly surprising, for at no other period of her life, except in the last six months of it, is there any note of merriment, and it is pleasant to know that there was this interlude of comedy bordering on farce at the Parsonage.

But another Brontë biographer has more than made up for Mrs. Gaskell's suppressions, and Miss Isabel Clarke, in her charmingly written book, *Haworth Parsonage,* has added to the Brontë-Saga so amazing a romance concerning Mr. Weightman and Emily Brontë that it, and the grounds on which it is based, must be briefly examined. The grounds are merely that Miss Robinson (Madame Duclaux) stated in her book on Emily Brontë that 'the first curate at Haworth (Mr. Weightman) was exempted from Emily's liberal scorn.' Miss Clarke suggests that the information was derived from Ellen Nussey, and on that somewhat bare stem proceeds to graft a sumptuously flowering romance which, as far as can be ascertained, is wholly imaginary. As follows:

Ellen Nussey on her visits to Haworth went for walks with Mr. Weightman, and to check his amorous attentions Emily was sent out with them, 'ostensibly in the capacity of chaperon, thereby earning for herself the nickname of the "Major."' But, Miss Clarke tells us,

while he walked and flirted with Miss Nussey, he glanced with admiration and something of wonder at the tall slight form of the 'Major.' He noticed her dark, soft kindling eyes, her thick hair, the strange, brooding, other-worldly look. He saw that this girl, destined to so tragic a doom, was not as the others. She loved him.

Now this is rather startling. All we actually know is that Emily did not dislike Mr. Weightman as much as she disliked the curates who succeeded him. Miss Clarke confesses that 'upon that subject Emily allowed no word to pass her lips. If she made a confidante of Anne the younger sister never betrayed that confidence, even after she had gone to her grave.' Nor does Charlotte in all her numerous allusions to Weightman ever even hint that Emily was attracted by him. She tells us that he made eyes at Anne in church, that he flirted desperately with the Misses Walton, Sugden and Dury, and for that reason (as Charlotte herself writes) she warns Ellen not to allow herself to fall under his charm, for he made love to every girl he met. But Miss Clarke tells us that this was not the real reason. These love affairs were, as Charlotte knew, 'merely ephemeral, for it was still Emily who held his heart.' Then he was in love with her too; Miss Clarke proves this triumphantly. She tells us 'that he loved her is undeniable, for she was the last woman in the world to give her love unsought.' In other words, having invented the idea that Emily was in love with him, Miss Clarke asks us to deduce that he must have been in love with Emily, because otherwise Emily would not have allowed herself to be in love with him, and with this firmly established and knit together, the romance proceeds blithely on its way. Why, if Emily was deeply in love with Weightman and he deeply in love with Emily, he did not tell her so and find that his passion was returned, it would evidently be profane to inquire; the main fact of their mutual passion is already proved. It follows, therefore, that when Emily wrote her poem, *If grief for grief can touch thee*, ending with the stanza

Yes, by the tears I've poured,By all my hours of pain,O, I shall surely win thee,Beloved, again.

these lines were addressed to Weightman. Again, when Charlotte took Emily to Brussels two years later, it was not, as the ignorant might suppose, on the evidence of Charlotte's letters, for the purpose of completing their education with a view to setting up a school, but that she might 'take her sister away from a position that his (Weightman's) gay philandering had rendered untenable.' Emily's unhappiness at Brussels again was not due to the acute heart-sickness which she always suffered from when she was away from Haworth, and which had caused her recall from Miss Wooler's school, but to the craving for the presence of Weightman. Weightman died while she was away, and so it is equally clear that when she wrote *Remembrance* it was he of whom she speaks as 'Sweet Love of Youth.' It is true that she also speaks of 'fifteen wild Decembers' having passed since his death, whereas there had been only three, but that, we are assured, was mere camouflage. Finally, to clinch the matter, Miss Clarke finds in *Wuthering Heights* passages that were 'indubitably wrought out of a passionately emotional experience which imagination alone could never have inspired.' 'Who else but Weightman,' she asks us, 'could it have been?' To that certainly there is no answer, but examine the evidence (or lack of it) as we may, we can find no sort of reason for supposing that it was anybody.

We have then two ardent Brontëites, the one of whom, in dealing with the 'affaire Weightman,' suppresses all hint of Charlotte's intense preoccupation and amusement with his numerous flirtations, while the other finds therein a proof of the deep attachment that existed between him and Emily. The middle way is perhaps the safest—namely, to accept what Charlotte says about him, and to reject her complete silence as being evidence for the existence of a romance of which she gives no hint.

II

During this period Charlotte's scheme for the educational career of her sisters and herself was for the present in abeyance. She had come back from Mrs. Sidgwick's, and six months later Anne gave up her situation as governess to Mrs. Ingham's children. The scheme of starting a joint school, possibly at the Parsonage, was already being discussed, but there could be no immediate prospect of that, and, during this winter of 1839-1840, she and Branwell, still allies, began their literary labours again—he on the work of translating the Odes of Horace into English verse, she on a Richardsonian novel of which she felt she had the material for half-a-dozen volumes. Early in 1840 Branwell found a tutorship in the family of Mr. Postlethwaite at Broughton-in-Furness, in Westmorland, and from there wrote a highly vigorous and unedifying letter to John Brown, the sexton at Haworth and President of the 'Lodge of the Three Graces,' which strongly resembles some of those letters which R. L. Stevenson wrote during his period of turbulent and intemperate adolescence at Edinburgh.

Old Knave of Trumps: Don't think I have forgotten you, though I have delayed so long in writing to you. It was my purpose to send you a yarn as soon as I could find materials to spin one with and it is only just now that I have had time to turn myself round and know where I am. If you saw me now you would not know me, and you would laugh to hear the character the people give me. Oh, the falsehood and hypocrisy of this world! I am fixed in a little retired town by the seashore, among wild woody hills that rise round me— huge, rocky and capped with clouds. My employer is a retired County Magistrate, a large landowner, and of a right hearty and generous disposition. His wife is a quiet, silent and amiable woman, and his sons are two fine spirited lads. My landlord is a respectable surgeon, two days out of seven is as drunk as a lord! His wife is a bustling, chattering, kind-hearted soul, and his daughter! oh! death and damnation! Well, what am I? That is, what do they think I am? A most calm, sedate, sober, abstemious, patient, mild-hearted, virtuous, gentlemanly philosopher—the picture of good works, and the treasure-house of righteous thoughts. Cards are shuffled under the table-cloth, glasses are thrust into the cupboard if I enter the room. I take neither spirits, wine, nor malt liquors, I dress in black, and smile like a saint or martyr. Everybody says 'What a good young gentleman is Mr. Postlethwaite's tutor!' This is a fact as I am a living soul, and right comfortably do I laugh at them. I mean to continue in their good opinion. I took a half-year's farewell of old friend whisky at Kendal on the night after I left. There was a party of gentlemen at the Royal Hotel and I joined them. We ordered a supper and whisky-toddy as 'hot as hell'! They thought I was a physician and put me in the chair. I gave sundry toasts, that were washed down at the same time, till the room spun round and the candles danced in our eyes. One of the guests was a respectable old gentleman with powdered head, rosy cheeks, fat paunch and ringed fingers. He gave 'The Ladies' ... after which he brayed off with a speech; and in two minutes, in the middle of a grand sentence he stopped, wiped his head, looked wildly round, stammered, coughed, stopped again and called for his slippers. The waiter helped him to bed. Next a tall Irish squire and a native of the land of Israel began to quarrel about their countries, and, in the warmth of argument, discharged their glasses, each at his neighbour's throat instead of his own. I recommended bleeding, purging and blistering, but they administered each other a real 'Jem Warder,' so I flung my tumbler on the floor too, and swore I'd join 'Old Ireland!' A regular rumpus ensued, but we were tamed at last. I found myself in bed next morning with a bottle of porter, a glass and a corkscrew beside me. Since then I have not tasted anything stronger than milk and water, nor, I hope, shall till I return at Midsummer; when we will see about it. I am getting as fat as Prince William at Springhead, as godly as his friend Parson Winterbotham. My hand shakes no longer, I ride to the banker's at Ulveston with Mr. Postlethwaite, and sit drinking tea and talking scandal with old ladies. As to the young ones! I have one sitting by me just now—fair-faced, blue-eyed, dark-haired, sweet eighteen—and she little thinks the devil is so near her!

I was delighted to see thy note, old Squire, but I do not understand one sentence—you will perhaps know what I mean. How are all about you? I long to hear and see thee again. How is the 'Devil's Thumb'? whom men call ——, and the 'Devil in Mourning,' whom they call ——. How are ——, and ——, and the Doctor, and him who will be used as the tongs of hell—he whose eyes Satan looks out of, as from windows, I mean ——, esquire? How are little ——, 'Longshanks' —— and the rest of them? Are they married, buried, devilled and damned? When I come I'll give them a good squeeze of the hand; till then I am too godly for them to think of. That bow-legged devil used to ask me impertinent questions which I answered him in kind, Beelzebub will make of him a walking stick! Keep to thy teetotalism, old squire, till I return, it will mend thy old body. Does 'little Nosey' think I have forgotten him? No, by Jupiter! nor his clock either. I'll send him a remembrance some of these days! But I must talk to some one prettier than thee; so goodnight, old boy, and believe me thine

The Philosopher.

Write directly. Of course you won't show this letter; and, for Heaven's sake, blot out all the lines scored with red ink.

Now this letter is certainly no uplifting document. It is full of drink and devil and cheap brag: the writer wished to exhibit himself as the deuce of a fellow, and it shocked Mr. Swinburne very much. Evidently Branwell was trying to be literary and impressive, and the style in consequence is monstrously pompous and pretentious, though we cannot deny that the description of the party at Kendal is vigorous and picturesque. The letter would not be worth reprinting at all, except that it furnishes us with an example of Branwell's style in narrative, and will be useful for subsequent reference. It is not, moreover, quite the letter we should have expected from one who was already supposedly besotted and ruined by drink and drugs, and this is borne out by the fact that Bramwell was now engaged in translating three books of Horace's Odes into English verse. While tutor to Mr. Postlethwaite's boys he met Hartley Coleridge, spent a day with him at Ambleside, and sent him, asking for his opinion, his translation of two of these books. What Coleridge thought of them there is no record, but Mr. John Drinkwater, who privately printed them in 1910, bestowed on them his high commendation. 'The first book,' he tells us, 'need, at their best, fear comparison with no other version.' He finds in them passages of clear lyrical beauty; he considers them 'excellent in themselves, and as good as any English version I know.'

Charlotte had abandoned poetry altogether. 'Once indeed,' she writes to Henry Nussey early in 1841, 'I was very poetical, when I was sixteen, seventeen, eighteen, nineteen years old, but now I am twenty-four, approaching twenty-five, and the intermediate years are those which begin to rob life of its superfluous colouring. I have not written poetry for a long while....' But in peace at Haworth she had been busy during 1839 on *Caroline Vernon* and on a Richardsonian novel, and just as Branwell and she, when they were children, had agreed to send their poetical compositions to Wordsworth and Southey, so now, clearly by arrangement, when Branwell sent his Odes to Hartley Coleridge, she sent the opening chapters of one of these stories to Wordsworth. She signed her letter to him 'C. T.', the initials of Charles Townsend under whose name she wrote *Caroline Vernon* and the unnamed story.

She received an answer from him, which is not extant, but the substance of it can be gathered from her reply to it. Wordsworth must have been at least as discouraging about her prose as Southey had been about her verse, and have recommended her to give up writing, for she answers him:

Authors are generally very tenacious of their productions, but I am not so much attached to them but that I can give it up without much distress. No doubt, if I had gone on, I should have made quite a Richardsonian concern of it.... I had material in my head for half a dozen volumes. Of course, it is with considerable regret I relinquish any scheme so charming as the one I have sketched.

She wishes she had lived fifty or sixty years ago, when the *Ladies' Magazine* was flourishing like a green bay tree.

In that case I make no doubt my literary aspirations would have met with due encouragement, and I should have had the pleasure of introducing Messrs. Percy and West into the very best society, and recording all their sayings and doings in double-columned, close-printed pages.

She decidedly resented Wordsworth's letter, for she continues, deeply sarcastic:

I am pleased that you cannot quite decide whether I am an attorney's clerk or a novel-reading dressmaker. I will not help you at all in the discovery; and as to my handwriting, or the ladylike touches in my style and imagery, you must not draw any conclusions from that—I may employ an amanuensis.

Evidently Wordsworth touched her on the raw on this question of her sex, just as in later years, when *Jane Eyre* had made Currer Bell famous, she bitterly resented any conjectures as to whether she was a man or a woman.

The notion of sending part of an immense novel to Wordsworth (of all arbiters!) was as infelicitous as his reply seems to have been, and, failing to win encouragement for the second time in the eyes of the mighty, Charlotte again gave up all idea of a literary career, and for the next five years, till the autumn of 1845, she never set pen to paper except to write her French exercises at Brussels and letters to her friends. To go out as a governess again seemed the only thing to do, and during this year (1840) she made one or two applications for posts of the sort, but they came to nothing. She paid visits to Ellen and Mary Taylor; Mary Taylor and her sister Martha came to Haworth, and with no alien faces to render her tongue-tied and miserable, her letters abounded in geniality and enjoyment, and in the intensest interest in Celia Amelia's amours. But the moment strangers came to Haworth, even though they were relations, she was quick to observe and to recount their deficiencies. Of such were some family connections from Cornwall, John Branwell Williams and his wife and daughter, and Charlotte's gimlet eye bored ruthlessly into their pretensions.

They reckon to be very fine folks indeed, and talk largely—I thought assumingly. I cannot say I much admired them; to my eye there seemed to be an attempt to play the great Mogul down in Yorkshire.... Mrs. Williams sets up for being a woman of great talents, tact, and accomplishment: I thought there was more noise than work. My cousin Eliza is a young lady intended by Nature to be a bouncing, good-looking girl: Art has trained her to be a languishing, affected piece of goods.

This visit seems to have been brief.

Branwell in the summer completed his engagement at Mr. Postlethwaite's and returned home with his Horatian Odes. Painting and poetry alike had failed, but he was anxious, or at least willing, to employ himself somehow, and in September he became the booking-clerk at a small station called Sowerby Bridge. It was a dismal *dégringolade* from the brilliant promise of his boyhood and from the bright hopes which Charlotte, above all, had entertained about his career, and there is more than a touch of sarcastic contempt in her announcement of this to Ellen Nussey. She writes (September 1840):

A distant relative of mine, one Patrick Boanerges, has set off to seek his fortune in the wild, wandering, adventurous, romantic, knight-errant-like capacity of clerk on the Leeds and Manchester Railroad.

So off went Branwell to his ticket-office, and the three girls remained at Haworth. Throughout Charlotte's voluminous correspondence during this year, we get no glimpse at all of their relations to each other, for Emily's name is never mentioned at all; Anne suffered from a cold, and Celia Amelia made eyes at her in church. As for Aunt Branwell, all we know of her is that she was vastly pleased with the knitting-needle case which Ellen sent her, and on more than one occasion was 'precious cross.' But the autumn winds blew across the hills, filling Charlotte with rapture.

I see everything [she wrote] *couleur de rose*, and am strongly inclined to dance a jig. I think I must partake of the nature of a pig or an ass—both which animals are strongly affected by a high wind. From which quarter the wind blows I cannot tell, for I never could in my life, but I should very much like to know how the great brewing tub of Bridlington Bay works, and what sort of yeasty froth rises just now on the waves.

Other causes besides the freedom and seclusion of Haworth contributed to this joyful serenity, for that hysterical religious disquiet arising out of her adolescent passion for Ellen had calmed down completely, and in her letters, now and henceforth, there is not the smallest trace of those spiritual aspirations and excitements. The blaze of that volcanic human attachment, which gave the other birth, had cooled down also, and a firm crust of friendship, never to be broken, had formed over these fires, and now, when Ellen consults her about her own matrimonial possibilities, it is indeed a grandmother (as Charlotte calls herself) who tells Ellen that 'the majority of these worldly precepts whose seeming coldness shocks and repels us in youth are founded in wisdom.' With a somewhat ponderous humour, she pictures herself advising Ellen's swain who, with a lover's diffidence, is slow to come to the point, and bids him

begin in a clear, distinct deferential, but determined voice. 'Miss Ellen, I have a question to put to you,—a very important question to put to you, Will you take me for your husband for better for worse? I am not a rich man, but I have sufficient to support us. I am not a great man but I love you honestly and truly. Miss Ellen, if you knew the world better you would see that this is not an offer to be despised, a kind attached heart and a moderate competency.' Do this, Mr. Vincent, and you may succeed. Go on writing sentimental love-sick letters to Henry and I would not give sixpence for your suit.

Then with a solemnity not less portentous she adjures Ellen not to wait for *une grande passion*.

My good girl, *une grande passion is une grande folie*.... No young lady should fall in love till the offer has been made, accepted, the marriage ceremony performed, and the first half-year of wedded life has passed away. A woman may then begin to love, but with great precaution, very coolly, very moderately, very rationally. If she ever loves so much that a harsh word, or a cold look, cuts her to the heart, she is a fool....

The poor grandmother, so calm, so edifying, so pathetically ignorant of the entire subject on which she was giving such comprehensive oracles from the secluded shrine of Haworth! Presently she was to become very much younger.

CHAPTER VII

Charlotte's determination that she and her sisters should teach, should have a career, should 'get on,' was not only due to special necessities in their individual case, but, not less, to her general principle that girls as well as boys should stand on their own feet and make their way in the world. The early Victorian view (and, indeed, the mid-Victorian view) was that marriage was the only career for them, but Charlotte was far in advance of her age. She wrote, for instance, a few years later to her friend Mr. Williams, saying: 'Your daughters, as much as your sons, should aim at making their way honourably through life. Do not wish to keep them at home. Believe me, teachers may be hard-worked, ill-paid and despised, but the girl who stays at home doing nothing is worse off than the hardest-wrought and worst paid drudge of a school.' Considering how miserable she had been in such situations, this is a most remarkable utterance. Charlotte was indeed the pioneer of the movement for the independence of women. No one before her, and none after her for at least fifty years, thus stated that girls would be better off if working in the most uncongenial surroundings than if they stayed at home.

So the caravans had to leave their oasis of peace, to travel once more across alien sands, and in the spring of 1841 both Charlotte and Anne went forth to new situations among strangers, while Emily remained at Haworth. Anne went as governess to the children of the Reverend Edmund Robinson, an invalid clergyman at Thorp Green, near York. Here she remained for over four years, coming home for the holidays, disliking the place from the first, but patiently and mildly enduring it without complaint, and solacing herself with the adventures of Gondaland, and secretly writing a story called *Solala Vernon's Life*. Hitherto Anne's literary efforts had been entirely poetical; some poems she had written under the name of Olivia Vernon. Of this story we know nothing, except that by July 1841 she was engaged on the fourth volume or notebook of it. Probably it was autobiographical.

Charlotte's situation was as governess to the two children, a girl of eight and a boy of six, of Mr. and Mrs. John White of Upperwood House, in the village of Rawdon, near Bradford. At once the misery that her shyness among strangers caused her began to descend on her. She expected them to behave shabbily to her; she was on the look out for slights and want of consideration, and within a day of her arrival she wrote to Ellen Nussey, 'I have *as yet* had no cause to complain of want of consideration or civility.' She hated her employment in itself. She immediately noted that her pupils were wild and unbroken, though apparently well disposed, and it does not bode well for the success of a governess if, as Charlotte writes, 'she finds it hard to repel the rude familiarities of children.' Her shyness was not less than an obsession, of which she was aware, but against which she was powerless.

I find it so difficult [she continues] to ask either servants or mistress for what I want, however much I want it. It is less pain to me to endure the greatest inconvenience than to request its removal. I am a fool. Heaven knows I cannot help it.

However, it was not so bad as Stonegappe. Charlotte liked Mr. White extremely; also Ellen's home was within nine miles of Rawdon, and meetings might be possible. But, rather ominously, she says, 'Respecting Mrs. White I am for the moment silent. I am trying hard to like her.' The effort was not successful. Charlotte asked her whether she might go to spend a couple of nights with Ellen during term time, and Mrs. White said '"Ye—e—es" in a reluctant cold tone,' adding that she had better go on Saturday and return on Monday, so that the children should not miss their lessons. That was enough: 'You *are* a genuine Turk' thought Charlotte, and it is evident there were no more efforts to like her. Ellen's brother drove her back to Rawdon on Monday, and because he did not go into the house Mrs. White got 'quite red in the face with vexation.' Instantly Charlotte perceived that Mrs. White's cook, when dressed, had much more the air of a lady than her mistress.

Well can I believe [she writes] that Mrs. White has been an exciseman's daughter, and I am convinced also that Mr. White's extraction is very low. I was beginning to think Mrs. White a good sort of body in spite of all her bouncing and boasting, her bad grammar and worse orthography, but I have had experience of one little trait in her character which condemns her a long way with me. After treating a person in the most familiar terms of equality for a long time, if any little thing goes wrong, she does not scruple to give way to anger in a very coarse, unladylike manner. I think passion is the true test of vulgarity or refinement.

Then Mr. White wrote to Mr. Brontë begging him to come and spend a week at his house. But Charlotte would not permit that: 'I don't at all wish papa to come; it would be like incurring an obligation,' and so papa did not come.

This ungraciousness, this acutely censorious eye, was the result very largely of her abnormal and invincible shyness, and the two throughout her life reacted on each other. She was ill at ease with strangers, and attributed the discomfort their presence caused her to their disagreeable qualities. No efforts on their part, however well-meaning, could deliver her from the prison of her unhappy temperament, and she sat silent and unapproachable while they abandoned themselves to their unfeeling gaieties, and noted their 'coarse imbecilities.' Her occupation, moreover, was most uncongenial; 'no one but myself,' she writes, 'is aware how utterly averse my whole mind and nature is to the employment,' and though she had chosen it for herself and for her sisters with a definite object in view and gallantly stuck to it, she found it invariably odious. No one was ever less suited to be a governess, for she took the same gloomy view of her charges as of their parents, and the little Sidgwicks were devils incarnate, and the little Whites 'noisy, over-indulged, and hard to manage.' The truth was that she did not like children, and repelled their 'rude familiarities'; in other words, when they manifested affection towards her, she did her best to shut them up. She had, it is true, a tenderness for Mrs. White's baby, but her admission of this softness takes the form of a confession. 'By dint of nursing the fat baby,' she writes, 'it has got to know me and be fond of me. I suspect myself of growing rather fond of it. Exertion of any kind is always beneficial.' Mrs. Gaskell and others have divined from this an exquisite tenderness in her nature towards the young; but was there ever a queerer expression of it than the admission that by *dint* of nursing the fat baby she had got fond of it, and that exertion is always beneficial? She was surprised that she was growing fond of it: it was odd to her.

Branwell meanwhile, after three months of ticket-collecting at Sowerby Bridge, had been transferred to another station on the Leeds and Manchester line called Luddenden Foot. Trains and passengers were few, the station buildings consisted of one wooden hut, and the staff of Branwell and a porter. Charlotte, writing to Emily, agrees that this '*looks* as if he was getting on at any rate.' What kind of progress might be expected of a young man of social tastes and alcoholic tendencies at a place where there was nothing for him to do and only a porter to talk to, she does not specify. A more disastrous environment could hardly be conceived.

After a while things shaped a little better at Upperwood House; Charlotte wrote to Henry Nussey, her ex-suitor, that her employers were 'kind, worthy people in their way,' and returned to Haworth on the last day of June for three weeks' holiday, after a tussle with Mrs. White, who thought ten days would be enough. She found it was Paradise to be at home again. Anne had already had her holiday and gone back to her situation, and a small black kitten of the Parsonage was dead; 'every cup,' Charlotte commented, 'however sweet, has its drop of bitterness in it.' But Aunt Branwell was in high good humour, and this just now was a most fortunate circumstance, for the project of the three girls setting up a school, long cherished in secret, especially by Charlotte, was now being discussed by their elders, and Aunt Branwell's help was necessary to supply funds to start their enterprise. She had an invested capital of about

£1,500, which brought her in £50 a year, and though Charlotte had always considered she was the last person who would offer a loan for the purpose in question, Miss Branwell was willing to advance a sum of £100 or £150, provided that a suitable situation for the school could be found and pupils were forthcoming; this offer Charlotte considered 'very fair.' At last, and at long last, there seemed a definite chance that the long-cherished scheme of setting up a school might be realised. She went back to Underwood House, after three weeks' holiday, full of new hope. A long time might yet elapse before it could be carried out, but sufficient capital was now forthcoming, and she began to consider where the school should be started.

At this point we get, owing to a rare felicity, something that has long been lacking—namely, a glimpse, vivid and authentic, into the life of the Parsonage as seen by those two inhabitants of it, hitherto so shadowy, Emily and Anne. It came to Mr. Clement Shorter in the shape of four folded pieces of paper sent him in a small box by Charlotte's husband forty years after her death. These papers were covered with the minute handwriting of Emily and Anne, two of each. As has been already seen, they formed a group among the four children, with secrets of their own and chronicles of Gondaland, and from these papers it appears that it was their habit every four years separately to write a summary of their doings and of the family affairs during that period, to be opened four years later on Emily's birthday, July 30. Thus in the year 1841 they wrote the two summaries which first concern us, and which would be opened on July 30, 1845. Again, on July 30, 1845, they wrote the summaries of the years 1841-1845 which, had they lived, would have been opened in due course. Emily's paper of 1841 is as follows:

> *A Paper to be opened*
> *when Anne is*
> *25 years old, or*
> *my next birthday after*
> *if*
> *all be well.*
> Emily Jane Brontë. July the 30th 1841.

It is Friday evening near 9 o'clock—wild rainy weather. I am seated in the dining room, having just concluded tidying our desk-boxes, writing this document. Papa is in the parlour—Aunt upstairs in her room. She has been reading *Blackwood's Magazine* to Papa. Victoria and Adelaide are ensconsed in the peat-house, Keeper is in the kitchen and Hero in his cage. We are all stout and hearty, as I hope is the case with Charlotte, Branwell and Anne, of whom the first is at John White Esq: Upperwood House, Rawdon, the second is at Luddenden Foot, and the third is, I believe, at Scarborough, inditing perhaps a paper corresponding to this.

A scheme is at present in agitation for setting us up in a school of our own, as yet nothing is determined, but I hope and trust it may go on and prosper, and answer our highest expectations. This day four years I wonder whether we shall still be dragging on in our present condition or established to our hearts' content. Time will show.

I guess that at the time appointed for the opening of this paper, we, *i.e.*, Charlotte, Anne, and I shall be all merrily seated in our own sitting room in some pleasant and flourishing seminary, having just gathered in from the midsummer lady-day. Our debts will be paid off, and we shall have cash in hand to a considerable amount. Papa, Aunt and Branwell will either have been or be coming to visit us. It will be a fine warm summer evening, very different from this bleak look-out, and Anne and I will perchance slip out into the garden for a few minutes to peruse our papers. I hope that either this or something better will be the case.

The Gondaland are at present in a threatening state, but there is no open rupture as yet. All the princes and princesses of the Royalty are at the Palace of Instruction. I have a good many books on hand, but I am sorry to say that as usual I make small progress with any. However, I have just made a new regularity paper! and I must *verb sap* to do great things. And now I close, sending from far an exhortation of courage, boys! courage, to exiled and harassed Anne, wishing she was here.

Certainly this document presents a cheerful picture: there is no hint of the tragic sibyl about the girl who so contentedly records the past, and looks forward to the next four years in so optimistic a fashion. She was alone with her aunt and her father, with a bulldog and a hawk, looking forward to the moment four years hence when she and Anne will 'peruse' the papers they 'indited' to-day, and Anne will know that four years ago she sent an exhortation of courage to the harassed exile. Charlotte was exiled too, and, as her letters so volubly testify, abundantly harassed by the vulgarities of the low-born, but to her sufferings Emily makes no allusion. It is just worth while to notice this, though without stressing it. The debts which she refers to and hopes will be paid when the school prospers are clearly those which may be incurred, owing to initial expenses. It has been suggested that they were debts incurred by Branwell, but for this there is no particle of evidence. It is, however, worth mentioning, since we abundantly find in the Brontë-Saga suggestions that the sisters went out as governesses and tried to start a school in order to pay his debts.

It is the complete reticence of Emily concerning the fire, mystical and rapturous and sombre, which we know inspired her, that strikes us most in this domestic record. Not the tip of a red tongue of flame nor any hot breath of the furnace escapes, nor yet the cold wind of the arctic night which encompassed her when only a few days before the date of this pleasant and contented chronicle she wrote that untitled poem beginning,

I see around me tombstones grey

Stretching their shadows far away.

Icy despair at the woes of this transitory life suffuses it, yet there glows in it lambent fire, the hot, passionate love of the Earth, as when, in *Wuthering Heights,* Catherine dreams that she was dead and so miserable in Heaven that in anger the angels threw her out, and she woke sobbing for joy to find herself once more in the heather of the moor. To the record of her inner life Emily gave access to none—not even to the secret eyes of Anne, who, four years later, as we shall see in the second group of these papers, said that she knew only that Emily was writing poetry, and wondered what it was about.

Herein we begin to see something of the vital difference between the nature of Charlotte and Emily, the abysmal, impassable gulf that separated the great talent of the one from the genius of the other. Charlotte in her novels used not once, but over and over again, both in motive and episode, the actual experiences of her life—its detested occupations, the relationship between employer and employed as she encountered them in her schoolings, bitterly caricaturing those who had offended her. Emily, on the other hand, save in a few commemorative poems, never drew from external experience—her inspiration, like that of the mystic, came wholly from within, and her work glowed and was fed by the fire and wine of the soul that dwelt apart.

Anne's corresponding paper, written at Scarborough, fills in the hitherto faint outline of her piety and gentleness. She does not like her present situation at Thorp Green and wishes to change it: owing to Charlotte's plans, she actually remained there for four years more. She gives almost precisely the same details about the past movements of the family as Emily does, adding the exact ages of them all in years and months. Charlotte's various situations are recorded in a short sentence, and about Emily she makes a comment which is surely significant: 'We are all of us,' she writes, 'doing something for our own livelihood, except Emily, who, however, is as busy as any of us, and in reality earns her food and raiment as much as we do.' We can certainly infer from this that there had been a feeling in someone's mind—and there is no need to ask in whose—that Emily should not be idling at home while her sisters were earning their living. With regard to the future, Anne too hopes that the idea of the joint school will materialise, but quotes from one of her own poems:

How little know we what we are,

How less what we may be.

... What will the next four years bring forth? Providence only knows. But we have sustained very little alteration since that time [*i.e.* of the last papers four years ago]. I have the same faults that I had then, only I have more wisdom and experience, and a little more self-possession than I then enjoyed. I am now engaged in writing the fourth volume of *Solala Vernon's Life*.

These papers, then, beyond what they present to us of domestic furnishings, are valuable as showing us Emily moving about content and cheerful, but silent as Wuthering Heights itself lying white beneath its winter snows about the things that truly concerned her, and of Anne, uncomplaining and patient, meekly accepting the decrees of Providence and busy, pathetically busy, over the fourth volume of *Solala Vernon's Life*, for neither in verse nor prose had she more than the most mediocre talent. These two sisters wrote solely for each other. Charlotte has no part in their secret papers, and both their pens seem to pass over her name without comment. But Emily sends a message of encouragement to Anne, and Anne speaks up on Emily's behalf, as if someone had unjustly reproached her for idleness.

Charlotte had gone back to Dewsbury Moor before these papers were written; now there came for her a letter from her friend Mary Taylor, who, with her sister Martha, was at school at Brussels, and the gift of a silk scarf and a pair of kid gloves. This letter first suggested to her an idea which proved to have a profound effect on her life. She wrote to Ellen about it:

Mary's letter spoke of some of the pictures and cathedrals she had seen—pictures the most exquisite, cathedrals the most venerable. I hardly know what swelled to my throat as I read her letter: such a vehement impatience of restraint and steady work, such a strong wish for wings—wings such as wealth can furnish: such an earnest thirst to see, to know, to learn: something internal seemed to expand boldly for a minute. I was tantalised with the consciousness of faculties unexercised: then all collapsed, and I despaired.

But the collapse was but momentary. Mary's letter immediately kindled in her a spark that should soon blaze high. It crept along in her mind and presently it united itself with the other fire that always burned there, namely, the school-keeping scheme. She began to wonder whether her longing to see the pictures and cathedrals of which Mary spoke could not be gratified in conjunction with the other. How much more likely she and her sisters would be to succeed with their school if a further education, the acquisition of a larger knowledge of French and German, could be acquired at Brussels!

But just then another opportunity came in view, and it looked as if the prospect of setting up a school (or rather of taking over one that already existed) was capable of instant realisation. Miss Margaret Wooler, at whose establishment at Dewsbury Moor Charlotte had been a teacher and Emily and Anne pupils, had now retired, leaving the place to be carried on by her sister. Now this sister intended to give it up, for it had not prospered lately, and Miss Wooler proposed to Charlotte that she should take it on and try to revive it, singly at first, then in conjunction with Emily and Anne; she also offered her the use of her furniture. Charlotte cordially accepted this very generous proposal, but pending its completion, she sat down to think. Her aunt had agreed to advance a loan up to £150 to meet initial expenses, but now, since the furniture of the house would be lent her, that loan might be used in other ways. Before Miss Wooler answered her letter of acceptance, she wrote to Aunt Branwell as follows:

A plan has been approved by Mr. and Mrs. White and others, which I wish now to impart to you. My friends recommend me if I desire to secure permanent success, to delay commencing the school for six months longer, and by all means to contrive by hook or by crook, to spend the intervening time in some school on the continent. They say schools in England are so numerous, competition so great, that without some such step towards attracting superiority we shall probably have a very hard struggle and may fail in the end. They say, moreover, that the loan of £100, which you have been so kind as to offer us, will perhaps not be all required now, as Miss Wooler will lend us the furniture; and that, if the speculation is intended to be a good and successful one, half the sum at least ought to be paid out in the manner I have mentioned, thereby insuring a more speedy repayment both of interest and capital.

I would not go to France or to Paris. I would go to Brussels in Belgium. The cost of the journey there, at the dearest rate of travelling, would be £5: living is there little more than half as dear as it is in England, and the facilities for education are equal or superior to any other place in Europe. In half a year I could acquire a thorough familiarity with French, and could improve greatly in Italian and even get a dash of German, *i.e.*, provided my health continued as good as it is now. Martha Taylor is now staying in Brussels, at a first-rate establishment there. I should not think of going to the Château de Kockleberg, where she is resident, as the terms are much too high; but if I wrote to her, she, with the assistance of Mrs. Jenkins, the wife of the British Consul, would be able to secure me a cheap and decent residence and respectable protection. I should have the opportunity of seeing her frequently, she would make me acquainted with the city, and, with the assistance of her cousins, I should probably in time be introduced to connections far more improving, polished, and cultivated than any I have yet known.

These are advantages which would turn to vast account, when we actually commenced a school—and, if Emily could share them with me, only for a single half year, we could take a footing in the world afterwards which we can never do now. I say Emily instead of Anne: for Anne might take her turn at some future period, if our school answered. I feel certain, while I am writing, that you will see the propriety of what I say: you always like to use your money to the best advantage, you are not fond of making shabby purchases: when you do confer a favour, it is often done in style, and depend upon it £50 or £100, thus laid out, would be well employed. Of course, I know of no other friend in the world to whom I could apply on this subject, except yourself. I feel an absolute conviction that, if the advantage were allowed us, it would be the making of us for life. Papa will perhaps think it a wild and ambitious scheme, but who can rise in the world without ambition? When he left Ireland to go to Cambridge, he was as ambitious as I am now. I want us *all* to get on. I know we have talents, and I want them to be turned to account. I look to you, aunt, to help us. I think you will not refuse. I know, if you consent, it shall not be my fault if you ever repent your kindness.

A more tactful and diplomatic letter could not be conceived. Charlotte had the support of the Whites and other friends for her suggestion. She congratulated her aunt upon the wise way in which she always laid out her money, a foe to shabby presents; she disarmed her father's possible opposition by the flattering reminder that he, too, in his day had been ambitious, or he, the son of an Irish peasant, would never have succeeded in getting a University education, and she made a powerful suggestion to her aunt that she was going to consent. Miss Branwell's answer, though there were points yet to be settled, was favourable enough to cause Charlotte to cancel her acceptance of Miss Wooler's offer. She did so apparently without much sense of gratitude for it, writing to Ellen:

I am not going to Dewsbury Moor as far as I can see at present. It was a decent friendly proposal on Miss Wooler's part, and cancels all or most of her little foibles in my estimation; but Dewsbury Moor is a poisoned place to me, besides I burn to go somewhere else. I think, Nell, I see a chance of getting to Brussels.... Dewsbury Moor was an obscure dreary place not adapted for a school.

She had finished with Dewsbury Moor.

Charlotte had now completely transformed the original idea of the school to be started with Miss Branwell's assistance, where the three sisters might be together, though that was to come later, with the prospect of the greater success that their improved educational equipment would give them. This entailed many changes in the first plan, which, with her masterly efficiency, she now proceeded to make, for the sake of the general object of them 'all getting on.' Emily, she settled with Miss Branwell's approval, was to accompany her to Brussels. 'I wished for one, at least, of my sisters,' she wrote to Ellen, 'to share the advantage with me. I fixed on Emily. She deserved the reward, I knew.' How far Emily appreciated that reward is another question: she had pined with home-sickness when she had been only three months from Haworth at Miss Wooler's school, and now she was to be transplanted to Brussels for six. Indeed, Charlotte's plans went far beyond that, now that Miss Branwell had sanctioned them so far, for in a few weeks she wrote to Emily, saying:

Before our half year in Brussels is completed, you and I will have to seek employment abroad. It is not my intention to retrace my steps home till twelve months if all continues well, and we and those at home retain good health.

Then there was Anne. A few months before, Charlotte had written to Ellen most tenderly about her, for Anne was unhappy in her situation as governess to the family of Mrs. Robinson:

I have one aching feeling at my heart. It is about Anne; she has so much to endure; far, far more than I have. When my thoughts turn to her, they always see her as a patient persecuted stranger. I know what concealed susceptibility is in her nature, when her feelings are wounded. I wish I could be with her to administer a little balm. She is more lonely, less gifted with the power of making friends even than I am.

Now there is a very sincere and affectionate anxiety in these words; of that there can be no doubt. But the Brussels plan, for the eventual benefit of them all, now overrode in Charlotte's mind all other considerations. 'Anne for the present,' as Charlotte wrote to Emily, 'seems omitted in it, but if all goes right I trust she will derive her full share of benefit from it in the end.' But why, we cannot help asking, should not Charlotte have arranged that Anne, over whose loneliness she mourned, longing to be with her, should accompany her to Brussels where they would be together, while Emily, who was abjectly miserable away from Haworth, remained at home? The answer seems plain: Emily was wasting her time at Haworth, she was doing nothing towards the project of the school, for which further education at Brussels would be of such assistance, and she was earning nothing. This seems to accord with Anne's gentle protest in her secret paper that Emily was as busy as any of them, and the implication that Charlotte thought otherwise. Anne, on the other hand, was gaining experience in teaching, and was earning her livelihood. So, much as she disliked the situation, and much as Charlotte longed to be with her and comfort her loneliness, it was better that Anne should remain at Thorp Green and continue, as Charlotte wrote in her notes on Anne's poems, 'to taste the cup of life as it is mixed for the class termed "governesses,"' while Emily came to Brussels. They all must get on, and all must work, at whatever personal sacrifice.

There were still many inquiries to be made about a suitable establishment at Brussels when the sisters were together again at Haworth for Christmas, 1841. Branwell was expected, but did not arrive; he had not been seen at Haworth for the last five months, though the station at Luddenden Foot, where he had gone in what Charlotte ironically called 'his wild, wandering, adventurous, romantic, knight-errant-like capacity of ticket collector,' was not more than a dozen miles off. When he did arrive in January 1842, it was because he had been dismissed from his high estate. He had made a habit of leaving the ticket-office in that solitary shanty in care of his colleague the porter, and had spent his days drinking heavily in hospitable farm-houses and pot-houses of the neighbourhood. His colleague had pocketed the money which he received for the tickets, and when the audit was made, the cash that should have been received by the ticket-collector was far from tallying with the price of the tickets that had been purchased. Though Branwell was not personally suspected of theft, his neglect and carelessness of his duties had been monstrous, and it was no wonder that the Leeds and Manchester Railway Company had no further use for him.

Meantime there had arisen the question as to whether better educational advantages would not be obtained at Lille than at Brussels, but further inquiries made by Mr. Jenkins (who proved not to be British Consul in Brussels, but chaplain to the British Embassy) led to the selection of the *pensionnat* kept by Madame Héger in the Rue d'Isabelle.

Emily and Charlotte, accompanied by their father, set off sometime during February 1842. Mr. Brontë remained in Brussels one night, and then returned to Haworth. He had prudently written out for himself a list of the French equivalents of the things he might be called upon to ask for during his return journey when he would be without interpreters. Charlotte's scheme had been carried out in bulk and detail. Just as her father had gone up to Cambridge at the age of twenty-five, *in statu pupillari* after being a master at an Irish school, so she at the same age, after being a mistress at Miss Wooler's and governess at Stonegappe and Underwood House, became a pupil again in Madame Héger's *pensionnat*.

CHAPTER VIII

The external features and internal arrangements of the *pensionnat* were reproduced by Charlotte with such accurate and photographic detail in *The Professor* and *Villette*, that it is unnecessary to describe them. Mrs. Gaskell says that there were eighty to a hundred pupils there at the time, but Charlotte in a letter to Ellen states that there were about forty day pupils and twelve boarders. The terms for board and tuition were 650 francs per annum, so that Miss Branwell's loan, even if it was only £50, not £100, easily covered the total expenses of the two girls for six months. The boarders all slept in one dormitory, at the far end of which, withdrawn behind a curtain, were Charlotte's and Emily's beds. Miss Branwell had paid something extra for this privilege, and Charlotte 'considered it kind' of her. It felt strange to her at first to be a pupil and once more 'to submit to authority instead of exercising it,' but she liked it. She had come here to learn, in order to fit herself for the future she had planned for herself and her sisters, and the life was congenial and delightful compared with that of a governess. The difference between the sisters and the other pupils in the matter of age, nationality, and religion caused her and Emily to be 'completely isolated in the midst of numbers,' but constant occupation andintense interest in it made the time pass only too quickly for her. The great chance was hers, and she meant to drain the utmost drop of profit from it.

Emily, on the other hand, was throughout her time here entirely wretched. She was always unhappy away from Haworth, the presence of strangers had a more appalling effect on her than even on Charlotte, and when the two on school holidays went to see Mary and Martha Taylor, who were being educated at the Château de Kockleberg, or visited Mrs. Jenkins, Emily sat dumb and miserable. M. Héger and she, Charlotte recorded, 'did not draw well together at all,' and otherwise in her letters scarcely mentioned her. But the account she gave of Emily in the prefatory memoir she wrote to her poems after her death is heartrending. She alluded to the misery Emily experienced when at school, and

now (at Brussels) the same suffering and conflict ensued, heightened by the strong recoil of her upright, heretic and English spirit from the gentle Jesuitry of the foreign and Romish system. Once more she seemed sinking, but this time she rallied through the mere force of resolution: with inward remorse and shame she looked back on her former failure, and resolved to conquer in this second ordeal. She did conquer, but the victory cost her dear.

It is possible that retrospective exaggeration tinges this account, but Brussels was evidently an inferno to the unhappy girl. Charlotte is strangely at error about Emily's age in this memoir; she says she was twenty when she went to Brussels, whereas, as a matter of fact, having been born in 1818, she passed her twenty-fourth birthday there.

During this first sojourn at Brussels, Charlotte wrote very few letters to Ellen. Being amongst strangers produced its invariable reactions, and she found the folk among whom she was thus isolated almost as disagreeable as those of her days of bondage as governess. Madame Héger came off best. She

is a lady of precisely the same cast of mind, degree of cultivation, and quality of intellect as Miss Catherine Wooler. I think the severe points are a little softened, because she has not been disappointed and consequently soured. In other words, she is a married instead of a maiden lady.

(Perhaps this is not so much appreciation of Mme. Héger as depreciation of Miss Wooler.) Then there were the three other mistresses—Mdlle. Blanche, Mdlle. Sophie, Mdlle. Marie:

The two first have no particular character. One is an old maid, the other will be one. Mademoiselle Marie is talented and original but of repulsive and arbitrary manners.

Then there is M. Héger:

A man of power as to mind, but very choleric and irritable in temperament: a little black being, with a face that varies in expression. Sometimes he borrows the lineaments of an insane tom-cat, sometimes those of a delirious hyena; occasionally but very seldom he discards these perilous attractions and assumes an air not above 100 degrees removed from mild and gentlemanlike.... The few private lessons M. Héger has vouchsafed to give us are, I suppose, to be considered a great favour, and I can perceive they have already excited much spite and jealousy in the school.

Brussels, she found, was a selfish city, and this a selfish school.

If the national character of the Belgians is to be measured by the character of most of the girls in this school, it is a character singularly cold, selfish, animal, and inferior ... their principles are rotten to the core.

Their religion was as vile as themselves.

My advice to all Protestants who are tempted to do anything so besotted as to turn Catholics is, to walk over the sea on to the continent; to attend Mass sedulously for a time; to note well the mummeries thereof; also the idiotic mercenary aspect of all the priests; and *then*, if they are still disposed to consider Papistry in any other light than a most feeble, childish piece of humbug, let them turn Papists at once—that's all.

In spite of these disagreeable companions and uncongenial surroundings, Charlotte found that Brussels was fulfilling her expectations; it is evident also that Monsieur and Madame thought highly of the abilities of both the sisters, for in an undated letter to Ellen, Charlotte writes:

I consider it doubtful whether I shall come home in September or not. Madame Héger has made a proposal for both me and Emily to stay another half-year, offering to dismiss her English master, and take me as English teacher: also to employ Emily some part of the day in teaching music to a certain number of the pupils. For these services we are to be allowed to continue our studies in French and German, and to have board, etc., without paying for it: no salaries, however, are offered.

It is clear that this proposal must have been accepted by Charlotte on behalf of Emily and herself, though by the original arrangement they would have returned to England in August, at the end of their six months, for they both stopped at Brussels, through the *vacances*, into the new term which opened in September, and Charlotte began giving English lessons to younger pupils and Emily was teaching them the piano. Emily was now 'drawing together better' with M. Héger, and Charlotte, with a dryness that contrasts curiously with the passionate and perhaps remorseful tenderness of her subsequent memoir, says that 'Monsieur et Madame Héger begin to recognise the valuable parts of her character, under her singularities.' Subsequently M. Héger spoke in the very highest terms of Emily's abilities, ranking them far above Charlotte's, both in mental grasp and in imaginative power.

The two sisters were therefore now installed as pupil teachers at the *pensionnat* for another half-year. Charlotte, it may be remembered, had told Emily she did not propose to come back to England under twelve months. Late in October, Martha Taylor, Mary's sister, died suddenly at the Château de Kockleberg; Charlotte wrote of her very tenderly in *Shirley* as Jessie Yorke. Then on November 2nd Charlotte got news of Miss Branwell's serious illness, and, on the next day, of her death. The sisters sailed from Antwerp on the 6th, arriving at Haworth two days afterwards, to find the funeral was over. Though Miss Branwell had supplied the funds wherewith Charlotte had realised her dream of going to Brussels, she had never had any affection for her aunt, and writing to Ellen immediately afterwards, she expressed neither sorrow nor gratitude. 'All was over,' she says. 'We shall see her no more. Papa is pretty well'; then a fortnight later, inviting her friend to Haworth, she says: 'Do not fear to find us melancholy or depressed, we are all much as usual. You will see no difference from our former demeanour.' There is no further allusion in her subsequent letters either to Miss Branwell or to Mr. Weightman, Celia Amelia, whose death had preceded Miss Branwell's by a few days.

Branwell throughout this year had been living at Haworth since his dismissal from Luddenden Foot. He had there made friends with a young engineer on the Leeds and Manchester line, Francis H. Grundy, who was immensely impressed, even as the commercial travellers at the 'Black Bull' had been, by the brilliance of Branwell's conversation, and was perfectly frank regarding his drunken habits. In his *Pictures of the Past* he tells us that Branwell, just before he made his acquaintance, had been in the habit also of taking opium, in emulation of De Quincey, but broke himself of it, though before the end of his life he resumed it again. There are several letters from Branwell to him during this year. Branwell had asked him if he could get him another appointment in the employment of the railway, but was not surprised to hear that there was no chance of it. He wisely rejected the idea of going into the Church, remarking that 'I have not one mental qualification, save perhaps hypocrisy, which would make me cut a figure in the pulpit.' He alone seems to have felt any regret for Miss Branwell's death, whose favourite he had always been, and refers to her, who, he said, had been his mother for twenty years, with sincere feeling. He cannot at this period have been the utter wreck which he is represented to have been, for after this year at Haworth he became tutor to Mr. Robinson's boys at Thorp Green, where Anne was already governess; they went there together directly after the Christmas holidays, and remained there for the next two years and a half. This Christmas of 1842, Mrs. Gaskell tells us, 'they all enjoyed inexpressibly. Branwell was with them; that was always a pleasure at this time.'

Mrs. Gaskell makes some curiously erroneous statements with regard to Miss Branwell's will and the disposition of her money. She states:

The small property which she had accumulated by dint of personal frugality and self-denial, was bequeathed to her nieces. Branwell, her darling, was to have had his share: but his reckless expenditure had distressed the good old lady, and his name was omitted in her will.

Subsequent biographers have followed her without troubling to verify her information, and we find Miss Robinson (Mme. Duclaux), for instance, closely paraphrasing Mrs. Gaskell. She says:

The little property she (Miss Branwell) had saved out of her frugal income was all left to her three nieces. Branwell had been her darling, her only son, called by her name, but his disgrace had wounded her too deeply. He was not even mentioned in her will.

These statements, which have passed into accredited Brontë-Saga, are so wide of the truth that it is worth while correcting their errors. The facts are these: Miss Branwell's will was drawn up at York on April 30, 1833, and it was this will, made more than nine years before, which was now proved. At the time when she made her will Branwell was fifteen years old, and it is quite impossible that at that age 'his reckless expenditure' or his 'disgrace' had caused his aunt to revoke a previous will, and cut him off from the share she had intended for him; nor is there the slightest reason to suppose that any such previous will ever existed. He was, moreover, mentioned in her will: she left of her personal effects an Indian workbox to Charlotte, her china-topped workbox and an ivory fan to Emily, her Japan dressing-box to Branwell, her watch and various trinkets to Anne. Again, she did not leave her capital to her three nieces, but to four nieces, the Brontë girls being three of them, the fourth, Anne Kingston, being the daughter of another sister. Her capital was proved at 'under £1500' (*i.e.* over £1400), and her income of £50 a year was derived from it, and was not the result of frugality; she had been left it by her father. A further provision in her will was that her property should be divided between her nieces when the youngest of them attained the age of twenty-one. Anne, the youngest, at the time of her death was twenty-two, and therefore as soon as the will was proved the three sisters each came into a sum of over £300.

On the sudden departure of Charlotte and Emily from Brussels owing to their aunt's death, M. Héger wrote a letter to Mr. Brontë, which they brought with them. He spoke in it of his great regret, due to more than one cause, at their leaving the school; and this letter certainly must have carried great weight in determining the decision which so profoundly affected Charlotte's future life and work. He wrote:

En perdant nos deux chères élèves, nous ne devons pas vous cacher que nous éprouvons à la fois et du chagrin et de l'inquiétude; nous sommes affligés parce que cette brusque séparation vient briser l'affection presque paternelle que nous leur avons vouée, et notre peine s'augmente à la vue de tant de travaux interrompus, de tant de choses bien commencées, et qui ne demandent que quelque temps encore pour être menées à bonne fin. Dans un an chacune de vos demoiselles eût été entièrement prémunie contre les éventualités de l'avenir; chacune d'elles acquérait à la fois et l'instruction et la science d'enseignement: ... encore un an tout au plus et l'œuvre était achevée et bien achevée. Alors nous aurions pu, si cela vous eût convenu, offrir à mesdemoiselles vos filles ou du moins à l'une des deux une position qui eût été dans ses goûts, et qui lui eût donné cette douce indépendance si difficile à trouver pour une jeune personne.... Nous savons, Monsieur, que vous pèserez plus mûrement et plus sagement que nous la conséquence qu'aurait pour l'avenir une interruption complète dans les études de vos deux filles; vous déciderez ce qu'il faut faire, et vous nous pardonnerez notre franchise, si vous daignez considérer que le motif qui nous fait agir est une affection bien désintéressée et qui s'affligerait beaucoup de devoir déjà se résigner à n'être plus utile à vos chères enfants.

The effect of so emphatic and so kindly a persuasion might easily and naturally have determined Charlotte to go back to Brussels, as M. Héger strongly advised; Madame also, who up till now was on excellent terms with her, wrote her a kind and affectionate letter. Indeed, on the face of it, there seemed to be every reason for so doing. Emily, who, as Charlotte says in her memoir, had barely with the utmost power of her resolution got through the ordeal of living away from Haworth, would remain at the Parsonage with her father, while she went back to complete the education through which all the sisters would jointly profit when their school was established. Moreover, there was now no difficulty about money; they had, all three of them, come into a sum of £300, left them by Miss Branwell; besides, as it turned out, Mme. Héger amended her original offer of merely granting Charlotte board and tuition free, in return for the English class she was to hold, and gave her in addition a salary of £16. As the charges for board and tuition were only £26 a year, Charlotte got food, lodging, and tuition for £10. Yet in spite of all this, in spite of the fact that it was strictly in accordance with her principles about all girls, not Brontës alone, making their way in the world, that she should return to Brussels, and that Anne should go back to her post as governess at Thorp Green, Charlotte subsequently wrote to Ellen, saying:

I returned to Brussels after aunt's death against my conscience, prompted by what then seemed an irresistible impulse. I was punished for my selfish folly by a withdrawal for more than two years of happiness and peace of mind.

Now these are strong expressions, and for many years controversy raged over them. It was hard to understand why it should have been against Charlotte's conscience to return there in accordance with M. Héger's very kind and competent advice, and continue the course which had been broken off by the purely extraneous circumstance of Miss Bramwell's death, or why it should have been 'senseless folly' so to do, or why this senseless folly, which apparently was so eminently reasonable and wise, should have resulted in so long a forfeit of happiness and peace of mind. The only conjecture that was made by those who knew Charlotte best, namely, her friend Ellen Nussey and her subsequent husband Mr. Nicholls, was that she felt she ought to have stopped at home to look after her father, for he, like Branwell, drank too much, and her firm presence at Haworth might have checked this tendency. Therein we are let into another grim secret of the life at the Parsonage, but, as revelations which came out more than fifty years afterwards proved, this conjecture was not the real reason.

Certain students of Charlotte's novels formed another theory. They knew (as who does not?) that she used in her books every possible scrap of personal experience: there was never an author of fiction who owed so much to her own actual life. Cowan Bridge School, her sufferings as governess, the curates, her friends Mary and Martha Taylor, her sister Emily, the scenery and setting of her books, and, above all, she herself are drawn often photographically and without disguise. These students, working on a sound principle, found in *Villette* numbers of such portraits of M. Héger and the rest; the *pensionnat* in the Rue d'Isabelle was presented with the most exact fidelity, down to minute details, and they conjectured that Lucy Snowe's passionate devotion to her teacher, Paul Emmanuel, was a fictional but faithful transcript of Charlotte's feelings for M. Héger. The whole of the book, so they rightly pointed out, was a slice carved from her life: it was reasonable to suppose that the central *motif* was carved from it too. Such a theory also explained the nature of 'the irresistible impulse' to return to Brussels, and why this 'selfish folly' had so disastrous an effect on her happiness: Charlotte would scarcely (so they argued) have applied 'irresistible impulse' to her desire to learn more German, nor, since this acquisition was to result in benefit for her sisters as well, was this scholastic ambition a selfish folly. There was something more. She knew, they suggested, that she was falling in love with M. Héger and could not resist that fatal and dangerous impulse to go back to him.

Such a notion, considered as degrading and disfiguring to the image of Charlotte as presented by Mrs. Gaskell, brought down on these theorists vials of scorn and opprobrium. Her champions felt it to be a monstrous outrage that she should be suspected of having fallen in love with a married man. No one had suggested that there was any semblance of an actual love-affair arising out of this situation, or that Charlotte's devotion to her professor was returned by him; but many ardent Brontëites, in no less ardent language, were unspeakably shocked by the mere suggestion that she loved him, and a furious indignation inspired their pens. They proved to their own satisfaction that not only was there no evidence to support so malevolent a notion, but that anyone who knew anything about Charlotte's puritanical uprightness must have known also that she was incapable of such a spontaneous surrender, and they proved it by a hurricane of arguments that swept all before it. Then, nearly sixty years after her death, came the conclusive evidence that all they had proved to be false was perfectly true.

Charlotte returned then to Brussels alone during the last week of January 1843. Madame Héger, she wrote to Ellen, received her with great kindness, and both she and her husband, for whom alone she felt regard and esteem, did all they could to make her at home, telling her to use their sitting-room as if it was her own, whenever she was not engaged in the schoolroom. She gave lessons in English to M. Héger and his brother-in-law, M. Chapelle, whose wife was the sister of M. Héger's first wife. They were both quick in learning, especially M. Héger, though the efforts they made to acquire an English pronunciation would have made Ellen 'laugh to all eternity.' Apparently there had been an idea that Ellen should have come out to Brussels with Charlotte, for she wrote again early in April, saying: 'During the bitter cold weather we had through February and the principal part of March, I did not regret that you had not accompanied me.' She was occasionally lonely, but happy, she affirmed, compared to what she had been when a governess. Then we infer that there must have been some badinage on Ellen's part, such as the two friends indulged in over the susceptible Mr. Weightman, for Charlotte denies with considerable asperity the report that had reached Ellen that she had gone back to Brussels 'in some remote hope of entrapping a husband.' She lives, she assures her, in 'total seclusion,' never speaking to any man except M. Héger, and seldom to him. Possibly, then, the English lessons had already come to an end.

By May Charlotte had already been in Brussels for twelve months altogether, and there must have been some idea that she would then return, but in answer to an inquiry of Ellen's, Emily wrote to tell her that 'Charlotte has never mentioned a word about coming home.' She adds a somewhat acid comment: 'If you would go over for half a year, perhaps you might be able to bring her back with you, otherwise she might vegetate there till the age of Methuselah for mere lack of courage to face the voyage.' Simultaneously Charlotte wrote to Branwell, saying: 'I grieve that Emily is so solitary; but, however, you and Anne will soon be returning for the holidays, which will cheer the house for the time.' Clearly, she had no intention of going home herself. Branwell, it may be noticed, who had now been four months with Anne at Thorp Green, must have been conducting himself decently, for Charlotte says: 'I have received a general assurance that you do well and are in good odour.'

It is now that the first signs of trouble and disquietude begin to manifest themselves. Charlotte, as she herself most truly says in this same letter of May 1 to Branwell, 'grows exceedingly misanthropic and sour.' She launches out into bitter diatribe against the Belgian world:

Amongst 120 persons which compose the daily population of this house, I can discern only one or two who deserve anything like regard. This is not owing to foolish fastidiousness on my part, but to the absence of decent qualities on theirs. They have not intellect or politeness or good nature or good feeling. They are nothing. I don't hate them—hatred would be too warm a feeling. But one wearies from day to day of caring nothing, fearing nothing, liking nothing, hating nothing, being nothing, doing nothing,—yes, I teach and sometimes get red in the face with impatience at their stupidity. But don't think I ever scold or fly into a passion.... Nobody ever gets into a passion here. Such a thing is not known. The phlegm that thickens their blood is too gluey to boil. They are very false in their relations with each other, but they rarely quarrel and friendship is a folly they are unacquainted with.

If this was not hate, it was surely a very fair imitation of it; then follows a significant passage about M. Héger, lately 'a delirious hyena,' and his wife, who had welcomed Charlotte back with such kindness.

The black swan, M. Héger, is the only sole veritable exception to this rule (for Madame always cool and always reasoning is not quite an exception). But I rarely speak to Monsieur now, for not being a pupil I have little or nothing to do with him. From time to time he shows his kind-heartedness by loading me with books, so that I am still indebted to him for all the pleasure and amusement I have.

Her bitter censoriousness of others, though now no longer strangers, did not decrease. A month later she wrote to Emily about the three teachers, Mdlles. Blanche, Sophie, and Marie Haussé, whom previously Charlotte regarded with comparative indifference. These ladies appear to have had less gluey phlegm in their blood than the rest; there is also a fresh sidelight on Madame Héger:

Mdlle Blanche and Mdlle Haussé are at present on a system of war without quarter. They hate each other like two cats. Mdlle Blanche frightens Mdlle Haussé by her white passions (for they quarrel venomously). Mdlle Haussé complains that when Mdlle Blanche is in fury, *'elle n'a pas de lèvres.'* I find also that Mdlle Sophie dislikes Mdlle Blanche extremely. She says she is heartless, insincere, and vindictive, which epithets, I assure you, are richly deserved. Also I find she is the regular spy of Mme Héger, to whom she reports everything. Also she invents—which I should not have thought. I have now the entire charge of the English lessons. I have given two lessons to the first class. Hortense Jannoy was a picture on these occasions, her face was black as a 'blue-piled thunder-loft,' and her two ears were red as raw beef. To all questions asked, her reply was *'Je ne sais pas.'* It is a pity but her friends could meet with a person qualified to cast out a devil. I am richly off for companionship in these parts. Of late days, M. and Mme Héger rarely speak to me, and I really don't pretend to care a fig for anybody else in the establishment. You are not to suppose by that expression that I am under the influence of warm affection for Mme Héger. I am convinced she does not like me,—why, I can't tell, nor do I think she herself has any definite reason for the aversion; but for one thing, she cannot comprehend why I do not make intimate friends of Mesdames Blanche, Sophie, and Haussé. M. Héger is wondrously influenced by Madame, and I should not wonder if he disapproves very much of my unamiable want of sociability ... consequently he has in a great measure withdrawn the light of his countenance.... Except for the loss of M. Héger's good will (if I have lost it) I care for none of them.

Now this is very bitter invective about her pupils and her colleagues, and though Charlotte was at all times censorious, such violence taken in conjunction with the spyings of Madame and the coldness of Monsieur would not unnaturally lead us to suppose a more intimate agitation than any contempt of Belgian phlegm and furies would warrant. It reminds us of bubbles coming up through dark waters, and just beginning to prick the surface; we seem to hear a clamour, almost hysterical, designed half-subconsciously to overscore, even for herself, disquieting whispers within. There is some hidden agitation, some tumult in the heart of the city.

But at present she had no thought of putting an end to the situation which was already beginning to wreck her happiness and peace of mind. In June she wrote a letter to her father, hoping that he and Emily were well:

I am afraid she will have a good deal of hard work to do now that Hannah [a servant at Haworth] is gone. I am exceedingly glad that you will keep Tabby, besides she will be company for Emily, who without her would be very lonely.

So Emily was left to do most of the housework and console herself for her loneliness with the society of an old servant of over seventy years of age, and Anne to continue in her situation at Thorp Green, which she detested. After that there is no further letter from Charlotte till August 6, a few days before the summer vacation, when the pupils would disperse and the Hégers leave Brussels for a five weeks' holiday. She was miserably home-sick, the prospect of being so much alone for all those weeks appalled her, and it is impossible to find any reason, now that Miss Branwell's legacy had put her in funds, why she should not have gone back to Haworth for the holidays, except that she foresaw difficulties in returning again to Brussels when the vacation was over. 'I will continue to stay (D.V.) some months longer,' she wrote, 'till I have acquired German.'

She wrote to Emily again on September 2, when the holidays were more than half over. Mlle. Blanche, who was Mme. Héger's spy, had returned.

But [writes Charlotte] I am always alone except at meal times, for Mdlle Blanche's character is so false and so contemptible, I can't force myself to associate with her. She perceives my utter dislike, and never now speaks to me —a great relief.

Then follows this passage:

... So I go out and traverse the Boulevards and streets of Bruxelles sometimes for hours together. Yesterday I went on a pilgrimage to the cemetery, and far beyond it to a hill where there was nothing but fields as far as the horizon. When I came back it was evening.

Now Mrs. Gaskell clearly saw this letter for, though she does not actually quote it, she describes Charlotte's days during the holidays as follows:

She went out and with weary steps would traverse the Boulevards and the streets sometimes for hours together.... Then up again ... anywhere but to the *pensionnat*—out to the cemetery where Martha lay—out beyond it to the hills, whence there is nothing to be seen but fields as far as the horizon. The shades of evening made her retrace her footsteps.

No coincidence can possibly account for the identity of phrasing. Mrs. Gaskell's narrative shows that she wrote this description with Charlotte's letter to Emily in front of her. But the actual letter from which with a bewraying fidelity Mrs. Gaskell paraphrased this paragraph, immediately proceeded to describe a very astonishing adventure, which she decided to omit, though it lay before her:

I found myself opposite to Ste. Gudule, and the bell, whose voice you know, began to toll for evening *salut*. I went in quite alone (which procedure you will say is not much like me), wandered about the aisles, where a few old women were saying their prayers, till Vespers began. I stayed till they were over. Still I could not leave the church or force myself to go home—to school, I mean. An odd whim came into my head. In a solitary part of the Cathedral, six or seven people still remained kneeling by the confessionals. In two confessionals I saw a priest. I felt as if I did not care what I did, provided it was not absolutely wrong, and that it served to vary my life and yield a moment's interest. I took a fancy to change myself into a Catholic, and go and make a real confession to see what it was like.... I approached at last, and knelt down in a niche which was just vacated. I had to kneel there ten minutes waiting, for on the other side was another penitent invisible to me. At last that (one) went away, and a little wooden door inside the grating opened, and I saw the priest leaning his ear towards me. I was obliged to begin, and yet I did not know a word of the formula with which they commence their confessions.... I commenced with saying I was a foreigner, and had been brought up a Protestant. The priest asked if I was a Protestant then. I somehow could not tell a lie, and said 'yes.' He replied that in that case I could not '*jouir du bonheur de la confesse*,' but I was determined to confess, and at last he said he would allow me because it might be the first step towards returning to the true church. I actually did confess—a real confession. When I had done, he told me his address, and said that every morning I was to go to the rue du Parc—to his house—and he would reason with me and try to convince me of the error and enormity of being a Protestant!!! I promised faithfully to go. Of course, however, the adventure stops there, and I hope I shall never see the priest again. I think you had better not tell papa of this.

That was certainly a wise precaution. Mr. Brontë's adamantine Protestantism would not have looked upon his daughter's going to a Catholic confessional as merely an 'odd whim'; he would have called it by a much harder name. So also at heart would she herself, for she had already expressed her contempt of the Catholic religion in abundantly emphatic terms; she had advised any Protestant who felt in danger of changing his faith to attend Mass and note the 'idiotic mercenary aspect of all the priests,' and, so Mrs. Gaskell tells us,

one of the reasons for the silent estrangement between Mme Héger and Miss

Brontë is to be found in the fact that the English Protestant's dislike of Romanism increased with her knowledge of it, and its effects upon those who professed it: and when occasion called for an expression of opinion from Charlotte Brontë she was uncompromising truth.

Yet in spite of her contempt for it, she now availed herself of one of its Sacraments. It is true that she avowed herself a Protestant, when kneeling in the Confessional, but for the sake of the relief which confession would bring her, she insisted on making it, and 'promised faithfully' to go and receive instruction from the priest, which promise, she states, she had not the slightest intention of carrying out. Was this confession then, so strangely made, merely an 'odd whim,' as she told Emily, that 'should yield a moment's interest'? It is impossible to believe that. She had something on her mind which, in her lonely, nervous, hysterical state, she must confide to somebody for the human relief that the mere communication of it would bring. What could it possibly have been that lay so heavily and unhappily on her troubled soul? Something serious, or she could never have had recourse to the benefits of an institution which she so thoroughly despised. But there must be no chance that this communication should be betrayed, and it must be made under the seal of confession. Knowing what we do now, after the publication of Charlotte's subsequent love-letters to M. Héger, we cannot doubt the nature of that confession. All points to the desire, which her essential uprightness of character abhorred, but which was terribly insistent and made the absence of M. Héger on holiday so intolerable.

Now Mrs. Gaskell having seen this letter (for she quotes from it) omits the incident, for in *Villette*, which minutely and accurately describes the *pensionnat* in the Rue d'Isabelle, which portrays under the name of Paul Emanuel the unmistakable lineaments of M. Héger, and under the name of Madame Beck those of Madame Héger, and her espionage, Lucy Snowe, though a Protestant, makes a precisely similar confession to a Roman Catholic priest, and no doubt it was better not to let it be known that that incident was a piece of authentic autobiography. It was discordant with Charlotte's strongly expressed views about Catholicism, and it was inconsistent with the reason Mrs. Gaskell had given for the coolness between Charlotte and Madame Héger. On all counts, then, it was wise to suppress the confessional, and especially so because her readers might conceivably begin to conjecture what heart's need drove Charlotte to make use of the benefits of a religion of which she was so contemptuous. It would have been too truly directed a pointer to regions best left unsuspected.

The Hégers returned during September, and the school reassembled again for the new term. Charlotte had determined (D.V.) to stop some months longer in order to acquire German, but the situation was beginning to break her, and early in October she wrote to Ellen:

I felt as if I could bear it no longer, and I went to Mme Héger and gave her notice. If it had depended on her, I should certainly have been soon at liberty; but M. Héger, having heard of what was in agitation, sent for me the day after, and pronounced with vehemence his decision that I should not leave. I could not, at that time, have persevered in my intention without exciting him to passion, so I promised to stay a little while longer....

How Charlotte, miserable though she was, must have adored his vehemence in forbidding her to go, and secretly, in the way of a woman's heart, have whispered to herself the interpretation which her reason told her it could not bear! For M. Héger naturally did not want to lose his English teacher at the beginning of the term; he was thinking of the pupils learning English, not of their instructor, and there is no more evidence for supposing that he was ever in the slightest degree in love with Charlotte than that Mr. Weightman had been in love with Emily. But now at last Charlotte began to suspect that Madame Héger had some inkling of her secret, for writing to Ellen she hints at it:

I have much to say—many odd little things, queer and puzzling enough—but which one day perhaps or rather one evening—if ever we should find ourselves by the fireside at Haworth or at Brookroyd with our feet on the fender, curling our hair—I may communicate to you.

In her next letter she became more explicit as to what these were: 'I fancy I begin to perceive the reason for this (Mme. Héger's) mighty distance and reserve; it sometimes makes me laugh and at other times nearly cry.'

December came and once more Charlotte wrote to Emily, saying that she had no thought of coming home yet; she lacked a 'real pretext' for doing so. There was indeed every reason why she should go home and begin on her project of starting the school, for the sake of which, and for the further education it would give her, she had originally come to Brussels for a period of six months. Now she had been here for nearly two years, and still she could find no pretext to leave! She longed to get away, she was wretched with this misbegotten passion, but she could not endure to cut herself off from the source of it. She saw vivid and minute, in calenture, what was going on this Sunday morning in the kitchen at the Parsonage:

I should like even to be cutting up the hash with the clerk and some register people at the other table, and you standing by, watching that I put enough flour, not too much pepper, and, above all, that I save the best piece of the leg of mutton for Tiger and Keeper, the first of which personages would be jumping about the dish and carving knife, and the latter standing like a devouring flame on the kitchen floor. To complete the picture, Tabby blowing the fire, in order to boil the potatoes to a sort of vegetable glue! How divine are these recollections to me at this moment!

But she intended to remain in Brussels, still clinging to the protestation that she must acquire more German, and feeding her soul with the sweet torture that racked her. Then, as was bound to happen, came the breaking point. She suddenly wrote to Emily saying that she had taken her determination and was coming home, assigning no cause. M. Héger, we gather, was vexed at her going, for subsequently she wrote to Ellen: 'I suffered much before I left Brussels. I think, however long I live, I shall not forget what the parting with M. Héger cost me; it grieved me so much to grieve him, who has been so true, kind and disinterested a friend.' It was a tradition in the Héger family that on parting with Mme. Héger she said '*Je me vengerai*'; but that is the kind of legend that may have arisen after the publication of *Villette*.

She arrived at Haworth on January 2, 1844.

CHAPTER IX

Branwell and Anne were home for the Christmas holidays, but presently went back to their situations as tutor and governess to Mr. Robinson's children at Thorp Green. Mrs. Gaskell says that 'agonizing suspicions' about Branwell's conduct there had been one of the causes why Charlotte returned from Brussels, but it seems impossible that this was the case, for Charlotte wrote to Ellen, after she got back to Haworth, to say 'that Branwell and Anne were both wondrously valued in their situations.' Though she had longed to get away from the daily renewal of the secret strain and struggle of her life at Brussels, she found the quiet of home, with her father and Emily as companions, unutterably flat and objectless. 'Something in me,' she wrote, 'which used to be enthusiasm is toned down and broken. I have fewer illusions: what I wish for now is active exertion.'

She took up again the scheme for starting a school with her sisters. Thanks to Miss Branwell's legacies there was now money enough. Emily's six months at Brussels and her own year and three-quarters there had greatly added to their qualifications, and M. Héger at parting had given her a diploma certifying to her abilities as a teacher, and attached to it was the seal of the Athénée Royal at Brussels where he was professor in Latin. But once more the scheme must be changed, for Mr. Brontë was growing old; he was threatened with the loss of his sight, also he was disposed to drink too much, and it was no longer feasible that they should all leave him. Miss Wooler's proposal had been possible while Miss Branwell was still alive, but not now. So with her indomitable courage Charlotte settled to turn the Parsonage into a school.

Before May she was seeking for pupils, and fixed the terms at £25 per annum for board and English education, subsequently raising them to £35. She made some personal applications, but these led to nothing. Mr. White, to whose children she had been governess, regretted that his daughter was settled elsewhere; Colonel Stott and Mr. Bousfeild were in the same predicament. As soon as she could get the promise of only one pupil, she proposed to issue a circular and begin making the necessary alterations in the Parsonage.

About this time she had, as she wrote to M. Héger, an offer of the post of head teacher in a girls' school at Manchester at the salary of £100 a year; she refused that because she had high hopes of this school at Haworth, where she hoped to take five or six boarders. In July, though she had not secured any pupils, she printed her circular and sent it round 'to all the friends on whom I have the slightest claim, and to some on whom I have no claim.' She was sure she would succeed, for she wrote to Ellen, saying: 'What an excellent thing perseverance is for getting on in the world. Calm self-confidence (not impudence, for that is vulgar and repulsive) is an admirable quality.'

The circular ran as follows:

THE MISSES BRONTËS' ESTABLISHMENT

FOR

THE BOARD & EDUCATION

OF A LIMITED NUMBER OF

YOUNG LADIES.

The Parsonage, Haworth,

NEAR BRADFORD.

Terms.

	£	s.	d.
Board & education, including Writing, Arithmetic, History, Grammar, Geography, and Needle Work per annum:	35	0	0
French, German, Latin (Each per Quarter)	1	1	0
Music, Drawing, each per Quarter	1	1	0
Use of Piano Forte, per Quarter	0	5	0
Washing, per Quarter	0	15	0

Each young lady to be provided with One Pair of Sheets, Pillow Cases, Four Towels, a Dessert and Tea Spoon.

A Quarter's notice, or a Quarter's Board, is required previous to the Removal of a Pupil.

Out went these circulars broadcast; Ellen had half a dozen for distribution, but never an answer, beyond sympathy and regrets, came to any single one of them. The months went on, and in October Charlotte wrote to her friend saying, 'Everyone wishes us well, but there are no pupils to be had.' She had done everything that careful thought and iron determination could accomplish. She had qualified herself and Emily by pupilage and teaching at Brussels, there was sufficient money, Mr. Brontë had consented to the scheme, and all was ready except the pupils, whom no effort of will or circularisation would produce.

Whether her sisters had still any enthusiasm for the idea is doubtful. Emily, in the private paper written on her birthday of 1845 for the secret eyes of Anne, exhibits none, making the following entry with regard to it:

I should have mentioned that last summer (1844) the school scheme was revived in full vigour. We had prospectuses printed, despatched letters to all acquaintances, imparting our plans and did our little all: but it was found no go. Now I don't desire a school at all, and none of us have any great longing for it.

Anne, in her corresponding paper, was equally lukewarm. She says:

When the last paper (1841) was written we were thinking of setting up a school. The scheme has been dropt, and long after taken up again, and dropt again, because we could not get pupils.

From the first the initiative and driving-power had been wholly Charlotte's, but now, in the autumn of 1844, she gave it up, because in spite of all her efforts no pupils would come. The abandonment of the school has, of course, been laid at Branwell's door, and one notable Brontë biographer asks: 'How could she (Charlotte) receive children at Haworth with this drugged and drunken wastrel in the house?' But at the time when it was finally abandoned Branwell was still in his situation at Thorp Green, and was at home only for his holidays. We hear no more about the school, for the sake of which she and her sisters had taken abhorred situations as governesses, and for which Emily had suffered a half-year's misery at Brussels. Anne was still 'in the house of bondage' at Thorp Green, where she remained till the summer of 1845.

Charlotte's disappointment was bitter, but she drew, on behalf of herself and her sisters, a moral lesson from it. 'They were not mortified at defeat. The effort must be beneficial, whatever the result may be, because it teaches us experience and an additional knowledge of the world.' Now in spite of her efforts without ruth to herself or them, the long-cherished idea for which she had worked for years had failed, and she recognised that it was hopeless. Never again did she attempt to revive it, or indeed allude to it.

Throughout this year, while the withered leaves of her ambition for herself and her sisters dropped from the tree, she had to bear, in addition to this disappointment, a disquietude of which she could speak to none. She had fallen in love with M. Héger, and she was writing to him in terms that wring the heart of those who can now read what she said in a few of these desolate and longing letters. Sometimes he replied to them, but usually she got no answer. The first of these letters that is extant was dated July 24, 1844, at the time when she was sending out her circulars for the school, but there had been others before, as these extracts from it show.

I am well aware that it is not my turn to write to you.... I once wrote you a letter that was less than reasonable because sorrow was at my heart: but I shall do so no more. I shall try to be selfish no longer, and even while I look upon your letters as one of the greatest felicities known to me, I shall wait the receipt of them in patience.

I am firmly convinced that I shall see you again some day. I know not how or when—but it must be for I wish it so much....

I should not know this lethargy if I could write. Formerly I spent whole days and weeks and months in writing, not wholly without result, for Southey and Coleridge, two of our best authors, to whom I sent certain MSS., were good enough to express their approval. Were I to write much I should become blind.... Otherwise I should write a book and dedicate it to my literature master.... The career of letters is closed to me,—only that of teaching is open....

Once more good-bye, Monsieur—it hurts to say good-bye even in a letter. Oh, it is certain I shall see you again some day: it must be so, for as soon as I have earned money enough to go to Brussels I shall go there—and I shall see you again if only for a moment!

There are one or two curious points about this letter. Charlotte was very short-sighted, but never did she have nor was even threatened with such trouble with her eyes as would prevent her from writing, and we must put this wail that the career of literature was closed to her *ad misericordiam*. Again, Southey had never expressed approval of the poems she sent him; indeed, his reply was such that Charlotte resolved to give up writing altogether. Wordsworth had been equally discouraging about the opening chapters of the novel she sent him, and it was Branwell not she who wrote to Hartley Coleridge for his verdict.

There was no answer returned to this letter; the next is dated three months later, October 24, 1844. She now took advantage of Mary Taylor's brother going to Brussels, and entrusted him to deliver it. In it she wrote: 'I would only ask of you if you heard from me at the beginning of May and again in the month of August,' Possibly she suspected that Madame had intercepted these two other letters. Yet still M. Héger gave no response, and once more she wrote to him on January 8, 1845:

Mr. Taylor has returned. I asked him if he had a letter for me. 'No, nothing.' 'Patience,' said I, 'his sister will be here soon.' Miss Taylor has returned. 'I have nothing for you from M. Héger,' says she, 'neither letter nor message.'

Day and night I find neither rest nor peace. If I sleep I am disturbed by tormenting dreams in which I see you always stern, always grim and vexed with me.... You will tell me perhaps: 'I take not the slightest interest in you, Mdlle Charlotte. You are no longer an inmate of my house. I have forgotten you.'

Well, Monsieur, tell me so frankly. It will be a shock to me. It matters not. It would be less dreadful than uncertainty.

The fourth letter that survives is dated 'Nov. 18,' without indication of the year. But doubtless the year was 1845, not 1844, for in this letter she says that her father's blindness has so increased that he can neither read nor write, and that in a few months' time he will have an operation on his eyes. This operation took place in the summer of 1846. She writes:

I have tried to forget you, for the remembrance of a person whom one thinks never to see again is too wearing to the spirit, and when one has suffered that kind of anxiety for a year or two one is ready to do anything to find peace once more.

It is humiliating to be the slave of a fixed and dominant idea which lords it over the mind!

For you to write will not be very interesting but for me it is life. Your last letter was stay and prop to me for half a year. When day by day I await a letter and when day by day disappointment comes to fling me back into overwhelming sorrow, and the sweet delight of seeing your handwriting and reading your counsel eludes me like a phantom vision, the fever takes me—I lose appetite and sleep and pine away.

These letters evoke our unstinted compassion and sympathy with the writer. She had fallen in love with this man many years her senior, who was a

Catholic, who had a wife and five children, and who had no interest in her save as a queer though clever pupil, and no feeling for her, as far as any evidence goes, except the *affection presque paternelle*, of which he had assured her father. They explain without need of any further comment thenature of the 'irresistible impulse' which took her back for the second time to Brussels against the warnings of her own conscience and common sense; they define the 'selfish folly' for which, as she wrote to Ellen, she was 'punished by a withdrawal for more than two years of happiness and peace of mind.' She knew the insanity of what she was doing, but she compounded with her accusing conscience, telling herself, perhaps more than half convincing herself, that she was going back to Brussels not for that reason at all, but in order to fit herself better, by a completer knowledge of French and German, for the school which she was determined to start with her sisters. Then there was M. Héger's letter to her father: he had strongly urged her to return, and by another year's work fulfil the remarkable progress she had already made; surely it would be unwise to disregard the advice of one so experienced. Such considerations were weighty; it would be missing a chance of future success not to act as she had done. But all the time her conscience told her not to go. She had gone, and at once the harvest which she had herself sown began to ripen. Her affection for him grew into a devotion and a surrender so abject, that when finally, after long procrastinations, she returned home she could not refrain from writing to him these love-letters, though all the time she knew that Madame had long suspected her feelings for him, and for months had spied on her. That gives the measure of her passion, and she risked anything sooner than not have the bitter consolation of writing to him and the eager suspense of waiting month by month for his rare replies. Once, knowing nothing of what she was talking about, she had been profuse in exhortations to Ellen, laying down with precision the manner in which a girl should prudently and without undue haste allow herself to fall in love with a man who wanted her, bidding her remember the importance of her keeping herself well in hand, and warning her of the monstrous folly of a *grande passion*. Now she had committed that monstrous folly in the most undesirable manner; she had fallen hopelessly in love with a man who felt nothing for her, and who could not possibly marry her. Bitter was wisdom.

Then we must look at the affair from the point of view of M. Héger and his wife. It was known to both of them, while Charlotte was still at Brussels, that she had formed this strong attachment to him, for from that arose Monsieur's coldness and Madame's spyings, and when these letters began to arrive it was necessary to act with circumspection. A girl who wrote in such a strain to the respectable father of a family might do something more embarrassing yet; indeed, she had threatened in one of them to visit Brussels again and see him. M. Héger behaved very properly. He did not always answer Charlotte's letters, but, when he did, he employed his wife as his amanuensis; this was no rare thing, for he much disliked writing himself. It was wise and prudent that she should know how he replied, and his answers, written by her, had thus passed the conjugal censorship. What these replies were is unknown, for either Charlotte destroyed them or her husband did so after her death, but we shall find reasons for feeling sure that they were careful and circumspect. M. Héger did not read to his wife Charlotte's letters to him, but tore them up and threw the pieces into the waste-paper basket. One he did not destroy, for he had noted on the back of it the address of a Brussels bootmaker. Then, we assume, he imagined he had lost it, and thought no more of it. That was M. Héger's share in the matter; Madame had a policy of her own, which was disclosed many years later.

Such was the superficial history of this correspondence, and there, as far as M. Héger was aware, the matter stayed till after Charlotte's death. But the inner and subsequent history of these four letters of Charlotte's which survived and which are now in the British Museum is so interesting and extraordinary that, though the story of them lies outside the immediate sphere of the affairs of the Brontës, it must be followed up, as revealed by Mr. Marion H. Spielmann, who obtained it from M. Héger's daughter, Mdlle. Louise Héger. An old lady of over seventy years of age when these letters were published in 1913, she was a girl of six when Charlotte left her mother's *pensionnat*. She remembered her quite well, 'a little person, extremely narrow of chest, with side-curls, large eyes (but not so large as in her portrait) and sadly defective teeth—somewhat ill-favoured indeed, and unattractive to look upon—and yet beloved by her.' The following is the account that Mdlle. Héger gave to Mr. Spielmann.

Madame Héger had looked upon Charlotte when she was at Brussels as a highly excitable, nervous girl, whom she did not at all understand. Her farewell words when she left, *Je me vengerai*, were not pleasant, and perhaps portended trouble; it was as well to bear them in mind. Then her letters began to arrive; her husband (as we have seen) tore them up after reading them, threw them into the waste-paper basket, and dictated his replies to his wife. One (the first of those that survive) he did not tear up, and his wife read it and kept it. Having found out in what terms Charlotte was writing to him, she felt that her general apprehensions as to what a hysterical girl like this might do were justified, and when other letters came and he tore them up, she rescued them from the waste-paper basket whenever she had the opportunity, pieced them together and kept them also. They confirmed what she had always thought, and in case there was trouble with Charlotte, it would be useful to have them. At least one of them, moreover, had been addressed to her husband, not at the *pensionnat* in the Rue d'Isabelle, but at the Athénée Royal, where he held a Latin class for boys. Then in course of time the letters ceased, for after two years Charlotte wrote no more, and as far as M. Héger then knew, no letter of hers to him was in existence, for he had put them into the waste-paper basket.

Over twenty years later, when the Brontës had become famous, there was a lecture delivered at Brussels by a literary Frenchman on the subject of 'The Brontës.' Mdlle. Louise Héger attended it, and was horrified to hear her father and mother held up to the execration of the audience for their cruelty and barbarity to the two sisters when at Brussels; the lecturer illustrated his remarks by quotations from *Villette*. She told her mother on her return home what had been said, and in answer Mme. Héger took her to her room, opened her jewel-case, and showed her the four letters of Charlotte to her father which she had pieced together and kept, bidding her read them. The devotion they showed towards him adequately disposed of the idea that he had treated her with barbarity, and shed an entirely new light on the situation. Mdlle. Louise understood, and the letters were then replaced in their *cache*.

Madame Héger died in 1889, leaving to Louise her jewel-case and its contents, among which were the letters. She took them to her father, who was engaged in going through and destroying papers of his wife's. He recognised them, and, astonished and ill-pleased to know that they were still in existence, threw them once more into the waste-paper basket. Louise thought that her father was not in the mood to give careful consideration to the fate of these letters which her mother had been at pains to preserve for so long; they should not be destroyed without due reflection, and presently, when her father had left the room, she did exactly as her mother had done forty-five years before, took them out of the waste-paper basket, and again kept them. Thus though M. Héger, when they were eventually published, was roundly abused (especially by those who had so conclusively proved that Charlotte was never in love with him) for having kept them at all, it turns out that, as far as his intention was concerned, he had twice destroyed them. Mdlle. Louise then consulted a French friend on the wisdom of keeping the letters. He strongly recommended her to do so, since they were now of the highest literary interest. After her father's death she showed them to her brother, Professor Paul Héger, and eventually a family council was held as to what should be done with them. One member of it maintained that such fervour of expression pointed to guilty intercourse between M. Héger and Charlotte, and it is certainly possible that this construction might be put upon them by those who did not know the circumstances. But neither Professor Héger nor his sister, to whom the letters belonged, wished to destroy them, and in 1913 they brought them to England to consult Mr. Marion Spielmann, whose judgment they trusted, about their fate. On his advice they consented to the publication, and presented the letters themselves to the British Museum.

Mdlle. Louise Héger's narrative, as here abridged, is obviously trustworthy; she alone knew the history of the letters, and there is no reason to suspect that it is other than completely reliable, and we can accept it without reservations. But there is one point which may already have struck the reader and which requires examination. It is this.

Mdlle. Louise was not the only person who read these letters during their incarceration in her mother's jewel-case. Mrs. Gaskell read them also, for in her *Life of Charlotte Brontë* she quotes verbatim from three of them, piecing together paragraphs of two of them, and giving a few sentences from a third. Nothing that she quotes gives the faintest hint of their essential contents, there is not a word that a girl might not with the utmost propriety have written to her master; Charlotte thanks him for his kindness to her, she sends messages to Madame and the children. But Mrs. Gaskell certainly read the letters, and since they had remained in Brussels from the time when they were written and posted at Haworth till they were brought to England in 1913, she must therefore have seen them when she went to Brussels in 1856 to collect materials and *mise en scène* concerning Charlotte's life at the *pensionnat*. But they were then, according to Mdlle. Louise's account, reposing in her mother's jewel-case, having been rescued by her from the waste-paper basket where M. Héger had thrown them, and pieced together. Who, then, showed them to Mrs. Gaskell? Not Madame Héger, for, knowing that she was a friend of Charlotte's, she refused to see her. It has always been supposed that it was the delineation of herself in *Villette* that led to this refusal, but the French translation of the book (Mme. Héger knew no English) had only just appeared, and it is a pure assumption to suppose that Mme. Héger had read it. But she had read Charlotte's letters to her husband, and she had no need to seek further for a reason for not consenting to see Mrs. Gaskell. In any case she did not, and, since she is ruled out, the only person who could have shown Mrs. Gaskell the letters was M. Héger himself. She had an interview with him; she liked and respected him, and they talked about his correspondence with Charlotte, for M. Héger begged her to read his letters to her; he felt sure she would have kept them, and they contained 'advice about her character, studies, mode of life.' M. Héger in fact, it becomes plain, showed Mrs. Gaskell Charlotte's letters (from which she made judicious extracts) and was anxious that she should see how properly he answered them. I therefore venture to suggest—it is a theory only, but one that solves our difficulty—that Mme. Héger's reason for not seeing Mrs. Gaskell was Charlotte's letters, and that she said, in effect, to her husband: 'Show them to Mrs. Gaskell and she will understand why I won't see her.' Out came the letters from the jewel-case, and, Mrs. Gaskell having read them they were returned there again.... This conjecture does not, however, invalidate the general credibility of Mdlle. Louise's narrative to Mr. Spielmann. M. Héger knew that in 1856 his wife was still keeping the letters, but it is no wonder that on her death thirty-three years later it was a matter of surprise to him that they were still in existence. Probably he had forgotten all about them.

It remains to consider Mrs. Gaskell's decision to omit from her *Life of Charlotte Brontë* the whole story of her having fallen in love with M. Héger, of her having written those letters which so indubitably prove it, and to exclude from her book any incident, any hint that might, in her opinion, have given rise to conjecture. It was an important decision, for she was the official biographer, and she must have thought that her book, a model of apparently exhaustive research, would probably remain for all time the final work on the family in general, and on Charlotte in particular, for so ample a *Life* would surely be definitive. But she must also have known that she was omitting not only the most profound emotional experience of her heroine herself, but one out of which sprang her best and noblest work, for there can be no doubt that without it *Villette* would never have been written. Nothing more important psychically or mentally ever happened to her, and Mrs. Gaskell, knowing all, decided to say nothing about it, and remove all traces of it. Nothing in her book suggests the possibility of such an entanglement; she even invents a reason for Mme. Héger's coldness to Charlotte. Some biographers, no doubt, if this decision had been presented to them, would have abandoned their work altogether, sooner than falsify its essential truth by such an omission; Mrs. Gaskell thought otherwise, and having formed her loyal and admiring conception of the figure she wished to present, scrapped (with or without compunction) what she knew was of first-rate importance for a faithful portrait.

But there is another side to the question. The disclosure which M. Héger made to her of Charlotte's letters not only must have been a great shock to her (so great that she could not biographically deal with it at all), but would be equally or more shocking to Charlotte's father and to her widower, at whose instance she had undertaken the work. They knew nothing, so far as we know, of the whole Héger episode, or, at the most, they had read the extremely proper answers which M. Héger had returned, in the handwriting of his wife, to the letters which Mrs. Gaskell alone had seen. She was full of enthusiasm for her task; she knew, rightly, that it was in her power to make a charming picture of the woman whose work she so admired, and for whom she had so genuine an affection. Though she did publish gossipy stories about Mr. Brontë which, owing to his justifiable indignation she was obliged to withdraw, it was quite another thing to publish far more serious matter which she was perfectly able to substantiate. It was better to say nothing at all about it, to delete anything that might point to it, to invent reasons why Mme. Héger disliked and distrusted Charlotte, to account for her unhappiness at Brussels by the supposition that Branwell was causing grave anxiety—to do anything and everything in order to conceal what she imagined would never be disclosed. The odds in her favour were enormous, but the hundred-to-one chance went against her, and to us to-day Charlotte Brontë is a vastly more human and interesting figure than she ever could have been if it had not.

CHAPTER X

For a year and a half after Charlotte's final return from Brussels, she and Emily were alone with their father at the Parsonage, Branwell and Anne coming there only for their holidays from Thorp Green. Her letters during this period are few, and they all betoken the deep disquiet and depression and the bitterness of heart that were growing on her. Indeed, the lights were turned very low: her literary ambitions for the time were dead (or, as she wrote to M. Héger, her failing eyesight made it impossible for her to write), not a line of a poem nor a page of prose seems to have been written by her during this period; her friend Mary Taylor, despairing of occupation for an energetic young woman in England, went out to New Zealand; Branwell, though still giving satisfaction in his situation, was making trouble at home, and though Charlotte says nothing definite we may assume that he was drinking. 'He has been more than ordinarily tiresome and annoying of late; he leads Papa a wretched life,' is one of her comments on the conduct of him with whom she had once been the most intimate ally. She had come home from Brussels admirably equipped, a competent scholar in French and German, but no pupil sought to learn of her; she had obtained a certificate with the seal of the Athénée Royal at Brussels, bearing witness to her efficiency as a teacher, and Constantin Héger had signed it, but his name there served only to sharpen her heart's hunger. She had begged for the crumbs that fell from his table to assuage it, but all she got was letters in the handwriting of his wife, advising her about her studies and her mode of life. Activity, some scheme, some ambition, over which she could employ the self-poisoned energies of her soul, was what she longed for; but the scheme that had occupied her for years was derelict, her ambitions were dead, and her heart emptily aching. There was only bitterness to look back on, and a blank to look forward to.

It is true that she had Emily with her, but in spite of the oft-reiterated statement that there was a bond of passionate devotion between the two sisters, we search in vain for any expression of it during Emily's lifetime. Once, when Charlotte was governess at Mrs. Sidgwick's, she wrote a letter to her sister beginning, 'Mine bonnie love,' but otherwise, until Emily's short and final illness, we can find no token in Charlotte's letters of the affection, nor yet of the love that involuntarily betrays itself. As Emily's and Anne's quadrennial papers show, it was they who were the united couple, and before now estranging circumstances had occurred between the other two. Emily who, as Charlotte knew, was wretched away from Haworth, had been taken to Brussels, where had it not been for Miss Branwell's death she would have remained for six months more; she had been desperately unhappy there, and the only allusions Charlotte had made to her was that she and M. Héger did not 'draw well together,' and that subsequently the Hégers began to recognise 'her good points below her singularities.' Then Charlotte had gone back to Brussels alone, and hearing of the burden of household work that lay on Emily's shoulders, had hoped that her father would soon get another servant. Emily was lonely, and she was glad that old Tabby had returned to the Parsonage—she would be a companion for her sister; but it did not occur to her to go back herself. Nor, on Emily's side, is there the slightest expression of affection for Charlotte: she hoped that Ellen might manage to go out to Brussels, otherwise Charlotte might stop on there all the days of Methuselah sooner than face the crossing. Emily, no doubt, was intensely reserved, and not even to Anne did she show her secret life, but to Charlotte she showed nothing at all. If she ever had any deep affection for her, it was so completely concealed that not even when the shadow of death was on her did she reach out a hand to her. At present, and indeed up to the end, before which further cause for estrangement had occurred, Emily's attitude towards Charlotte was one of resentful indifference. Such are the only conclusions we can draw from their meagre references to each other.

Throughout this year and a half there is no sign that Emily's companionship was any consolation for the deadness of Charlotte's whole life. They walked on the moors together, they sewed shirts, the little cat died and Emily was sorry. But otherwise, as Charlotte wrote to her friend towards the end of this period:

I can hardly tell you how time gets on at Haworth. There is no event whatever to mark its progress. One day resembles another, and all have heavy, lifeless physiognomies. Sunday, baking day, and Saturday, are the only ones that have any distinctive mark. Meantime life wears away. I shall soon be thirty, and I have done nothing yet. Sometimes I get melancholy at the prospect before and behind me. Yet it is wrong and foolish to repine. Undoubtedly my duty directs me to stay at home for the present. There was a time when Haworth was a very pleasant place to me; it is not so now. I feel as if we are all buried here. I long to travel, to work, to lead a life of action.

It was now that Charlotte began to take notice, for future use in *Shirley*, of the famous curates. Including Mr. A. B. Nicholls, of whom she eventually became the devoted wife, there were four of them, though only two were Mr. Brontë's curates, and she viewed them all with the most unfavourable eye, very different from that with which she had observed that arch-flirt William Weightman, whose susceptibility had supplied such thrilling interest to her and Ellen. He had died while Charlotte was spending her first year with Emily at Brussels, and his successor was James William Smith, who appears in *Shirley* as Peter Augustus Malone. She at first suspected him, as she had suspected Mr. Weightman, of having matrimonial designs on Ellen, and she alludes to him as the Rev. Lothario Smith. He had said in reference to Ellen: 'Yes, she is a nice girl—rather quiet; I suppose she has money.' Charlotte thought these words spoke volumes—'they do not prejudice me in favour of Mr. Smith.' Mr. Brontë shared these misgivings: they both thought 'that Mr. Smith is a very fickle man, that if he marries he will soon get tired of his wife, and consider her as a burden, also that money will be a principal consideration with him in marrying.' He went for a six weeks' holiday to Ireland: 'Nobody regrets him, because nobody could attach themselves to one who could attach himself to nobody.... Yet the man is not without points that will be most useful to him in getting through life. His good qualities, however, are all of the selfish order.' While he was gone Joseph Brett Grant (Mr. Donne of *Shirley*), master of the Haworth Grammar School, took his duty for the time, and 'filled his shoes decently enough—but one cares naught about these sort of individuals, so drop them.' Then Mr. Smith left Haworth, took a curacy at Keighley, four miles off, and was succeeded by A. B. Nicholls (Mr. Macarthey of *Shirley*). A respectable young man: Charlotte hoped he would give satisfaction. But those hopes were disappointed, for six months afterwards she wrote to Ellen, saying: 'I cannot for my life see those interesting germs of goodness in him you discovered, his narrowness of mind strikes me chiefly. I fear he is indebted to your imagination for the hidden treasure.' Nor did he rise at all in her esteem, for in 1846, in answer to some sort of badinage on Ellen's part with regard to a rumour that Charlotte might be going to marry him, she told her that there was nothing but a 'cold, far away sort of civility between them,' and that he and 'all the other curates are highly uninteresting, narrow and unattractive members of the coarser sex.' As for his parochial efficiency, we learn that when he went to Ireland on a holiday 'many of the parishioners express a desire that he should not trouble himself to recross the Channel. This is not the feeling that ought to exist between shepherd and flock.'

The fourth, James Chesterton Bradley (figuring in *Shirley* as David Sweeting), was curate at Oakworth, a hamlet not more than a mile from Haworth. Three of them thus lived close to the Parsonage, and, so Charlotte writes to Ellen, 'God knows there is not one to mend another': curates seemed to her 'a self-seeking, vain, empty race.' Indeed, they were a sore trial.

The other day [we read] they all three accompanied by Mr. Smidt (of whom by the way I have grievous things to tell you) dropped or rather rushed in unexpectedly to tea. It was Monday (baking day) and I was hot and tired, still, if they had behaved quietly and decently I would have served them out their tea in peace, but they began glorifying themselves and abusing Dissenters in such a manner that my temper lost its balance, and I pronounced a few sentences sharply and rapidly, which struck them all dumb. Papa was greatly horrified also. I don't regret it....

A rather dreadful little scene; she was hot and irritated, and having lost her temper and shocked her father, felt that she had nothing to blame herself with. But she was saving up these experiences of the empty-headed race.

All contacts chafed her: she went to stay with her friends the Taylors at Hunsworth, and during the visit she suffered from headache and listlessness of spirits, and was sure that everyone except perhaps Mary was glad when she departed. She found that Mary's brother had sadly deteriorated. Eight years ago she would have been '*indignant*' if anyone had accused him of 'being a worshipper of mammon,' now she laughed at her vanished illusion about him.

The world with its hardness and selfishness has utterly changed him. He thinks himself wiser than the wisest ... his feelings have gone through a process of petrification which will prevent them from ever warring against his interest, but Ichabod! all glory of principle and much elevation of character is gone!

This bleak censoriousness of others was coupled with utter pessimism regarding the future and the past, and she did not believe that the world held happiness in store for anyone. She looked on people and prospects alike from the standpoint of her own hopelessness of anticipation, and miserably regretted that 'irresistible impulse' out of which had come those abject and yearning letters she wrote to Brussels and the sickness of deferred hope with which she awaited the coming of the barren post-hour.

The summer of 1845 arrived. In June Anne left her situation at Thorp Green for good, after being there for four and a half years, and went off with Emily for a jaunt to York: these were the only two nights that Emily spent away from Haworth from the time of her return from Brussels in 1842 until her death. They played at Gondals all the time, and Emily in her secret paper of July records how they impersonated Ronald Macalgin, Henry Angora, Julia Augusteena, and many other mystical folk 'escaping from the palaces of instruction to join the Royalists who are hard driven at present by the victorious Republicans.' She was writing a work on the First Gondal War, and Anne a book under the name of 'Henry Sophona.' Anne, though not quite so enthusiastic (for she found the Gondals were not 'in first-rate playing condition'), records that: 'The Unique Society, about half a year ago, were wrecked on a desert island as they were returning from Gaul.' She mentions also that Emily was writing poetry, and wondered what it was about. Branwell had come home for the holidays with Anne, while Mr. and Mrs. Robinson and the family went to Scarborough, and, as at present arranged, he would return to his post when the holidays were over. Charlotte, when her sisters had got back to Haworth, went off for a three weeks' visit to her friend Ellen at Hathersage. She found when she returned that the curtain had already risen on a drama which is surely among the grimmest of domestic chronicles.

She wrote next day to Ellen:

It was ten o'clock at night when I got home. I found Branwell ill: he is so very often owing to his own fault. I was not therefore shocked at first, but when Anne informed me of the immediate cause of his present illness, I was greatly shocked. He had last Thursday received a note from Mr. Robinson sternly dismissing him, intimating that he had discovered his proceedings, which he characterized as bad beyond expression, and charging him on pain of exposure to break off instantly and for ever all communication with every member of his family. We have had sad work with Branwell ever since. He thought of nothing but stunning or drowning his distress of mind. No one in the house could have rest. At last we have been obliged to send him from home with someone to look after him: he has written to me this morning, and expresses some sense of contrition for his frantic folly; he promises amendment on his return, but so long as he remains at home, I scarce dare hope for peace in the house.

Now Mrs. Gaskell, in the first edition of her *Life of Charlotte Brontë*, makes narrative of the above letter, and defines the reason for Branwell's dismissal. He had been dismissed by his employer because of his guilty intrigue with his wife. Her account ran as follows:

All the disgraceful incidents came out. Branwell was in no state to conceal his agony of remorse, or, strange to say, his agony of guilty love, from any dread of shame. He gave passionate way to his feelings, he shocked and distressed those loving sisters inexpressibly: the blind father sat stunned, sorely tempted to curse the profligate woman who had tempted his boy—his only son—into the deep disgrace of deadly crime.

All the variations of spirits and of temper—the reckless gaiety, the moping gloom of many months were now explained. There was a reason deeper than any mean indulgence of appetite to account for his intemperance; he began his career as an habitual drunkard to drown remorse.

The pitiable part, as far as he was concerned, was the yearning love he still bore to the woman who had got so strong a hold upon him. It is true that she professed equal love; we shall see how her profession held good. There was a strange lingering of conscience, when meeting her clandestinely by appointment at Harrogate some months afterwards, he refused to consent to the elopement which she proposed: there was some good left in this corrupted, weak young man, even to the very last of his miserable days.... A few months later (I have the exact date but for obvious reasons withhold it) the invalid husband of the woman with whom he had intrigued, died. Branwell had been looking forward to this event with guilty hopes. After her husband's death, his paramour would be free. Strange as it seems the young man still loved her passionately, and now he imagined the time was come when they might look forward to being married, and might live together without reproach or blame. She had offered to elope with him; she had written to him perpetually, she had sent him money—twenty pounds at a time—she had braved shame and her children's menaced disclosures for his sake, he thought she must love him: he little knew how bad a depraved woman can be. Her husband had made a will, in which what property he left her was bequeathed solely on the condition that she should never see Branwell Brontë again. At the very time that the will was read, she did not know but that he might be on his way to her, having heard of her husband's death. She despatched a servant in hot haste to Haworth. He stopped at the 'Black Bull' and a messenger was sent up to the Parsonage for Branwell. He came down to the little inn and was shut up with the man for some time. Then the groom came out, paid his bill, mounted his horse and was off. Branwell remained in the room alone. More than an hour elapsed before sign or sound was heard; then those outside heard a noise like the bleating of a calf, and, on opening the door, he was found in a kind of fit, succeeding to the stupor of grief which he had fallen into on hearing that he was forbidden by his paramour ever to see her again, as, if he did, she would forfeit her fortune. Let her live and flourish! He died, his pockets filled with her letters, which he had carried about his person, in order that he might read them as often as he wished.... When I think of him, I change my cry to heaven. Let her live and repent!

As soon as this was brought to Mrs. Robinson's notice, she determined to sue Mrs. Gaskell for libel, but consented not to do so if these passages and all other reference to her were omitted from future editions, and a public apology and retraction of them was made. This appeared in the advertisement pages of the *Times* of May 26, 1857, in the form of a letter from Mrs. Gaskell's solicitors to Mrs. Robinson's:

DEAR SIR,—As solicitor for and on behalf of the Rev. W. Gaskell, and of Mrs. Gaskell his wife, the latter of whom is authoress of the *Life of Charlotte Brontë*, I am instructed to retract every statement contained in that work which imputes to a widowed Lady, referred to but not named therein, any breach of her conjugal, of her maternal, or of her social duties, and more especially of the statement ... which imputes to the lady in question a guilty intercourse with the late Branwell Brontë. All those statements were made upon information believed to be well founded, but which, upon investigation, with the additional evidence furnished to me by you, I have ascertained not to be trustworthy. I am therefore authorized not only to retract the statements in question, but to express the deep regret of Mrs. Gaskell that she should have been led to make them.

I am, dear Sirs, yours truly,
WILLIAM SHAEN.

There followed on this apology some exceedingly pungent remarks in the *Athenæum*, which had previously spoke in high praise of Mrs. Gaskell's book, on the wantonness of publishing 'a gratuitous tale so dismal as concerns the dead, so damaging to the living, unless it was severely, strictly true.' Even then, the writer might have added, such sacerdotal comminations are as ludicrous as they are irrelevant to the story of Charlotte Brontë's life.

Now there is always a possibility that an author may be wise to withdraw libellous matter from his book with apologies, not because it is not true, but because he is unable to substantiate the truth of it, and will thus inevitably lose his case if an action is brought against him. But before we attempt to ascertain whether such was the case with Mrs. Gaskell, with regard to the main libellous matter, we must look into the rest of her story by way of test. We find it bristles with inconsistencies and inaccuracies. She states, for instance, that Mr. Robinson by his will bequeathed his property to his widow solely on the condition that she should never see Branwell again. Now Mr. Robinson died in May 1846, eleven years before Mrs. Gaskell's book appeared, and his will was proved in September of the same year. An inspection of it, or a copy of it, would have shown her that it contained no such condition, and that Branwell's name does not appear in it at all. Mrs. Robinson, therefore, would have been free to marryhim had she wished to do so, without pecuniary loss, other than that consequent on her marrying again at all. Again, there is the story that Mrs. Robinson sent her groom to Haworth to see Branwell and acquaint him with this provision; the result of the interview was that Branwell was found in a fit, bleating like a calf. But apart from the fact that no one but a demented woman would have sent a groom to talk over affairs with her lover, and tell him he must never see his paramour again, Mrs. Robinson could have sent no such message, since the will did not contain any such provision. Again, the supposed meeting of Branwell and Mrs. Robinson at Harrogate and her proposal to him to elope (which, if he had accepted it, would quite assuredly have deprived her of her inheritance) are utterly inconsistent with her refusal to see him after her husband's death, when she was at liberty to marry him. As for the story that on Branwell's death his pockets were found to be full of Mrs. Robinson's letters, we can only conclude that this was derived from some such source as that which gave Mrs. Gaskell so many details about Mr. Brontë's violent habits; and it was contradicted by the Parsonage servant, Martha Brown, who was in the room when Branwell died; there were no such letters. In the face of such glaring inconsistencies, it looks at first sight as if the whole of Mrs. Gaskell's account was a farrago of unverified gossip.

But looking closer, we must acquit Mrs. Gaskell of any very culpable carelessness in compiling an account which, though far better omitted altogether, was evidently derived from Charlotte herself, and by Charlotte from Branwell. He was making no secret, when she returned from her visit to Ellen in July 1845, of the cause of his dismissal, he was drinking and crying out on fate with the unmanliest lamentation, and we can infer for certain what he told his sisters from a letter he wrote three months afterwards to his friend Francis H. Grundy:

This lady (Mrs. Robinson), though her husband detested me, showed me a degree of kindness which, when I was deeply grieved one day at her husband's conduct, ripened into declarations of more than ordinary feeling. My admiration of her mental and personal attractions, my knowledge of her unselfish sincerity, her sweet temper, and unwearied care for others, with but unrequited return where most should have been given ... although she is seventeen years my senior, all combined to an attachment on my part, and led to reciprocations which I had little looked for. During nearly three years I had daily 'troubled pleasure, soon chastised by fear.'

A shabbier avowal of all that a man is usually silent about (especially if there is truth in what he says) can scarcely be conceived, and clearly this was the version which Branwell gave his sisters, and which Charlotte passed on to Mrs. Gaskell when subsequently they met and became friends. Branwell, too, was the author of the fiction about Mr. Robinson's will, for he wrote to his friend Grundy in a letter for which the contents supply the date:

The gentleman with whom I have been is dead. His property is left in trust for the family, provided I do not see the widow; and if I do, it reverts to the executing trustees with ruin to her.

What he thus wrote it is reasonable to suppose he raved about to his sisters, and in this particular we have the connecting-link between him and Mrs. Gaskell's narrative in the shape of a letter that Charlotte wrote to Ellen in the month following Mr. Robinson's death:

Shortly after came news from all hands that Mr. Robinson had altered his will before he died, and effectually prevented all chance of a marriage between his widow and Branwell, by stipulating that she should not have a shilling of it if she ever ventured to reopen any communication with him....

Whatever 'we hear from all hands' means, it is clear enough from Branwell's letter to his friend that one of these hands was his, and can infer with sufficient completeness that Charlotte supplied the information upon which Mrs. Gaskell's account was founded, and that this in turn rested entirely on Branwell's allegations and tipsy maunderings. He made of himself a stricken and bawling martyr to the cruel fate which parted impassioned lovers by the obstacle of a selfish and unsympathetic husband, and when that obstacle was removed and it was clear that his mistress (if she had ever been his mistress) had no intention of marrying him, he invented the story of the will, adding to it that she was distracted by these sorrows and anxieties to the verge of insanity. But as she married Sir Edward Scott three years later, as soon as the death of his wife in 1848 left him free, we must suppose that she had her sane intervals. All that actually remains of the whole story is that Branwell was summarily dismissed from his tutorship by Mr. Robinson on account of some improper behaviour, and the reasonable conclusion is that he had made love to his wife, who very properly had told her husband. All the rest is directly traceable to Branwell's unsupported assertions, for which no tittle of evidence could be found.

Charlotte, then, on her return to Haworth to find Branwell drinking heavily and bemoaning his stricken existence, took the same hopeless view of him as she took just now of everything. He was in such a state, she wrote, that it was necessary that he should leave home for a week with someone to look after him; the choice of this attendant was a strange one, for he was Branwell's boon companion, John Brown, the 'Old Knave of Trumps,' and President of the 'Lodge of the Three Graces,' which met at the 'Black Bull' to drink whisky and discuss women. While he was gone Emily's birthday came round, and as usual she and Anne wrote their secret papers for each other, to be opened (on this occasion after three years) on July 30, 1848. In contrast with Charlotte's pessimistic outlook Emily, though Branwell's disgrace was so recent, appeared to be in exceedingly good spirits. She gives a short *résumé* of events, barely mentioning Charlotte, and a long account of her expedition with Anne and the doings of the Gondals. She says that in spite of all efforts the idea of the sisters keeping a school was 'no go,' and that she, personally, did not want it at all, thereby emphasising that it was Charlotte's scheme all along; she says that the family were all well, but for Mr. Brontë's trouble with his eyes, and for Branwell,

who I hope will be better and do better hereafter. I am quite contented for myself; not as idle as formerly, altogether as hearty, and having learnt to make the most of the present and (not) long for the future with the fidgetiness that I cannot do all I wish; seldom or (n)ever troubled with nothing to do, and merely desiring that everybody could be as comfortable and as undesponding, and then we should have a very tolerable world of it.

Anne's corresponding paper, though not pitched in so robust a key, betokens a very tranquil mind. Her news in the main is much the same as Emily's; her mention of Branwell almost verbally identical, though she possibly alludes to him again when, speaking of her situation at Thorp Green, she said that she had 'some very unpleasant and undreamt-of experience of human nature.'

Then there follows an interesting entry: 'Charlotte is thinking about getting another situation. She wishes to go to Paris.' But was it Paris that was her ultimate aim in wanting to go abroad again? Six months before she had written to M. Héger saying, 'As soon as I have earned enough money to go to Brussels I shall go there,' and later Dr. Paul Héger (M. Héger's son) revised and passed an obituary notice of his father in *L'Etoile Belge*, which stated that Charlotte had written to the *pensionnat* asking leave to return there, and was refused. Possibly Charlotte's wish to go to Paris cloaked another destination.

Then we learn that Anne had begun the third volume of *Passages in the Life of an Individual*. 'Volume,' as we have noticed before, means no more than 'notebook,' but Anne by this time had certainly got some way into the writing of the book which eventually appeared as *Agnes Grey*. These few items of real information are islands in an ocean of the merest chatter, which however gives us a minute little still-life picture of this 'dismal, cloudy wet evening' at the Parsonage.

Charlotte is sitting sewing in the dining-room. Emily is ironing upstairs. I am sitting in the dining-room in the rocking-chair by the fire with my feet on the fender. Papa is in the parlour. Tabby and Martha are, I think, in the kitchen. Keeper and Flossy are, I do not know where. Little Dick is hopping in his cage.... (Charlotte) has let Flossie in, by the by, and he is now lying on the sofa.... This afternoon I began to set about making my grey figured silk frock that was dyed at Keighley. What sort of a hand shall I make of it? E. (Emily) and I have a great deal of work to do. When shall we sensibly diminish it? I want to get a habit of early rising. Shall I succeed?

Thus the gentle narrative rambles mildly on, telling of minute happenings and of the general outlook on life of this quiet soul, and helping us perhaps to understand that her apparent colourlessness is not due to our imperfect knowledge of her, but was a quality in her character, as indeed *Agnes Grey* abundantly testifies. But neither Anne's paper with its figured silk, its resolve to get up early, its information about the canary and the dogs, nor the cheerful contents of Emily's, justify Mrs. Gaskell's lurid estimate of the doom which Branwell had wrought in the lives of his sisters—'The premature death,' she tells us, 'of two at least of the sisters,—all the great possibilities of their lives snapped short—may be dated from Midsummer 1845.' Indeed, it is impossible to conjecture what she means by the snapping short of all their great possibilities (unless she alludes to the school scheme which had already been given up a year before, as no pupils could be obtained), for the great possibilities of their lives, all the achievements without which the name of Brontë would be unknown to this day, were as a matter of fact just about to be manifested.

Charlotte, as we have seen, could not take the same cheerful view as her sisters; all her plans had failed, she was prey to a miserable devotion, and now there was this fresh trouble about Branwell. From the moment of her arrival at Haworth to find him discharged with ignominy from his tutorship at Thorp Green, down to the day of his death, rather more than three years later, she held him in unmitigated hatred and contempt, which, so far from keeping to herself, she constantly expressed in her letters to her friend. No word of pity for her brother, no faintest indication of sympathy for the grievous pass into which his weakness and self-indulgence had already brought him oozed from her pen, but regularly and succinctly, month by month, she sent Ellen the stark bulletins of his deterioration. He came back from his trip with John Brown, and already in August she writes:

My hopes ebb low indeed about Branwell. I sometimes fear he will never be fit for much. His bad habits seem more deeply rooted than I thought. The late blow to his prospects and feelings has quite made him reckless. It is only absolute want of means that acts as any check to him. One ought, indeed, to hope to the very last; but occasionally hope, in his case, seems a fallacy.

Later in the same month she records that his health and temper have been a little better, but only 'because he has been forced to abstain.' Next month she tells Ellen that 'Branwell makes no effort to seek a situation, and while he is at home, I will invite no one to come and share our discomfort.' In November, however, he tried through his friend Francis Grundy to get employment again on the railway, but could not obtain it, and Charlotte again wrote, saying that

Branwell still remains at home, and while he is here—you shall not come. I am more confirmed in that resolution the more I know of him. I wish I could say one word to you in his favour, but I cannot. Therefore I will hold my tongue.

To Miss Wooler she gave the same reason why she could not ask her to Haworth; and again she writes to Ellen in December, saying: 'You say well that no sufferings are so awful as those brought on by dissipation: alas! I see the truth of this observation daily proved.' Bitter had been her disappointment with him, and deep was her disgust. Once he had been her chosen ally; she had seen in front of him a brilliant career in art or letters, but nothing of that was realised owing to the instability of his character. The artist had degenerated into a ticket-collector at a wayside station, and had proved himself entirely untrustworthy. Thereafter his downward course had been swift, and now he was a drunken, good-for-nothing philanderer, unfit for any employment that demanded reasonable steadiness.

Now Charlotte's view of the moral hopelessness of her brother thus early expressed was amply justified: he ruined his health by drink as he had ruined his position as tutor by his conduct (whatever it was) towards Mrs. Robinson. For publicans and sinners, for the weak, the self-indulgent, and the erring, Charlotte had no compassion nor any fellow-feeling, and she included her brother in her pitilessness. There was a special reason, apart from his sottishness, why she should do so. A woman of a nature less righteous than hers, and less austere, might have found in that reason a bond of sympathy with him; it was otherwise with her, and her experience of a hopeless attachment, intimate and her own, and somewhat similar to that in which Branwell had found himself, must vastly have added to her contempt for him when she contrasted her conduct with his. For she had been and still was in love with another woman's husband, and she had not taken to drink, but had done her best to start a school. She had not committed any 'frantic folly'; she had not raved about the hunger of her heart to her father and her sisters, but had refrained from mentioning to them even the name of M. Héger. How should she not then despise her brother for this unmanly lamentation and his sottish consolements? Hard and composed, with set mouth and unsoftening eyes, she wrote to Ellen that November bulletin, saying that she wished she could say one word in Branwell's favour, but could not.... Then there was another letter, for it was three months since she had written to Brussels and had yet received no answer; and her eyes softened, and the stern mouth relaxed, and her head was bowed low over the paper, as by the light of the dining-room fire she told M. Héger how humiliating it was 'to be the slave of a fixed and dominant idea which lords it over the mind.' She entreated him to write again, for his last letter had been stay and prop to her for half a year, and she tells him how day by day she awaits the post hour to see if it will bring anything from him, and day by day disappointment flings her back into overwhelming sorrow, when the sweet delight of seeing his handwriting fails her, and fever takes her and she loses appetite and sleep and pines away.

But these were private appeals for the eye of M. Héger alone. What would have happened, we cannot help wondering, if, when Madame had rescued these letters from the waste-paper basket and carefully pieced them together, she had sent even one of them to Mr. Brontë? Pitiable for their very abjectness, for their utter surrender of that womanly pride, which she had counselled Ellen always to preserve, they really reveal a folly not less frantic than that for which she so bitterly blamed her brother. What would her sisters and her father and her brother have thought of her and her determination not to leave Brussels till she had got a grip of German?

Of all the members of that tragic family, now collected under the roof of the Parsonage in this autumn of 1845, there to remain together till, one by one, the brother and two of the three sisters were beckoned forth by the finger of death, we must look on Charlotte as being the loneliest and the most wretched. She was the continual prey of this torture of the nerves, and it is to that she refers when, a year later, remission had come.

Assuredly, [she writes] I can never forget the concentrated anguish of certain insufferable moments, and the heavy gloom of many long hours, besides the preternatural horror which seemed to clothe existence and nature, and which made life a continual waking nightmare. Under such circumstances the morbid nerves can know neither peace nor enjoyment. Whatever touches pierces them, sensation for them in suffering.

Emily and Anne, according to their secret papers, were very tolerably content, Branwell had the consolation of the 'Black Bull' and the luxury of his own lamentations, while Charlotte whose scholastic programme, for which she had schemed at such ruinous cost to her own peace, had utterly failed, whose literary ambitions were dead, whose heart bled with secret self-torture, whose righteousness was hard and pitiless and without consolation for her, was burning away with the sense of talents unused and abilities thwarted of their due fruition. But Anne was working at her *Passages in the Life of an Individual*; Branwell was working at a story also, with which by September he had filled, in a handwriting as minute as Charlotte's, one notebook. Emily, for diversion, was writing the Gondal romance, *The Emperor Julius's Life,* and, for happiness, her poems, which were her secret life, full, not of hunger-heart and bitterness, but of the all-sufficient rapture of a mystic who waited the coming of the spirit when the house was still, even as the prophet waited for the temple to be filled by night with the glory of the Lord. Even so, she set her light in the window to show she was alert and ready.

Burn then, little lamp, glimmer straight and clear—

Hush! a rustling wing stirs, methinks, the air;

He for whom I wait thus ever comes to me;

Strange Power! I trust thy might, trust thou my constancy.

But in Charlotte's secret garden there were none of these night-flowering fragrances, and bitter alike to the mouth and to the belly were the herbs that grew for the succour of her solitude. She was the most sundered of them all, for Emily and Anne had their private alliance, and whereas she had turned her back on Branwell and gone by on the other side, Emily maintained a sisterly friendliness towards him that made yet another cause for distance and estrangement between Charlotte and her, and whatever private commerce she may have had with him, Charlotte had no more part in it than in Emily's affairs with Anne. Something to plan, something to manage, a scheme to mature, an ambition to strive for—any of this would have given alleviation to this weight of unbroken joyless nothingness, made more unbearable by the authentic sense of power and vitality and energy boiling within her, by the absence of any engine into which to direct its driving force, and by the continual besotted presence of an intolerable brother.

Then one day in this dreary autumn of 1845 Charlotte saw an opportunity and took hold of it with a grip of iron. Knowing from her letters and the secret papers of Emily and Anne the habit of life at Haworth, we may, without the aid of imagination, picture how it came to her.

Charlotte had been reading the daily paper one morning to her father, who was now very nearly blind; presently Mr. Nicholls came in to talk over parish affairs, and the rest of the day lay empty and objectless before her. Emily was making bread in the kitchen, for the day was Monday; there was a book propped up in front of her as she kneaded the dough, and her bulldog, Keeper, was lying by her. Anne was in the dining-room cleaning out the canary's cage; her spaniel Flossy lay on the sofa. Of Branwell there was no sign; most likely he had gone out to the 'Black Bull' for a morning dram. Very soon Anne's task was done and she went out quietly, to join Emily in the kitchen, and Charlotte was left alone in the dining-room, where once all four of them had been used to sit when the sewing tasks were done and Aunt Branwell gone up to bed, scribbling at poem or story, or walking round the table, discussing each other's work. For years there had been no such councils in literature. Anne, Charlotte knew, was writing a story of some kind; Emily, she knew, wrote poems still, but there was now no exchange of confidences between them; she knew nothing of what her sisters were writing, and as for herself, ever since she first went to Brussels three and a half years ago, she had written nothing except letters to Ellen and a few friends, and to M. Héger.

The two desks in which Emily and Anne kept their private papers were lying on the side-table. Idly, almost accidentally, Charlotte opened Emily's desk, and on the top of the papers within lay one of the notebooks of which Charlotte had filled so many. She took it up; it was full of those poems which she knew Emily wrote, but which neither she nor Anne had ever seen. They were surprising, they were more than surprising—she found them 'condensed and terse, vigorous and genuine,' not like the usual run of women's poems. While she was still at it, Emily's baking was finished and she came in and found Charlotte deep in her reading.

Emily was furious at this invasion of her privacies; 'it took hours,' Charlotte put it, 'to reconcile her to the discovery I had made.' The words 'My discovery,' if she used them, must have been peculiarly irritating, for what she had discovered was Emily's inviolable and guarded treasure, and not otherwise does a burglar 'discover' some pearl of great price in the jewel-chest of the house he has entered. Nor did Charlotte mean to let go of that pearl, when its indignant owner demanded it back, for after Emily was reconciled to the discovery another surrender was demanded of her. Not only her sister but the public must see those condensed and terse poems; they must be published; they were remarkable. Over that Emily fought harder: it took days, Charlotte tells us, to persuade her, but she 'knew that a mind like hers could not be without some spark of honourable ambition and refused to be discouraged.'

Though all our private sympathy is with Emily over this stern invasion of her secret life, which she had so firmly withheld from her sisters, we are unable not to thank God that Charlotte had no scruples about that, but wore down her opposition by the unyielding determination of her will. But for that, the world would perhaps never have seen Emily's poems at all, and possibly none of the great Brontë novels; *Wuthering Heights* and *Jane Eyre* and *Villette* might never have been written. For the 'discovery' struck the spark from which the old flame was rekindled, and all three of the sisters began to burn again with those ambitions for a literary career which had so long lain covered with the ashes of discouragement. Charlotte raked the ashes off and blew on the coal. Once again there was something to do, something to work for, and, as before, when a scholastic career was contemplated, Charlotte took charge for the joint advantage of her sisters and herself. This time Anne was not left out, for seeing that Emily's poems had pleased her sister she produced some of her own, and Charlotte found in them 'a sweet sincere pathos.' Hence arose the scheme, for Charlotte in her girlhood had written many poems herself, and she decided that they must bring out a joint volume. Branwell had written a good deal of verse too, of a quality certainly not inferior to Charlotte's or Anne's, but he was not asked to contribute, and neither he nor Mr. Brontë was told anything about the project. A selection of the poems was made, sufficient to run to 165 pages, and the pseudonyms of Currer, Ellis, and Acton Bell were chosen, thus preserving the initials of the three authors, and avoiding publicity. The 'ambiguous choice of these names,' Charlotte states, 'was dictated by a sort of conscientious scruple at assuming names positively masculine.' This scruple was but ephemeral, for after the book appeared she wrote thanking the editor of the *Dublin University Magazine* for a favourable review in the name of herself and her brothers.

The first difficulty was to get any answer at all from the publishers to whom Charlotte offered the book, though some warned her against publishing poems at all. Eventually, in January 1846, she got into practical touch with Messrs. Aylott & Jones of Paternoster Row, who agreed to publish the book on payment by the authors of thirty guineas, which was subscribed, we may suppose, between them. She went with untiring precision into questions of format, of type and of paper; she was anxious to correct all proof sheets herself, since the printer had set up 'tumbling stars' instead of 'trembling stars,' which threw 'an air of absurdity over the whole poem'; and she conducted correspondence with the firm under her own initial and surname on behalf of the three 'Bells,' receiving replies addressed to 'C. Brontë, Esq.' Then some mistake occurred (did Branwell, perhaps, seeing a male address open an envelope of proof sheets?) and future letters were addressed to 'Miss Brontë.' Then there came the question of binding, of the periodicals to which advance copies were to be sent, and of the price of the book. Charlotte thought five shillings would be suitable, but if that was excessive for so slender a volume, four shillings. From a letter of hers to Mrs. Gaskell in 1850, we find that this was the price at which it was published. An additional sum of £5 was sent to defray the further cost and £10 for purposes of advertising, so that in all the sisters paid £46 10s.

The spirit of God had moved upon the face of those dark and stagnant waters, and there dawned the light that while English literature endures will know no wane. Long before the poems were even selected and offered to Messrs. Aylott & Jones, all three sisters blazing with the resuscitated flame of authorship were, during the autumn of 1845, each engaged on a novel. Anne, when she returned from Thorp Green, was already filling her third notebook with *Passages in the Life of an Individual*, which subsequently appeared as *Agnes Grey*. Charlotte began on *The Professor*, and Emily was engaged on *Wuthering Heights*. By what date these three books were finished is not quite clear, for Charlotte gives irreconcilable pieces of information about it. Speaking of the book of poems she says: 'Ill-success failed to crush us, the mere effort to succeed had given a wonderful zest to existence, it must be pursued. We each set to work on a prose tale....' This implies that the sisters did not begin their novels till the venture in poesy had failed. But this was not the case; they must have begun to write their novels (and written fast, too) in the autumn of 1845, while the poems were being selected and a publisher sought for, for we find Charlotte writing in April 1846 to Messrs. Aylott & Jones, who were then printing the poems, saying that 'C., E., and A. Bell are now preparing for the press a work of fiction, consisting of three distinct and unconnected tales which may be published either together as a work of three volumes ... or separately as single volumes.' The three stories, therefore, must have been complete or nearly so before the poems were published at all.

Again, giving us another date for their completion, she tells us that these MSS. (*Wuthering Heights, Agnes Grey,* and *The Professor*) 'were perseveringly obtruded on various publishers for the space of a year and a half' before any of them were accepted. But *Wuthering Heights* and *Agnes Grey* were accepted for publication not later than July 1847; they must therefore have been finished and going out on the dreary round by January 1846. In either case the sisters must have been writing their novels during the autumn of 1845, and I suggest, as a possible explanation of these discrepancies in date, that *Agnes Grey,* already far advanced in the summer, was finished by January 1846, and began its fruitless journeys then, and that *The Professor* and *Wuthering Heights* were ready a few months later. As to the implication that the 'prose-tales' were not begun till the ill-success of the poems was proved, the established dates make this quite impossible, for all the first three stories had been finished long before, and *Jane Eyre,* Charlotte's second story in point of composition, was approaching completion.

The inception and the progress of these three novels was, like that of the poems, kept secret. Charlotte, in her constant and detailed letters to Ellen Nussey, in which she records the phases of Branwell's deterioration, gives not the slightest hint that any literary project was on the board, and it is equally certain from what happened after the publication of *Jane Eyre* (which was the first of the novels to appear) that Mr. Brontë, sitting in the parlour more sundered now every week from the visible world by reason of his failing eyesight, for which an operation was being mooted, knew nothing whatever of these renewed activities: whether Branwell knew is a question that will presently require a more detailed investigation. Nor was there less silence and secrecy between the authors themselves, and we must picture them busy but wholly uncommunicative to each other about their progress, in spite of Mrs. Gaskell's fascinating account of how they read new chapters of *Jane Eyre* and *Wuthering Heights* to each other, as they came hot from the glowing workshops. She says:

The sisters retained their old habit which was begun in their aunt's lifetime, of putting away their work at nine o'clock, and commencing their study, pacing up and down the sitting-room. At this time, they talked over the stories they were engaged upon, and described their plots. Once or twice a week, each read to the others what she had written and heard what they had to say about it ... the readings were of great and stirring interest to them all.

But to out infinite chagrin we find that nothing of the sort took place, for Charlotte, referring to the writing of these very books, says:

Formerly we used to show each other what we wrote, but of late years this habit of communication and consultation had been discontinued: hence it ensued that we were mutually ignorant of the progress we might respectively have made.

Nothing unfortunately can be clearer than that, and though we must abandon the delightful idea of these readings we are left with a reality far more characteristic of the isolation of the three in their common aim.

They still wrote chiefly in the evening, for there was housework to do, and how long were the busy silences! Anne would be sitting to-night at the table in the dining-room with her desk in front of her. She was getting towards the end of *Agnes Grey*. Emily had gone to give the dogs their supper, and they had heard her go upstairs, for she often did her writing in her bedroom. Mr. Brontë had just looked in to say good-night and tell them not to sit up late. He wound up the clock as, now nearly blind, he groped his way upstairs to the room where he and Branwell slept together. Charlotte sat on the hearth-rug, writing by the firelight. She had a board on her knees, and she wrote in her minute hand on scraps of paper which next day she copied out for her finished manuscript. She was getting on well with *The Professor*. Then the long silence would be broken by the sound of the opening of the front door; so Branwell was back from the 'Black Bull,' and he stumbled as he shuffled along the passage. To-night he looked into the dining-room and came and sat close to Charlotte to warm himself, for it was a cold night, and the north wind blew, specked with snow, from the moor. Charlotte had nothing to say to him; she did not even look up, but stiffened and drew a little away from him, for he kept coughing, and his breath was foully sweet with whisky. He would have liked to ask Charlotte what she was writing, but he was afraid of her, and she might say something biting in return. So as his reception was not encouraging, he soon left them: Emily was gone upstairs, and he tapped at the door of her room—that slip of a room just over the front door—to have a few words with her, if she was not yet gone to bed, for he had an idea in his head to talk about. He stumbled off, forgetting to shut the door.

Not a word did the two sisters exchange about him: silence descended again, and, when the clock struck midnight, Anne put her papers into her desk—perhaps locking it—and left Charlotte still absorbed in her work, her face close to the paper. For the last day or two she had been thinking much about Branwell and his frantic folly, his making love to a woman in her husband's house, and the disgusting creature he was, with his foul breath and his tipsiness and his maudlin lamentations. To-night she was engaged on the twentieth chapter of *The Professor,* and she had been describing how William Crimsworth was leaving the Professor's house, 'where a practical modern French novel seemed likely to materialise.'

I had once [he reflected] the opportunity of contemplating, near at hand, an example of the results produced by a course of interesting and romantic domestic treachery. No golden halo of fiction was about this example, I saw it bare and real: and it was very loathsome. I saw a mind degraded by the habit of perfidious deception, and a body depraved by the infective influence of the vice-polluted soul. I had suffered much from the forced and prolonged view of this spectacle....

But it was late and the fire was burning low. Charlotte went upstairs, pausing before she entered the room, once Aunt Branwell's, now occupied by her and Anne, for she heard Branwell's voice coming from Emily's room. It was strange that she could tolerate his disgusting presence.

CHAPTER XI

In the spring of 1846 (or at the beginning of the year, if Charlotte's statement about the three books vainly seeking a publisher for a year and a half is correct) *Wuthering Heights* was finished; it is necessary to go into the much-derided suggestion that Branwell was the author of it. It was published under the *nom de plume,* Ellis Bell, which Emily had already adopted for her contribution to the joint volume of poems, and Charlotte tells in the Biographical Notice to the 1850 edition of *Wuthering Heights,* how 'Ellis Bell produced *Wuthering Heights,* Acton Bell, *Agnes Grey,* and Currer Bell also wrote a narrative (*The Professor*) in one volume.' That would certainly seem to settle the question once and for all, and no doubt Charlotte believed that Emily was the sole and entire author of the book. Moreover, she wrote after Branwell's death to Mr. W. S. Williams of the firm of Smith, Elder & Co., making the following statement concerning her brother's complete ignorance of all the buzz of literary activity that was going on at the Parsonage:

My unhappy brother never knew what his sisters had done in literature—he was not aware that they had ever published a line. We could not tell him of our efforts for fear of causing him too deep a pang of remorse for his own time misspent and talents misapplied.

Now it is frankly impossible to accept that statement. For the last two years of Branwell's life printed proofs were constantly arriving for the sisters, one packet of which was perhaps opened by Branwell himself by mistake: six presentation authors' copies, Charlotte tells us, were sent to Emily and Anne on the publication of their books, and to her also, as well as multitudes of reviews which she always insisted on seeing. Mr. Brontë, when *Jane Eyre* had begun to boom, was informed by Charlotte that she was the author; Charlotte and Anne went up to London more than a year before Branwell died, to disclose themselves to Smith, Elder & Co.; Mrs. Gaskell tells us how, when Charlotte had sent the manuscript of *The Professor* to a publisher, and had received no acknowledgment, she consulted Branwell himself as to the reason of his silence. For all these reasons it is ludicrous to suppose that Branwell knew nothing about his sisters' publications; the most we can believe, but that readily, is that Charlotte, who found it difficult to remain in the same room with him or to speak to him at all, never herself said a word to him about them. As for the reason she assigned for his not being told of them, because the sense of his own wasted life in comparison with his sisters' would cause him remorse, it is better, considering her implacable treatment of him, to refrain from comment altogether.

Returning, then, to the main question as to whether or no Branwell was responsible in whole or in part for *Wuthering Heights*, there is so much queer and seemingly strong evidence that he not only knew about it, but had something to do with it, that it would be a mere dishonesty to disregard it entirely, or to dismiss it unexamined. The principal documents are as follows:

(1) On September 10, 1845 (that is, at the beginning of the autumn when the literary activity of the three sisters started again), Branwell wrote thus to his friend J. B. Leyland the sculptor, who executed the bas-relief profile of his head, seen by Mrs. Gaskell at Haworth:

I have, since I saw you at Halifax, devoted every hour of time, snatched from downright illness, to the composition of a three volume novel, one volume of which [notebook?] is completed, and, along with the two forthcoming ones, has been really the result of half a dozen long-past years of thoughts about, and experience in, this crooked path of life. I feel that I must rouse myself to attempt something, while roasting daily and nightly over a slow fire, to while away my torments.

(2) Mr. William Dearden, author of *The Demon Queen* and other poems, published in the *Halifax Guardian* in June 1867 a remarkable story concerning himself and Branwell. They agreed to hold a sort of poetic tournament at the Cross Roads Inn, near Haworth, each reading his own poem. J. B. Leyland was appointed umpire in this contest. Dearden continues:

I read the first act of *The Demon Queen,* but when Branwell dived into his hat —the usual receptacle of his fugitive scraps, where he supposed he had deposited his MS. poem, he found he had by mistake placed there a number of stray leaves of a novel on which he had been trying his 'prentice hand.... Both friends earnestly entreated him to read them, as they felt a curiosity to see how he could wield the pen of a novelist. After some hesitation, he complied with the request and riveted our attention for about an hour.... The scene of the fragment which Branwell read, and the characters introduced in it,—so far as then developed,—were the same as those in *Wuthering Heights*, which Charlotte confidently asserts was the production of her sister Emily.

(3) Mr. Edward Sloane, a friend of Branwell's and of Mr. William Dearden's, declared to the latter that 'Branwell had read to him, portion by portion, the novel as it was produced at the time, insomuch that he no sooner began the perusal of *Wuthering Heights* when published than he was able to anticipate the characters and incidents to be disclosed.'

(4) Branwell's friend, Mr. F. H. Grundy, who first made his acquaintance when he was ticket clerk at Luddenden Foot Station in 1842, and paid at least two visits to him at Haworth, wrote in his memoirs:

Patrick Brontë declared to me, and what his sister Emily said bore out the assertion, that he wrote a great portion of *Wuthering Heights* himself. Indeed it is impossible for me to read that story without meeting with many passages which I feel certain *must* have come from his pen. The weird fancies of diseased genius with which he used to entertain me in our long talks at Luddenden Foot reappear in the pages of his novel, and I am inclined to believe that the very plot was his invention rather than his sister's.

Now much of this evidence was not published till twelve years at least after Charlotte's death. It is therefore remote from the events of which it treats. But there is one dated and contemporary document, namely, Branwell's letter of September 10, 1845, to J. B. Leyland, which states that he had then written the first volume of a novel, and the rest of the evidence (the reading of the opening chapters of it to Mr. Dearden and Leyland, the recognition of what had then been read, when *Wuthering Heights* was published, and so forth) is in accordance with it. Unless, then, we assume that these gentlemen, Messrs. Dearden, Sloane, and Grundy, were confederated liars of remarkable constructive imagination, it must be confessed that there is a *prima-facie* case for Branwell's having had knowledge of the book before it was published, and for his having had a hand in its writing. The case is carried further by certain internal evidence in the story itself.

First come one or two verbal points of little importance in themselves, but contributory:

(1) In a letter of Branwell's (already quoted) addressed to 'Old Knave of Trumps' we find the rather remarkable phrase: '... he whose eyes Satan looks out of as from windows'; and in *Wuthering Heights* we find Nellie Dean admonishing Heathcliff as follows about his sulky face:

Do you mark ... those thick brows, that instead of being arched, sink in the middle; and that couple of black fiends, so deeply buried, who never open the windows boldly but lurk glinting under them like devil's spies?

Again Isabel, speaking of Heathcliff, says: 'I stared full at him and laughed scornfully. The clouded windows of hell flashed a moment towards me.'

This is nothing in itself. Branwell's letter to 'Old Knave of Trumps' was written in 1841, and he may easily have used the image of Satan looking out of a man's eyes as from windows in Emily's hearing, and she, struck with it, have twice closely paraphrased it. But the coincidence is curious, and Miss Robinson, who scouted the idea of Branwell having had anything to do with *Wuthering Heights*, certainly found it so, for in her admirable book *Emily Brontë* she quotes Branwell's letter otherwise entire to show what a degraded wretch he was, but omits these few words.

(2) In a letter of Branwell's after his dismissal from his tutorship, in consequence of his conduct concerning Mrs. Robinson, he writes: 'My own life without her will be hell. What can the so-called love of her wretched sickly husband be compared with mine?'

In *Wuthering Heights* Heathcliff says to Nellie Dean:

Two words would comprehend my future—*death* and *hell*; existence after losing her would be hell. Yet I was a fool to fancy for a moment that she valued Edgar Linton's attachment more than mine. If he loved with all the power of his puny being, he couldn't love in eighty years as I could in a day.

This latter verbal coincidence is far more significant than the other, for *Wuthering Heights* was nearing completion when Branwell wrote the corresponding letter, and it looks therefore as if he must have been cognisant of the passage in *Wuthering Heights*. Taken in conjunction with his statement that he had written part of a novel, and the statement of three other witnesses that what Branwell on one occasion read them, and on another occasion told them, enabled them, when *Wuthering Heights* appeared, to recognise in it a story of which already they knew the outline and had heard a part, these coincidences support the suggestion that he had something to do with the book, and, as author, or collaborator, or confidant, knew about it.

But apart from and vastly outweighing the sum of such minor points, apart from but curiously confirming the stubborn external evidence of other witnesses, comes the internal evidence, both as regards composition, verbal expression, and general texture, that *Wuthering Heights* is the work of two authors. The work of the first was merely a handicap, though a serious one, on that of the second, and is a very small portion of the whole, and in the 'fire and the mighty wind' of the second we recognise the wild and visionary and mystical power which inspires Emily's poems. In that Branwell had no part at all, and it would be as ludicrous to suppose that he was in any real sense the author of the book as that Charlotte was. It was supposed by some when the book first came out that it was an early and immature work of hers, but she indignantly repudiated such a suggestion.

To turn then to the book itself, which is among the greatest works of fiction the world has ever seen, the composition and construction are inconceivably awkward, and this awkwardness is entirely due to the manner in which it begins. It opens—dated 1801—with the first-hand narrative of Mr. Lockwood, the tenant of Thrushcross Grange, who goes to visit his landlord Heathcliff at Wuthering Heights, and it is clear that the intention of the writer was to make him a personage in the story. He pays a second visit next day and is immensely struck with the younger Catherine, whom he has not seen before. He pities her for being buried alive with these savages: he thinks she is Hareton's wife.

She has thrown herself away on that boor [he reflects] from sheer ignorance that better individuals existed! A sad pity—I must beware how I cause her to regret her choice. The last reflection may seem conceited: it was not. My neighbour struck me as bordering on repulsive; I knew through experience that I was tolerably attractive....

It is impossible to imagine a clearer indication of the writer's intention to make a *motif* out of Catherine's beauty and Lockwood's complacent susceptibility. But nothing happens; the intention was scrapped. Lockwood returns to Thrushcross Grange next morning, after some bitter nocturnal experiences, and asks his housekeeper Nellie Dean to tell him more about this strange family. Thereupon she becomes the narrator, and talks to him that day for eighty pages. Next day he falls ill, and is a month in bed. When he gets better, she resumes her narrative, he merely listening. She began it from her earliest years and now completes it up to the date at which the story opens, giving him the entire history of the Earnshaws, of the Lintons, and of Heathcliff. We lose sight of Lockwood altogether; he only listens to Nellie Dean as she repeats verbatim long conversations, telling this voluminous history at first hand as she witnessed it. She reads him a letter of eleven pages, which Lockwood reproduces word for word; she oversees, she overhears, and it is not till page 367, quite near the end of the book, that the original narrator appears again to tell us that Mrs. Dean's story, which has lasted for twenty-seven chapters, is over. Then Lockwood narrates one chapter, describing his third visit to Wuthering Heights, and leaves the district. After a break he dates his next chapter 1802, and when he visits the Heights once more, Nellie Dean again tells him what has happened while he has been away. From first page to last he has had nothing whatever to do with the story to which, instead of narrating it himself, as he began to do, he is merely audience, and writes down what Nellie Dean has told him. He has no more to do with it than the occupant of a stall in the theatre has to do with the action on the stage.

No single author could have planned a book in so topsy-turvy a manner. It begins, in point of time, nearly at the end, the original narrator drops completely out, and the actual narrator, whose story forms the bulk of the book, tells it to him. But supposing that, for some reason, the first few chapters had to be retained, this complete change of plan, though productive of endless awkwardnesses, was necessary in order to tell the story at all. Lockwood, the newly arrived tenant who auto-biographically opens the book, could not know the previous history of Heathcliff and the rest. So Nellie Dean must recount it to him, and it takes so long that he must needs fall ill so that his convalescence may be beguiled with it. Nobody planning a story from the first could have begun with an episode so misplaced that such an awkward device must be resorted to. Moreover, though from first to last Lockwood has nothing to do with the story at all, there are those sure indications in the early chapters that he was meant to play a part in it. He warns himself that he must not make himself *too* attractive, and cause the enchanting Catherine (married, so he fancies, to the boorish Hareton) to fall in love with him.

Now in September 1845, as we have seen, Branwell wrote to J. B. Leyland that he was writing a story. He gave an hour's reading of the beginning of it to Leyland and Dearden: Dearden, when *Wuthering Heights* was published, recognised that the opening was what Branwell had read them. Branwell also read pieces to Sloane, who similarly recognised them; he affirmed to Grundy that he had written 'a great portion' of the book (which we decline to believe), and Grundy, when it came out, similarly recognised stories which Branwell had told him when a clerk at Luddenden Foot. My suggestion is that Messrs. Dearden, Leyland, Sloane and Grundy were not independent liars, who happened to hit on the same lie, but that Branwell planned with Emily a considerable part of the book and that he wrote and read to Leyland and Dearden the opening chapters, which make so awkward a misfit with the rest. We must also remember as a matter of evidential importance that Branwell's letter to Leyland, saying that he had completed a volume—notebook—of his story, was dated September 10, 1845. Charlotte made the 'discovery' of Emily's poems in the autumn of that year, and it was that which set going again the literary activities of the sisters. Emily (hitherto occupied with the Gondal History of the Emperor Julius) then took *Wuthering Heights* in hand with the connivance and collaboration of Branwell, retaining the first two chapters that open the book, which Branwell had already written.

Dates, then, support the idea that what Branwell read his friends was the earliest chapters of *Wuthering Heights*. A more effective support is derived from the contents of those chapters which led to such awkwardnesses in the composition of the whole, and, in especial, from the style of them. Lockwood, at present the narrator, writes with the identical pomposity with which

Branwell wrote to Southey, to Blackwood, and was now writing to his friends: he uses elaborate expressions and journalistic phrases, he employs a vast number of words derived from the Latin and Latin words; he displays a scholastic pretentiousness. Such sentences as these, all culled from those first two chapters, are characteristic of his style:

I had no desire to aggravate his impatience previous to inspecting the penetralium.

I detected a chatter of tongues and a clatter of culinary utensils.

Imagining they (the dogs) would scarcely understand tacit insults, I unfortunately indulged in winking and making faces at the trio, and some turn of my physiognomy so irritated madam....

Swayed by prudential considerations of the folly of offending a good tenant, he (Heathcliff) relaxed a little in the laconic style of chipping off his pronouns and auxiliary verbs.

'Wretched inmates,' I ejaculated mentally, 'you deserve perpetual isolation from your species for your churlish inhospitality.'

You are the favoured possessor of the beneficent fairy.

A mingled guffaw from Heathcliff and Hareton put the cope-stone on my rage and humiliation.

I ordered the miscreants to let me out, with several incoherent threats of retaliation that in their indefinite depth of virulency smacked of King Lear.

Such extracts are typical of Lockwood's style of writing when he opens the story of *Wuthering Heights*. Then he vanishes and is a mere listener to the lucid narrative of Nellie Dean. At the end of the book, when he takes up the story again, we should naturally expect him to resume the narrative style of the beginning; but what do we find?

I lingered round them under that benign sky, watched the moths fluttering among the heath and hare-bells, listened to the soft wind breathing through the grass, and wondered how anyone could ever imagine unquiet slumbers for the sleepers in that quiet earth.

Both the first two chapters and the end are supposedly Lockwood's writing, but it is incredible that the same hand held the pen. The hand that wrote the pompous, swashbuckling but picturesque letter to John Brown beginning 'Old Knave of Trumps,' might easily have written the first two chapters of *Wuthering Heights* as narrated by Lockwood, Style 1, but never the conclusion by Lockwood, Style 2. No hand but one could have written that, or the narrative of Nellie Dean, or the wild moorland passion of the book, fierce and devouring, yet with hardly a touch of the flesh in it, and that was hers (not Branwell's nor Charlotte's), which had written thus of the power that possessed it:

He comes with western winds, with evening's wandering airs,

With that clear dusk of heaven that brings the thickest stars.

Winds take a pensive tone, and stars a tender fire,

And visions rise and change, that kill me with desire.

To Branwell, then, we may assign these first two chapters, pompous and monstrous in style, with their Lockwood *motif* which once announced is heard no more, and then Emily took charge, but still in consultation with him. The 'ruffianly bitch' was his perhaps, so also, certainly, was the material for the half-savage country folk, such as Zillah and Joseph, whom he calls the 'surly indigenæ.' Charlotte herself, though fully believing that Emily wrote the book, as indeed she did, felt the difficulty of accounting for the intimate knowledge which she showed of Branwell's indigenæ, for in her preface to the 1850 edition she says:

I am bound to avow that she had scarcely more practical knowledge of the peasantry amongst whom she lived than a nun has of the country people who sometimes pass her convent gates ... except to go to church or take a walk on the hills, she rarely crossed the threshold of home.

How then could she have been able to draw them with that firm, minutely-etched delineation of their talk and their gestures that make them move and live before us in speech and habit and soul? But Branwell knew them; they were just the folk with whom he had always consorted at the 'Black Bull,' at the meetings of the 'Lodge of the Three Graces,' over interminable whisky-toddies, and his was the clay which he brought for Emily's fashioning. He made his contributions too, as in the verbal coincidences already noted, the devil-eyes of Heathcliff, and Heathcliff's ravings about the force of his love for Catherine compared with Linton's, for just so did he rave about his passion for Mrs. Robinson, compared with her invalid husband's tepidity and indifference. But of all this collaboration Charlotte knew nothing, just as she had known nothing about Emily's poems till she had rifled her desk. The others had their secrets together, Emily and Anne played at Gondals, Emily and Branwell talked over *Wuthering Heights*. Branwell had begun it, and they retained those first two chapters, though that handicap entailed endless awkwardnesses in the rest of the telling.

And Charlotte was the most solitary of them all. She had her heart's secret which she shared with none, and, while her soul was filled with loathing for

Branwell's tipsy maunderings about the married woman for whom he had committed some 'frantic folly,' she could scarce help contrasting the indecency of such gabble with her own silent tortures of expectation when the post-hour drew near and the silent despair which followed, when it brought her no reply from M. Héger.

CHAPTER XII

Early in January 1846 there was a railway panic, following a railway boom. New companies had been floated with insufficient capital, and many unfortunate shareholders were ruined. The legacies which the three Brontë sisters had inherited from their aunt had been invested by Emily during Charlotte's second sojourn in Brussels in the York and Midland Railway. This was a well-managed line with a sound financial basis, and in spite of the panic the capital value of the shares had been maintained. Charlotte was anxious that they should sell their shares and re-invest, though at a lower rate of interest, in something safer, but her sisters disagreed, and sooner than hurt Emily's feelings she agreed to let her money stop where it was. 'Disinterested and energetic (Emily) certainly is,' so she wrote to Miss Wooler,' and if she be not quite so tractable or open to conviction as I could wish, I must remember perfection is not the lot of humanity.' A few years later Charlotte's misgivings were justified, and she lost some considerable part of her legacy.

A dreary account of Branwell follows in this letter, for to Miss Wooler as well as Ellen, Charlotte wrote her grim bulletins.

He never thinks of seeking employment, and I begin to fear he has rendered himself incapable of filling any respectable station in life; besides, if money were at his disposal he would only use it to his own injury: the faculty of self-government is, I fear, almost destroyed in him.

She had already written to Ellen this month in the same strain. 'Branwell offers no prospect of hope, he professes to be too ill to think of seeking for employment.' And so throughout the spring it goes on, till one wearies of these incessant girdings, and bleeds for the unpitied brother more than for the pitiless sister. That complaint that he would not get a situation and thus rid Haworth of his odious, scarcely supportable presence, is always to the fore.

I am thankful that papa is pretty well, though often made very miserable by Branwell's wretched conduct. There—there is no change but for the worse,... You ask if we are more comfortable. I wish I could say anything favourable, but how can we be more comfortable so long as Branwell stays at home, and degenerates instead of improving? It has lately been intimated to him that he would be received again on the railroad where he was formerly stationed if he would behave more steadily but he refuses to make an effort; he will not work —and at home he is a drain on every resource—an impediment to all happiness....

Intolerable as Branwell must have been, it is strange to find that his sister would sooner he went back to Luddenden Foot, where he had no companion of any sort but a porter, nor the slightest stimulus, ineffective though it seemed to be, of home and of relations to keep him from going more quickly and finally to ruin, than that he should be such an impediment at Haworth to all happiness. Nor was she right in saying that he made no effort to get employment, or that any such post had been offered him. Three times during this period did he beg his friend Grundy, an engineer on the line, to get him reappointed to some post, and each time his application was refused.

No doubt in spite of the ruthlessness of her letters Charlotte tried to be more charitable towards him, but just as he was bound in those detestable chains that his weakness had so strongly wrought for him, so the very uprightness of her nature, the stern Puritanism of her principles, her revolt at the injustice of them all being made to suffer for his bestiality, fettered her capacity for pity. Something of this—this striving on both sides to do better than the self-indulgence of the one and the righteousness of the other permitted—appears in a certain statement which Branwell wrote down and read to his friend, Mr. George Searle Phillips, who came to see him at Haworth. The half-tipsy, self-pitying sentimentality of it is obvious and odious enough, but equally obvious is its underlying authenticity: nobody could have invented such a story. This is Mr. Phillips's account:

One of the Sunday-school girls in whom he and his house took much interest fell very sick, and they were afraid she would not live. 'I went to see the poor little thing,' Branwell said, 'sat with her half an hour and read a psalm to her, and a hymn at her request. I felt very like praying with her too,' he added, his voice trembling with emotion, 'but, you see, I was not good enough. How dare I pray for another who had almost forgotten how to pray for myself! I came away with a heavy heart, for I felt sure she would die, and went straight home, where I fell into melancholy musings. I often do, but no kind word finds its way ever to my ears, much less to my heart. Charlotte observed my depression and asked what ailed me. So I told her. She looked at me with a look I shall never forget—if I live to be a hundred years old—which I never shall. It was not like her at all. It wounded me as if somebody had struck me a blow in the mouth. It involved so many things in it. It was a dubious look. It ran over me, questioning and examining, as if I had been a wild beast. It said, "Did my ears deceive me, or did I hear aright?" And then came the painful baffled expression, which was worse than all. It said, "I wonder if that's true!" But as she left the room, she seemed to accuse herself of having wronged me, and smiled kindly upon me, and said, "She is my little scholar, and I will go and see her." I replied not a word, I was too much cut up. When she was gone I came over here to the "Black Bull," and made a note of it in sheer disgust and desperation. Why could they not give me some credit when I was trying to be good?'

The reader's first feeling, no doubt, is of nausea at this 'nobody-loves-me' attitude, at the maudlin self-pity, at the writer's going straight to the 'Black Bull' to console himself in the usual manner and 'make a note' of his sister's cruelty. But he writhed under her whips: her attitude to him is what we should gather from her letters to Ellen. And yet, sickened to the soul at him, she was trying to do better.

Then there was Anne. Anne's sincere piety, her gentleness, her sense of duty, made a strange harvesting from her brother's failings. As soon as she had finished *Agnes Grey* she at once set to work on her second novel, *The Tenant of Wildfell Hall*, which is largely concerned with a drunken monomaniac: of its genesis and the history of its production Charlotte gives a full account.

The choice of subject was an entire mistake. Nothing less congruous with the writer's nature could be conceived. The motives which dictated the choice were pure, but, I think, morbid. She (Anne) had, in the course of her life, been called on to contemplate near at hand and for a long time, the terrible effects of talents misused and faculties abused ... what she saw sank very deeply into her mind, it did her harm. She brooded over it till she believed it to be her duty to reproduce every detail ... as a warning to others. She hated her work, but would pursue it. When reasoned with on the subject she regarded such reasonings as a temptation to self-indulgence. She must be honest; she must not varnish, soften or conceal. This well-meant resolution brought on her misconstruction and some abuse....

There can be no question as to whom Anne contemplated 'near at hand' and 'for a long time'; the 'talents misused' were his whose 'talents misapplied' Charlotte lamented after Branwell's death, and we picture Anne, pious and gentle, industriously, from a sense of duty, making copy out of Branwell. Nor can there be any question who misconstructed her motives and abused her. Not Charlotte, who understood her motives, though she thought her choice of subject morbid, but Emily.... Again the picture of the quiet dining-room at the Parsonage outlines itself with a little terrible detail added.

The three sisters were together to-night in the dining-room, and Anne had just told Emily who was the model for the drunken wastrel in her new book. She sat silent, conscious of the rectitude and high moral aim of her intentions, while Emily stormed at her for the brutality of it. Charlotte, too, was dissuasive; she thought she was morbid to dwell on such a theme. When they had finished, Anne merely said she knew she was doing right—they must not tempt her—and patiently resumed her work. The words came easily to-night, for there had been a horrid scene with Branwell, who came back reeling and hiccoughing from the 'Black Bull.'

Charlotte escaped sometimes from the home which, if we may judge from her letters, had become to her, from various causes, so dark an abode of hate and misery, and on which soon far blacker shadows were to fall. This spring she spent a fortnight with Ellen, and heard encouraging news about the operation for cataract. On her return she went to see her father, who was now nearly blind, and cheered him up by telling him how successful the operation now was, for he dreaded the idea; also it was a relief to him to know that he might wait for a few months yet before he need submit to it. Charlotte's letter to Ellen continues:

I went into the room where Branwell was, to speak to him, about an hour after I got home; it was very forced work to address him. I might have spared myself the trouble, as he took no notice, and made no reply: he was stupefied. My fears were not in vain. I hear that he had got a sovereign from papa while I have been away under pretence of paying a pressing debt; he went immediately and changed it at a public house, and employed it as was to be expected. Emily concluded her account by saying that he was a hopeless being: it is too true. In his present state it is scarcely possible to stay in the room where he is.

This letter contains a sentence on which much has been built. It has been argued that, because Emily called her brother 'a hopeless being,' she gave him up with the same completeness as Charlotte had done. This view is shared by Mr. Clement Shorter, who concludes that 'by now (March 1846) Branwell had reached that stage of physical and moral wreckage when even his most broadminded sister had to give him up.' He refers again to this expression of Emily's and says: 'The fact is that Branwell's state at that time was such that Emily, being only human, could not possibly have been more tolerant,—and rightly so—than her two sisters....' Now it is with the greatest reluctance that one differs from Mr. Shorter, whose patient and careful research and whose fair treatment of all available data about the lives of the Brontës makes him so eminent an authority, but surely this conclusion, built on so slender a foundation, is unwarranted. We rather picture Emily telling Charlotte how Branwell had got a sovereign under false pretences from his father and spent it in the usual way, adding, merely cursorily, 'Oh, he's a hopeless being!' Such an interpretation seems more likely than to ascribe to Emily, on this phrase alone, a fixed and justifiable determination to have nothing more to do with him. It does not seem consistent with the nature of one who was 'full of ruth for others,' or who was indignant with Anne for using Branwell as a model for the drunken Huntingdon in *The Tenant of Wildfell Hall,* now on the stocks. Moreover, there is rebutting evidence that rests on a more solid foundation than this surmise.

Miss A. Mary F. Robinson (Madame Duclaux) published, in 1889, a book called *Emily Brontë*. It contains the following passage about Emily's relations with her brother:

There was one woman's heart strong enough in its compassion to bear the daily disgusts, weaknesses, sins of Branwell's life, and yet persist in aid and affection. Night after night, when Mr. Brontë was in bed, when Anne and Charlotte had gone upstairs to their room, Emily still sat up waiting. She often had very long to wait in the silent house before the staggering tread, the muttered oath, the fumbling hand at the door, bade her rouse herself from her sad thoughts and rise to let in the prodigal, and lead him in safety to his rest. But she never wearied in her kindness. In that silent house, it was ever the silent Emily who had ever a cheering word for Branwell; it was Emily who remembered that he was her brother, without that remembrance freezing her heart to numbness.

Then follows a spirited account of a fire that broke out in Branwell's room one night. He had gone to bed and fallen into a drugged or drunken sleep, and his candle had upset, setting his sheets alight. Emily dashed downstairs for a couple of pails of water, extinguished the flames and rescued her brother. Miss Robinson's account is too full of vivid but impossible details to be accepted entirely. We cannot, for instance, believe that while Emily went to fetch water from downstairs Charlotte, Anne, and the servant 'stood huddled together in amazed horror' against the wall of the passage outside without making the slightest attempt to pull Branwell off the burning bed, or see what could be done with the water-jug, but Miss Robinson has stated that she derived the information that Emily befriended and tried to help Branwell until the end, and that she did thus rescue him when his bed was on fire, from Ellen Nussey herself. This disposes of the suggestion that, because Emily allowed that her brother was a 'hopeless being,' she therefore abandoned him, and that this story of the fire was a mere myth incubated from the similar incident in *Jane Eyre* in which Jane rescues Rochester from the bed to which his lunatic wife had set fire. Indeed, considering how invariably Charlotte wove into her novels pieces of personal experience, the fact that an identical scene occurs in her book points to its being derived from the actual incident for which Ellen Nussey is the source. We are thus also enabled to date this rescue by Emily of her brother as having occurred before *Jane Eyre* was begun in the summer of 1846. Nature would otherwise be imitating Art with an almost indecent fidelity. A further confirmation of this date is supplied by our knowledge that for two years before his death Branwell slept in the same room as his father: at the time of the fire he must still have been occupying a room to himself.

Finally, as regards Emily's unbroken friendship and pity for Branwell during these appalling years when the other sisters watched him, with aversion or to point a moral, being wrecked by self-indulgence and dying of consumption, we have only to read her poem *The Wanderer from the Fold*, which was the last she ever wrote and was composed between Branwell's death in September 1848 and her own in December of the same year. It is not questioned that it refers to him:

How few of all the hearts that loved,

Are grieving for thee now:

And why should mine to-night be moved

With such a sense of woe?

Too often thus, when left alone

Where none my thoughts can see,

Comes back a word, a passing tone

From thy strange history.

Sometimes I seem to see thee rise,

A glorious child again;

All virtues beaming from thine eyes

That ever honoured men;

Courage and truth, a generous breast

Where sinless sunshine lay:

A being whose very presence blest

Like gladsome summer day.

Oh, fairly spread thy early sail,

And fresh and pure and free

Was the first impulse of the gale

Which urged life's wave for thee!

Why did the pilot, too confiding,

Dream o'er that ocean's foam,

And trust in Pleasure's careless guiding

To bring his vessel home?

For well he knew what dangers frowned,

What mists would gather dim;

What rocks and shelves and sands lay round

Between his port and him.

The very brightness of the sun,

The splendour of the main,

The wind that blew him wildly on

Should not have warned in vain.

An anxious gazer from the shore—

I marked the whitening wave,

And wept above thy fate the more

Because—I could not save.

It recks not now, when all is over:

But yet my heart will be

A mourner still, though friend and lover

Have both forgotten thee!

In May 1846 occurred Mr. Robinson's death. 'It served Branwell,' wrote Charlotte, 'for a pretext to throw all about him into hubbub and confusion with his emotion, &c. &c.' Of that sufficient has already been said; all that is solid about it is that the year before he had doubtless made love to the woman, and that very properly she told her husband about it, who dismissed him and told him not to hold any communication with her. Probably she was sorry for him and had friendly feelings towards him, as a perfectly respectable woman may towards a man who has tried to make love to her, for more than once subsequently Charlotte records that Branwell had been sent presents of money from 'the old quarter,' which is sufficiently explicit. All the rest we may confidently consider a fiction on Branwell's part, composed with the object of making himself a love-lorn and tragic figure. Unfortunately Charlotte believed, though with hesitation, his fantastic tale, for her letters to Ellen contain several most bitter allusions to Mrs. Robinson, as if it was she who, by making advances to Branwell and then throwing him over, was responsible for his degradation. With that we may dismiss the rest of the sordid episode as being in the main a drunkard's imaginings, since every detail of it can be directly traced to Branwell himself.

Early in June 1846, to judge by the date of reviews in the *Critic* and *Athenæum*, the joint book of poems by the three sisters was published. The *Critic* gave it a very good notice; the *Athenæum* declared that Ellis Bell had a 'fine quaint spirit'; but for the present only one copy was actually purchased, fourteen being sent out for review.

Meanwhile the three novels were going their weary journeys, and after long intervals returned to their authors with uncommenting refusals; and Mr. Brontë's eyes were getting worse. He could grope about still, but no longer could he see the face of his watch which he took with him into the pulpit on Sunday to regulate the length of his discourse; from habit, however, he still preached for a precise half-hour. But his eyes were now ripe for the operation, and in August Charlotte accompanied him to Manchester, having with admirable efficiency made all arrangements with the surgeon and having engaged lodgings for herself and him. She was racked with toothache which kept her awake at night; she had no idea how to cater for the nurse who would attend her father after the operation, and on the very morning when it took place a fatal parcel arrived which she knew to be the manuscript of *The Professor*, which, like the dove, had once more found no resting-place. At her father's wish she was present in the room throughout the operation, and during the days that followed, when he had to remain in the dark in charge of the nurse whom, as a stranger, she disliked and distrusted, she set to work on a new novel, *Jane Eyre*.

It would be hard to find an instance of a more indomitable pluck, a more iron determination not to be overborne by any phalanx of adverse circumstances. There was nothing whatever in prospect at home: there was a drunken brother for whom she felt nothing but loathing and contempt; every scheme which she had made for the career of herself and her sisters had crumbled, their poems were still-born, their novels found no publisher; life was passing away, she was earning nothing, and those acquirements for teaching which she had won at such cost to her peace were rusting in disuse. Most keenly and most bitterly and with an ever-growing pessimism did she feel these tribulations, but her will and the fire of her imagination flamed up unquenched through the smoke and the damp smouldering; indeed, she found fuel in what would have finally extinguished a less ardent soul. She stoked up the fires of her imagination and threw into them the bitterness of heart with which she wrote of her schooldays at Cowan Bridge and the death of her sisters. A year had already elapsed since her 'discovery' of Emily's poems had kindled, after long ash-covered smouldering, the flame of literary ambition, and though that year had brought forth nothing but disappointment, it burned unquenched. Hermetically secret about it, never a word or hint did she vouchsafe to Ellen about what she had written, what she and her sisters had published, or what she was now writing.

But she confided to Ellen a certain resolution she had made, of sufficient importance to be printed in capitals in one of her letters: 'And if I were ever again to find myself among strangers I should be solicitous to examine before I condemned.' This confession is striking. She was aware of her censorious habit, she knew it led her into erroneous conclusions, and yet it seemed an integral part of her character. She was too much of a fighter to rank herself with the non-combatants who suffer long and are kind; she was ever harshly critical of those who made her suffer. Strangers made her suffer, and the first thing she looked for in them was faults. She was abnormally shy of them; her shyness to the end of her days was torture to her, and she attributed her discomfort to their odious qualities. It was from this largely that her censoriousness sprang, but it was also due to her constitutional pessimism which, always expecting to find blemishes in others, was seldom disappointed. She was alert to detect faults, she was extreme to mark what was done amiss. Indeed this practice seemed rather to be a principle of hers, for she deprecated any sort of optimism about others.

I believe you are prone [she wrote a year or two later to Mr. W. S. Williams] to think too highly of your fellow-creatures in general—to see too exclusively the good points of those for whom you have a regard. Disappointment must be the inevitable result of this habit.

There is a certain cynical truth in her comment, but what she did not perceive was that her own habit of being over-eager to see faults was exactly what caused her *not* to arrive at a regard for others; nor did she perceive that those who go through life as she did, prone to think disparagingly of her fellow-creatures, lose more than they gain by saving themselves such inevitable disappointments, for they miss the vastly outweighing rewards which come to the kindlier disposition which is on the look-out for amiable qualities. Her instinct was always to judge, and this deprived her of all the unreflecting enjoyment which is part of the natural equipment of a normal human being: the light touch, the indulgence for herself and others which is like yeast in the otherwise heavy dough of existence, never seem to have been hers, nor that sense of humour that makes human failings endearing rather than culpable. This rigidity, pessimistic and puritanical, had the defects of its qualities, and it resulted in that absence of charity which revealed on all sides a multitude of sins, and it was the root of much of her unhappiness. Not until the last months of her life did she find the only possible antidote to it.

An alleviation to the monotonous gloom of the Parsonage this autumn was the recovery of Mr. Brontë's eyesight. By November he was in full harness again, and capable of taking three Sunday services by himself. That was a matter for thankfulness, but it passed into routine, and in the winter she writes to Ellen that nothing pleasant happens at Haworth, and the only thing that has 'stung us into life' was the arrival of a sheriff's officer for Branwell, 'inviting him either to pay his debts or take a trip to York.' Bitterness was about her path, and when Ellen tells her about a new white dress which she looks forward to wearing, while Charlotte commends her frankness in telling her of her pleasure, she warns her against indiscriminate frankness, and hopes that 'an overdose of vanity will not spoil this blessing and turn it into a misfortune.' She sends Ellen a piece of lace, but hopes that the Bradford Post Office will not steal it—for the officials there usually open letters that seem to contain something interesting. Then, though she had been firmly resolved that Ellen should not come to Haworth while Branwell was there, she now invites her, for

Branwell is quieter now and for a good reason; he has got to the end of a considerable sum of money, and consequently is obliged to restrict himself in some degree. You must expect to find him weaker in mind and a complete rake in appearance.

But the visit fell through: Ellen's sister had already arranged to be away from home, and she could not leave her mother. Upon which vials of wormwood and gall are outpoured: Charlotte says that she may find it more difficult next time to arrange for Ellen to come. This entirely unreasonable letter she subsequently withdrew with apologies.

By the summer of 1847 the book of poems had been out for a year, and in spite of favourable notices in the *Critic*, the *Athenæum*, and the *Dublin University Magazine*, only two copies in all had been sold. Before the remainder were scrapped Charlotte sent copies to Wordsworth, Tennyson, Lockhart, and De Quincey, with an identical letter of homage to each, in the name of the three authors, referring to the painful efforts their publishers must have made in getting rid of even two copies. To-day either of these would fetch at least a hundred pounds in the auction room. Southey, it may be noticed, who nine years before had very decidedly discouraged Charlotte from attempting to write verse, was not sent one. The poetical career for herself and her sisters had closed, and there was nothing to be done but to send the rest of the slender volumes to the trunk-makers for a paper lining to their boxes. But we cannot help wondering what would have been their fate if these volumes had been slenderer still, and had contained only Emily's poems. As it was, these were sandwiched between the work of her two sisters, and that work, to speak quite frankly, is destitute of all poetical quality and distinction. There is not a stanza or even a line in it all which gleams or sings. Charlotte, in after days, at any rate, knew that herself: she says, 'All of it that merits to be known are the poems of Ellis Bell.' It is strange that, when first she was arranging for the publication, that should not have struck her, and that her business sense should not have perceived how terribly Emily's work was handicapped by being wedged in between plain, pious, ponderous pages by herself and Anne. No doubt the glamour of the joint ambition dazzled her.

Ellen's deferred visit took place in August 1847: she came, she stayed, and she went away again in complete ignorance of all the excitement that raged beneath the peaceful surface at the Parsonage. For by now *Wuthering Heights* and *Agnes Grey* had both been accepted by the publisher Mr. T. C. Newby, after their pedlar-pilgrimages, and though *The Professor* made yet one more unsuccessful journey to Messrs. Smith, Elder & Co., it came back on Charlotte's hands not with the 'two hard hopeless lines' that had up till now accompanied its return, but, though refused, with a critical letter of two pages, showing, as Charlotte quaintly put it, 'a discrimination so enlightened that this very refusal cheered the author better than a vulgarly expressed acceptance would have done.' The firm also intimated that a manuscript of a three-volume novel would receive careful reading. *Jane Eyre*, begun just a year ago, at Manchester, when Mr. Brontë was lying in a dark room after his operation, was now nearly finished, and it was sent off to the publishers on August 24.

The reader for the firm, Mr. W. S. Williams, was enthusiastic about the book, so also was Mr. Smith, and it was at once accepted for publication in the autumn. Only a few weeks ago the prospect had been absolutely blank: two copies only of the joint volume of poems had been sold, and the three novels begun in the autumn of 1845 had journeyed wearily from publisher to publisher, returning always to Haworth. Now each sister had found a market for her wares, and among them was a book of supreme and matchless passion and *Jane Eyre*. Had it not been for Charlotte's discovery of Emily's poems two years before, and for the failure of her scheme to set up school, it is possible that neither of them would have been written. The Misses Brontë would have had a boarding-school for girls at Haworth Parsonage, and it would have kept them busy.

CHAPTER XIII

This visit of Ellen's to Haworth in August was returned by a visit of Charlotte's to Brookroyd the next month. Proofs of *Jane Eyre* were coming in fast, for it was being hurried through the Press, and Charlotte sat at the same table as her friend, with the printed galleys in front of her, yet not a word of question or volunteered information passed between them. Charlotte peered into her proofs and Ellen, with that excellent tact which characterised her, was completely blind to what was going on under her eyes. She must have been perfectly aware that Charlotte was correcting proofs and had therefore written a book, and the image of these two intimate friends sitting there in silence with this so highly exciting evidence sprawling on the table between them makes a pleasing picture.

She returned to Haworth and found her boxes stuffed with presents from her kindly friend. There was an eye-screen for Mr. Brontë, a peck of apples and a collar for Emily, who was pleased but astonished, a 'crab cheese' for Anne, that soothed her cough, a cap for Tabby, and a jar of preserves for Charlotte, for all which bounties Ellen got duly scolded. Other news from Haworth was that Mr. Nicholls was on holiday in Ireland, and that Anne's delicate chest found the east winds troublesome. Mr. Grant, the master of Haworth Grammar School, as yet unconscious that Charlotte was taking note of his behaviour, and that he was to figure among the curates of her next book, was full of unintelligible apologies for not having made more of Ellen during her visit to Haworth. The foolish creature! 'Why apologise for conduct which caused no suffering whatever?...' But what about Miss Amelia Ringrose, a young lady who had lately developed a *schwärm* for Ellen? Charlotte had never seen her, and had never been more interested about a total stranger. Of Branwell not a word, and not a word of *Jane Eyre*.

Currer Bell's book was published on October 16, and was an instant success not only with the ordinary fiction-reading public, but with the literary world. Thackeray's praise, conveyed in a letter to the publishers, was particularly pleasing to Charlotte, for she already admired his work (*Vanity Fair* was at the time coming out in parts), and his admiration of *Jane Eyre* accentuated her belief in his judgment. 'No author,' she wrote, 'seems to distinguish so exquisitely as he does dross from ore, the real from the counterfeit. I believed too he had deep and true feelings under his seeming sternness. Now I am sure he has....'

The popular enthusiasm over *Jane Eyre* as well as that of the literary world was not to be wondered at. The plot, though wholly incredible, is highly exciting; it teems with the stimulating impossibilities of shockers and best sellers. Mr. Rochester for years kept a lunatic wife on the third floor of his country-house, in charge of a gin-drinking maid, instead of putting her in an asylum, and none of the other servants nor Jane Eyre, who was governess to Mr. Rochester's illegitimate child, knew anything about it. The house resounded with her demoniac laughter: she attempted to burn her husband in his bed, she bit her brother, and on the eve of the wedding of Jane Eyre to

Rochester, she came to her room in the middle of the night and tore her bridal veil in half. No scruple about committing bigamy ever entered Rochester's head; he blandly proposed to marry the eighteen-year-old governess of his illegitimate child, and his intention was only thwarted by the intervention at the marriage-service itself of his brother-in-law and his lawyer. He then suggested to Jane Eyre that, since he had been prevented from tricking her into a bogus marriage, she should become his mistress. This she refused to do, and, though still madly adoring him and unresentful of his monstrous deception, ran away, and after spending her last penny on a coach fare, left her belongings in the coach, and scoured the country on foot for two days. Finally she dropped, dripping and exhausted, on the threshold of the house where her three first cousins happened to live, of whose existence she was not aware, but who were the only relations she had in the world. She then found that she was the heiress of an uncle who had died leaving her £20,000, which she divided up between her cousins and herself. Her male cousin, Rev. St. John Rivers, who was going out to be a missionary in India, decided that she must accompany him. It would cause scandal if they were not married, and so he told her that, though they were not in the least in love with each other, she must become his wife. Previously she had felt not the slightest interest in anything connected with missions, but she consented to go out with him, though not as his wife, and for that purpose learned Hindustanee. He still insisted on marriage, and she was on the point of yielding when she heard a phantom voice coming from the moonlit night calling 'Jane, Jane!' She knew it to be the voice of Edward Rochester, and ran out into the garden exclaiming, 'Where are you?' No answer came, and she commented: 'Down superstition. This is not thy deception nor thy witchcraft, it is the work of nature. She was roused and did—no miracle—but her best.' So she hurried back to Thornfield, and found that Mrs. Rochester had again set fire to the house, that a burning beam had fallen on her husband when he tried to rescue her, and that he was stone blind. The maniac had jumped off the roof and was killed. So Jane Eyre sought him out and married him. He recovered his sight and they had a baby.

Such is the mere plot of *Jane Eyre*, a tissue of violences, absurdities, and coincidences, not less ludicrous than those glimpses of high life, in which Blanche Ingram of the 'raven ringlets and the oriental eye' addresses her mother as 'Baroness Ingram of Ingram Park,' and says to the footman, 'Cease thy chatter, blockhead, and do my bidding.' The didactic passages, of which there are many, the hortatory passages (as when Jane Eyre draws a picture of herself in chalks, 'smoothing away no displeasing irregularity,' and then an imaginary and ideal portrait of Miss Ingram, in order to cure herself of her vain aspirations towards Mr. Rochester) are written in a style of incredible pomposity:

Order! No Snivel—no sentiment—no regret! (thus she addresses herself) I will endure only sense and resolution. Recall the august yet harmonious lineaments, the Grecian neck and bust; let the round and dazzling arm be visible, and the delicate hand; omit neither diamond ring nor gold bracelet ... call it 'Blanche, an accomplished lady of rank.'

But over all such extravagances the greatness of the book rises triumphant and supreme by reason of its beauty and its white-hot sincerity: all its faults are consumed in that furnace. Never before in the history of English fiction had there been anything to approach this picture of pure passion, not only of a man for a woman, but of a woman for a man. To the delicacies and pruderies of the early Victorian age the shock must have been terrific, but high and low, rich and poor, found that it was no use being shocked; they had to read it, and it was its fiery splendour rather than the shock of it that left them gasping. It was in no sense a designed revolt against the conventions of the day in literature and living: it merely disregarded them, was unconscious of them. Charlotte was not preaching, she was telling a story about an insignificant little woman who knew what she meant when she spoke of love, its sufferings and its fiery quality which burns up like dross all sentimentality and softness. The message in her book spoke direct to the soul of humanity, and instantly it had its architectural place in the literature of the world, weight-bearing and massive. Often and often in herself the larger vision, the sweep of the serene sky, was obscured as with clouds and peevish squalls, with censoriousness and bitterness, with want of compassion and decrying judgments, with the desire to preach and to scold, but behind was this clear shining.

Naturally, as is always the case when something new and startling and disturbing leaps to light, there were bitter criticisms of her work which, as was equally natural in one of her temperament, she bitterly resented. But she insisted on seeing all unfavourable reviews, and though her avowed object was to profit by them, the real effect of them was to make her blood boil with a sense of their injustice and stupidity.

It would take a good deal to crush me [she robustly wrote to Mr. Williams], because I know in the first place that my intentions were correct, that I feel in my heart a deep reverence for religion, that impiety is very abhorrent to me; and in the second I place firm reliance in the judgment of some who have encouraged me.

In fact, so far from being crushed, adverse criticism only caused her to take the gloomiest views of the character of those who expressed it.

I was aware [she wrote to her old mistress, Miss Wooler] that some persons thought proper to take exception to *Jane Eyre*, and that for their own sakes I was sorry, as I invariably found them individuals in whom the animal largely predominated over the intellectual, persons by nature coarse, by inclination sensual.

Most of all she resented any speculation as to the sex of Currer Bell; that seemed a most unwarrantable prying into her private affairs and she could not see that such a curiosity was legitimate. She believed that a woman novelist was not taken seriously either by the public or the critics; she did not have a chance, and Charlotte wanted her work to be judged as if it were the work of a man. Besides, there was the secret of Currer, Ellis, and Acton Bell to keep, and though her publishers suspected Currer Bell was a woman, she did not yet reveal herself even to them.

It was not till December, when the success of *Jane Eyre* had made it what we now call 'the novel of the season,' that her sisters induced Charlotte to tell Mr. Brontë of her fame. She gave Mrs. Gaskell an account of the announcement in a delicious bit of dialogue.

'Papa, I've been writing a book.'

'Have you, my dear?'

'Yes, I want you to read it.'

'I am afraid it will try my eyes too much.' [Charlotte wrote a microscopic hand.]

'But it is not in manuscript; it is printed.'

'My dear! You've never thought of the expense it will be. It will be almost sure to be a loss, for how can you get a book sold? No one knows you or your name.'

'But, papa, I don't think it will be a loss; no more will you if you will just let me read you a review or two, and tell you more about it.'

This was done, and he came in to tea, and said, 'Girls, do you know Charlotte has been writing a book and it is much better than likely?'

Evidently, then, Mr. Brontë knew nothing about the joint book of poems, or about *Wuthering Heights*, and *Agnes Grey*, which also came out in December 1847. The sisters had paid £50 for the printing and publishing of 350 copies, but it appears that the publisher only printed 250 copies. There was journalistic speculation as to the actual authorship of *Wuthering Heights*; it was suggested that it was an earlier and immature work by the author of *Jane Eyre*, but Charlotte at present took little heed of such attributions: 'the critics,' she wrote to Mr. Williams, 'are welcome to confuse our identities as much as they choose.'

Wuthering Heights appears to have sold decently, but it attracted no critical homage for many months yet, and Charlotte's occasional allusions to it in her letters show how little appreciation she herself had of it, and how profoundly she misunderstood it and the savagery of its supreme genius. Writing, for instance, of Heathcliff, that masterpiece of wild pagan passion, she says: 'The worst of it is some of his spirit seems breathed through the whole narrative, in which he figures, it haunts every moor and glen, and beckons in every fir-tree of the Heights.' She did not see that the terrific and appalling impression that moor and glen and fir-tree are permeated by Heathcliff is not 'the worst of it,' but that in this very point, namely, that he is somehow incarnate of the wild moorland, there lies the proof and the very seal of the genius of the book. She unmistakably sounds a note of apology, of excuse for Emily.

Ellis [she informed Mr. Williams] has a strong original mind, full of strange though sombre power. When he writes poetry that power speaks in language at once condensed, elaborated and refined, but in prose it breaks forth in scenes which shock more than they attract. Ellis will improve, however, because he knows his defects.

But she thought that neither poetry nor fiction were really Ellis's *forte*, for to the same correspondent she writes, 'I should say Ellis will not be seen in his full strength till he is seen as an essayist.' It seems scarcely credible that she was writing about the author of *Wuthering Heights*, and one vainly and impotently wonders what sort of essay it would be and on what subject, that would reveal the full strength of Emily Brontë which*Wuthering Heights* only partially disclosed. Still, sticking up for her sister, Charlotte says she would not be ashamed to have written it. Her maturer reflections about *Wuthering Heights*, when she re-read it, belong to a later period. Of *Agnes Grey* all she says is that it is the mirror of the mind of the writer. From this judgment it is impossible to differ.

With the publication and success of *Jane Eyre* the twilight of nothingness, to which at one time there had seemed to Charlotte to be no end but the complete darkness of age and death, had given place to the most brilliant dawn. Her horizons and possibilities had endlessly expanded, the tonic of success had vivified her. In January 1848 a second edition of *Jane Eyre* was issued, and she wrote a militant preface to it, in which her views about her critics were expressed with singular directness. She thanked the public and her publishers, and portions of the Press, namely, the 'select reviewers' who 'had encouraged her as only large-hearted and high-minded men know how.' Then there were some resounding smacks for 'the timorous and carping few who doubted the tendency of such books as *Jane Eyre*.' She reminded them that: 'Conventionality is not morality. Self-righteousness is not religion. To attack the first is not to assail the last. To pluck the mask from the face of the

Pharisee is not to lift an impious hand to the Crown of Thorns.' Then followed a panegyric on Thackeray, to whom she dedicated this second edition. He was an eagle compared with that carrion-feeding vulture Fielding: he came before high Society like the son of Imlah before the Kings of Israel and Judah, and hurled at it the Greek fire of his sarcasm and the levin bolt of his denunciation: they had better attend to him if they wished to escape a Ramoth-gilead. Thackeray, she was afraid, did not much care for this dedication—which seems probable, for, when thanking her for it, he told her that he, like Mr. Rochester, had a mad wife, and people said that *Jane Eyre* was written by his governess.

This second edition sold well, and soon after there arose the question of its dramatisation and production at some minor theatre. Charlotte shuddered at the thought of seeing it, but steeled herself to endure the 'rant and whine, strut and grimace for the sake of the useful observations to be collected in such a scene.' Nothing apparently came of this, but a year afterwards it was dramatised by John Brougham and produced in New York.

Among those who had been immensely struck with *Jane Eyre* was G. H. Lewes, who wrote to her that he intended to contribute a review of it to *Fraser's Magazine*. Charlotte had not heard of him before, but she now got his novel *Ranthorpe*, which she highly praised, and subsequently *Rose Blanche and Violet*, of which the 'didactic passages profound and acute' pleased her best. The correspondence between them is chiefly notable for her views on Jane Austen. Lewes had held her up as a master of technique, so Charlotte got *Pride and Prejudice* on his recommendation. It was a matter of amazement to her that anyone could admire it. She only found

an accurate daguerreotyped portrait of a commonplace face: a carefully fenced highly cultivated garden with neat borders and delicate flowers: but no glance of a bright vivid physiognomy, no open country, no fresh air, no blue hill, no bonny beck. I should hardly like to live with her ladies and gentlemen, in their elegant but confined houses.

Shrewd and discreet Jane Austen might be, but nothing more. Lewes tried again: he conceded that Jane Austen had no poetry, 'no sentiment,' but told Charlotte that she '*must* learn to acknowledge her as one of the greatest artists, of the greatest painters of human nature, and one of the writers with the nicest sense of means to an end that ever lived.' But that lack of poetry condemned her to Charlotte's sense: Miss Austen might be sensible, she might be real, but she could not be great. Years after she tried *Emma*, but it was quite hopeless: her final conclusion was that Jane Austen was a 'very incomplete and rather insensible (not senseless) woman.' The explanation of her entire want of appreciation, as has been already suggested, seems to be that Charlotte was, in actual fact, entirely devoid of any subtle sense of humour, and therefore could not understand Jane Austen's.

In her contract with Messrs. Smith, Elder for *Jane Eyre*, Charlotte had promised them to give them the refusal of two further novels. *Jane Eyre* must have been scarcely out before she set to work again, for less than two months afterwards she had made three attempts to start a fresh book, none of which satisfied her. One of these, probably, was the fragment of thirty-six pages, unpublished in her lifetime, called *The Moores*. It is usually assigned to a later date, *circa* 1852, but it is unlikely that after the publication of *Shirley*, in which the Moores figure so largely, she should have chosen such a title. She then read over the discarded *Professor* again, finding the beginning very feeble, and noting its deficiency in incident. 'Yet the middle and latter portion of the work,' so she wrote to Mr. Williams, 'all that relates to Brussels and the Belgian school, etc., is as good as I can write.' She therefore proposed to recast it and make a three-volume novel of it, but asked Mr. Williams's advice on the subject, for *The Professor* had already been refused by his firm. We gather that he was against it, for Charlotte dropped the idea and at once began on *Shirley*, taking up, probably, one of her previous three attempts. It is interesting to observe that the idea of doing something with *The Professor* had already entered her mind. She was right enough in her depreciation of it, as it stood, and she was eminently right in realising that the Brussels section contained the germ of a masterpiece. Again she put it back to simmer in her mind and made it the stock-pot for *Villette*.

With all these new interests and correspondences to occupy her, Charlotte's letters to Ellen were few; perhaps she found it difficult to write to so old a friend and refrain from any allusion to what filled her mind and energies. She had bitter things to say about Mrs. Robinson. 'That woman is a hopeless being: calculated to bring a curse wherever she goes, by the mixture of weakness, perversion and deceit in her nature.' The reason for this outburst was evident, for in another letter of close date she says:

Branwell has, by some means, contrived to get more money from the old quarter, and has led us a sad life with his absurd and often intolerable conduct. Papa is harassed day and night; we have little peace: he (Branwell) is always sick, has two or three times fallen down in fits, what will be the ultimate end, God knows. But who is without these drawbacks, these scourges, these skeletons behind the curtain?

We gather that Miss Ringrose's devotion to Ellen still flourished, for she had written to Charlotte almost entirely about her, with 'a kind of gentle enthusiasm of affection enough to make one at once smile and weep—her feelings are half truth, half illusion. No human being could be what she supposes you to be.' The two friends exchanged birthday letters in April, for their anniversaries fell on the same day, and Charlotte, now thirty-two, felt that youth was irrevocably over; over also was her own youthful devotion to Ellen which had once gilded her with all the perfections that Miss Ringrose so pathetically found in her still.

Then Ellen, who, some six months before, had seen Charlotte correcting the proof sheets of *Jane Eyre* under her very eyes, and who therefore must have known all along that Charlotte had a book in the press, summoned up her courage to break silence, and wrote that a report had reached her that Charlotte had written a book. The vehemence of Charlotte's reply probably carried conviction that this report was perfectly true, for under cover of an indignant virtual denial she never denied anything at all.

I have given *no one* [she wrote] a right either to affirm or hint, in the most distant manner, that I am 'publishing'—(humbug!). Whoever has said it,—if anyone has, which I doubt—is no friend of mine. Though twenty books were ascribed to me, I should own none. I scout the idea utterly. Whoever, after I have distinctly rejected the charge, urges it upon me, will do an unkind and an ill-bred thing. The most profound obscurity is infinitely preferable to vulgar notoriety and that notoriety I neither seek nor will have. If therefore any Birstallian or Gomersallian should presume to bore you on the subject,—to ask what 'novel' Miss Brontë has been 'publishing'—you can just say with the distinct firmness of which you are perfect mistress, when you choose, that you are authorized by Miss Brontë to say that she repels and disowns every accusation of the kind. You may add, if you please, that if any one has her confidence, you believe you have, and she has made no drivelling confession to you on the subject....

Surely the lady protested too much; had she not written a novel, she could never have shown such heat in repelling the accusation.

It is difficult to determine when Ellen was told: Charlotte did not want it to be known in the neighbourhood, and it was a secret in which her sisters shared. But such discretion need not be observed with Mary Taylor in New Zealand, and Charlotte sent her a copy of *Jane Eyre,* making no mystery about it, before these strenuous disclaimers.

But soon a certain acknowledgment of authorship became necessary. Anne having finished her second novel, *The Tenant of Wildfell Hall,* sent it to Mr. T. C. Newby, who had brought out *Wuthering Heights* and *Agnes Grey,* and he had been offered a high price for it by an American publisher as being a new work by the author of *Jane Eyre*. He believed (so he said) that the three Brontë novels already published were by one hand—in fact, that Currer Bell had really written them all. Meanwhile Messrs. Smith, Elder, with whom Charlotte had contracted for her next book, had promised it to another firm in America, and now found that what purported to be Currer Bell's next book (*The Tenant of Wildfell Hall*) was already being negotiated for there by Newby. Upon which Mr. Smith naturally wrote to Currer Bell asking for explanations. It was necessary, therefore, in order to establish their separate entities and prove their good faith, that Charlotte and Anne should show themselves to the firm, the one as the author of *Jane Eyre,* the other of *Agnes Grey* and the forthcoming *Tenant of Wildfell Hall*. Without wasting time the two sisters packed a small box and walked through a snowstorm (the month being July) to Keighley and took the night train for London. They washed and breakfasted at the Chapter Coffee House, Paternoster Row, where Charlotte had stayed in her journey to Brussels, and then set off on foot for 65 Cornhill.

An extremely dramatic scene, quite in the style of Euripidean recognition, followed. They asked for Mr. Smith, giving no names, and were after some delay shown up to his room. A tall young man received them, and Charlotte, having made sure that it was he, gave into his hand the disquieting letter she had received from him the morning before, directed to Currer Bell. He looked at it and asked where she had got it. Then came the recognition: the little lady in spectacles, who now gave her name as Miss Brontë, was Currer Bell, author of *Jane Eyre,* and the other one was Acton Bell. They all cursed the perfidious Newby, and Mr. Williams, with whom Charlotte had been in effusive correspondence, was introduced. He was pale, mild and fifty, and there was a long nervous shaking of hands all round.

The business part of the expedition being thus accomplished, a whirl of socialities followed. With a passion for further incognito the sisters called themselves the Misses Brown for introduction to Mr. Smith's friends, and wearing their 'plain high-made country garments' they went that evening to the opera.

Fine ladies and gentlemen [wrote Charlotte] glanced at us with a slight graceful superciliousness quite warranted by the circumstances. Still, I felt pleasantly excited in spite of headache and sickness and conscious clownishness, and I saw Anne was calm and gentle as she always is.

Next morning, the day being Sunday, they went to church with Mr. Williams, and afterwards Mr. Smith and his mother took them out to their 'splendid house' in Bayswater, six miles from Cornhill; there was a fine dinner but no appetite. On Monday there were visits to the Royal Academy and the National Gallery, another dinner with Mr. Smith, and then tea at Mr. Williams's 'comparatively humble but neat residence' with his family of eight children, about one of whom Charlotte had already counselled him, as to her becoming a governess. There was singing by a daughter of Leigh Hunt's, and on Tuesday morning they returned to Haworth laden with books. It had all been highly successful and exciting, but very exhausting; social pleasures and the presence of strangers had wrecked Charlotte.

A more jaded wretch than I looked, when I returned, [she wrote] it would be difficult to conceive. I was thin when I went, but was meagre indeed when I returned; my face looked grey and very old with strange deep lines ploughed in it, my eyes stared unnaturally....

But successful though that expedition had been, and pleased though Charlotte was at terminating with her publishers a mystery that had become irksome, she found that in her disclosure of identities to Mr. Smith she had gone too far, and when she returned to Haworth she was made aware of it. For not only had she revealed herself and Anne as being Currer and Acton Bell, but she had revealed Emily as being Ellis Bell. Once more, as by the 'discovery' of her poems, she had invaded her sister's privacy and Emily strongly resented it. In consequence Charlotte wrote to Mr. Williams:

Permit me to caution you not to speak of my sisters when you write to me; I mean do not use the word in the plural. Ellis Bell will not endure to be alluded to under any appellation other than the *nom de plume*. I committed a grand error in betraying his identity to you and Mr. Smith. It was inadvertent—the words 'we are three sisters' escaped me before I was aware. I regretted the avowal the moment I had made it: I regret it bitterly now, for I find it is against every feeling and intention of Ellis Bell.

This incident is significant. At the least it accentuates our sense of the estrangement and misunderstandings between the two sisters, which must have been rendered more acute by Emily's befriendings of Branwell in these three years, during which Charlotte had recorded, in bulletins to her friends, his growing degradation and her horror of him. To see more in it than that is perhaps a mistake, though those who believe, not without cause, that Branwell had something to do with *Wuthering Heights*, argue from it, plausibly and ingeniously, Emily's repudiation of sole authorship: she knew, though Charlotte did not, that there had been a collaboration between her and the outcast brother. But Emily's exasperation about Charlotte's original raid on her private papers is sufficient to account for her resentment now against this second disclosure.

For six months Charlotte had issued no news of Branwell, but in July 1848 she wrote to Ellen: 'Branwell is the same as ever and his constitution seems shattered. Papa, and sometimes all of us, have sad nights with him, he sleeps most of the day, and consequently will lie awake at night.' This letter contains, as did the one in which she last spoke of her brother in January, another fierce attack on Mrs. Robinson. Her daughters, in almost daily correspondence with

Anne, were about to make, says Charlotte, loveless marriages in obedience to her wish. 'Of their mother,' she writes: 'I have not patience to speak, a worse woman, I believe, hardly exists; the more I hear of her, the more deeply she revolts me.' This repeated coupling of Branwell's deterioration with such expressions about Mrs. Robinson perhaps implies the belief that she was originally responsible for Branwell's ruin, but Charlotte does not definitely state that, nor does she show the slightest softening towards him.

But the house was soon to be rid of its 'scourge and its skeleton behind the curtain.' He was a complete wreck, and no longer to be accounted sane.Consumption was making rapid inroads into a frame already hopelessly debilitated by drink and drugs, and all the summer he had been failing fast. We have but one glimpse more of him, which must be given chiefly because it throws light on what his sisters and father must have gone through during the past three years, living in the house with him.

His friend Francis Grundy came to Haworth to see Branwell two days before his death. He ordered dinner at the 'Black Bull,' and sent a message up to the Parsonage to ask him to come. Mr. Grundy's account proceeds:

Whilst I waited his appearance his father was shewn in. Much of the Rector's old stiffness of manner was gone. He spoke of Branwell with more affection than I had ever heretofore heard him express, but he also spoke almost hopelessly. He said that when my message came, Branwell was in bed, and had been almost too weak to leave it: nevertheless he had insisted upon coming, and would be there immediately. We parted and I never saw him again.

Presently the door opened cautiously and a head appeared. It was a mass of red, unkempt, uncut hair, wildly floating round a great gaunt forehead, the cheeks yellow and hollow, the mouth fallen, the thin white lips not trembling, but shaking; the sunken eyes once small, now glaring with the light of madness—all told the sad tale but too surely.... He glanced at me a moment and muttered something of leaving a warm bed to come out into the cold night. Another glass of brandy, and returning warmth gradually brought him back to something like the Brontë of old. He even ate some dinner, a thing which he said he had not done for long: so our last interview was pleasant though grave. I never knew his intellect clearer. He described himself as waiting anxiously for death—indeed longing for it, and happy, in his sane moments, to think that it was so near. He once again declared that death would be due to the story I knew, and to nothing else.

When at last I was compelled to leave, he quietly drew from his coat-sleeve a carving knife, placed it on the table, and holding me by both hands, said that having given up all thoughts of seeing me again, he imagined when my message came, that it was a call from Satan. Dressing himself, he took the knife, which he had long secreted, and came to the inn with a full determination to rush into the room and stab the occupant. In the excited state of his mind he did not recognise me when he opened the door, but my voice and manner conquered him, and 'brought him home to himself,' as he expressed it. I left him standing bareheaded in the road, with bowed form and dripping tears. A few days afterwards he died.

Now doubt has been cast on this piteous story, because, if Branwell was dying, he could not have left his bed; but, as Charlotte wrote to Ellen Nussey, he was in bed for only one complete day, and went into the village two days before his death, without doubt for this meeting with Grundy. He died on September 24, 1848.

Charlotte neither felt nor made pretence of feeling any personal grief. She wrote to her friend Mr. Williams:

We have buried our dead out of sight. A lull begins to succeed the gloomy tumult of last week. It is not permitted us to grieve for him who is gone as others grieve for those they love. The removal of our only brother must necessarily be regarded by us in the light of a mercy rather than a chastisement.

She told him that religion and principle had never meant anything to Branwell, and it was not till within a few days of his end that he believed in them at all, and then came 'conviction of their existence and worth,' and it was a 'strange change.' He said 'Amen' to the last prayer Mr. Brontë recited by his bedside. 'How unusual that word appeared from his lips, of course you, who did not know him, cannot conceive.' Charlotte felt she could now forgive all the wrong he had done and the pain he had caused her, and adds, 'If man can thus experience total oblivion of his fellow-creatures' imperfections, how much more can the Eternal Being who made man, forgive His creatures?' It is on her forgiveness of her brother that she chiefly dwells, and to Ellen and her sister she repeats that. 'All his vices were and are nothing now. We remember only his woes....' It was perhaps to be regretted that she had not remembered some of his woes a little sooner, and given him a glance of pity while he was able to receive it. Indeed she had more compassion for the profligate and the insane wife of Mr. Rochester in *Jane Eyre* than she had for Branwell in his lifetime, for she wrote to Mr. Williams with greater charity about her: 'Mrs. Rochester indeed lived a sinful life before she was insane, but sin is itself a species of insanity—the truly good behold and compassionate it as such.'

The shadow which for the last three years had darkened and embittered life for Charlotte was gone, and she put all thought of him from her; only three times in her very voluminous correspondence did she make further mention of

Branwell. Once she says that Mr. James Taylor, who, three years later, proposed marriage with her, was markedly like him, adding that when he looked at her 'her veins ran ice'; once she fears that Joe Taylor is going the same way as Branwell, and that a prospective marriage between him and Amelia Ringrose must end in hopeless misery; once she says that if she had a brother living she would not let him read Thackeray's lecture on Fielding, for it made light of such serious vices as drunkenness. His name was added to those of his mother and his sisters Maria and Elizabeth on the tablet in Haworth Church, and *The Tenant of Wildfell Hall*, which Anne had written to warn others concerning the wages of sin, went into a second edition.

CHAPTER XIV

Charlotte had been taken ill and was confined to bed for a week immediately after Branwell's death, and she could not go to his funeral, nor, to her great regret, be of use in comforting her father, who 'cried out for his loss like David for that of Absalom.' But hardly was the gloom which had darkened the Parsonage for three years removed, and the prospect of comfort restored, when death, instead of life, eclipsed the sunshine again. Branwell's funeral was the last occasion on which Emily left the house. She had a bad cold and cough, which grew worse, and before the end of October it was clear that she was seriously ill. She would not let a doctor see her, she would answer none of Charlotte's questions, she would take no medicine. In every letter that Charlotte wrote during these two months before Emily's death she wailed about this barrier that her sister had set between them, agonising that she was not permitted to approach her.

Her reserved nature occasions me great uneasiness of mind.... To put any question, to offer any aid, is to annoy.... You must look on and see her do what is unfit to do, and not dare to say a word.... She will not give an explanation of her feelings, she will scarcely allow her illness to be alluded to.... Would that my sister added to her great qualities the humble one of tractability.... She neither seeks nor will accept sympathy:—

such sentences as these occur everywhere. Stoical and secret as Emily was by nature, it is impossible not to see in so rigid an isolation of herself some special token of an estrangement which she would not suffer to be reconciled, and she fenced herself against any invasion even of sympathy. More than once her privacy had been broken into, and she would brook no further interference. For the last three years, too, there had been that silent daily antagonism over Branwell growing between Charlotte and her, and for these three months between his death and hers, the memory of their brother stood between them. Charlotte had had no pity for a publican and a sinner, and Emily, 'full of ruth for others,' would not accept for herself the compassion that had been withheld from him, nor allow her sister to pass the barrier which her ruthlessness had helped to build. Yearn and agonise as she might for the love and confidence which, partly by her own hardness, she had forfeited, they were not to be granted her now. Her very uprightness, the stern Puritanism of her nature, no doubt had invested her hardness with the garb of duty, just as Anne, in order to save others from such a career of profligacy and bestial self-indulgence as had brought her brother to ruin, had felt it a matter of conscience to make copy of him in the book that had come out a few months before his death. That, too, had been monstrous in Emily's eyes. Anne no doubt, like Charlotte, could forgive her brother now, but Emily, lover of the moor and the wild things there, would not accept sympathy from these stern moralists, nor soften to their appeal.

She went about her household work as long as her panting lungs would suffer her to mount the stairs or knead the bread. She wrote her requiem for her brother, and she revised and copied out her own salute to death. Refusing till the end to stop in bed, she rose daily at seven, dressed herself and came down, remaining there every night till ten o'clock, and then once more she dragged herself upstairs, and set her lamp in the window looking out over the snow-wreaths where once she had waited for the rustle of wings that betokened the coming of the 'Strange Power' that inspired her, and where now she waited for the sound of the wings of the Angel of Death. It was cold weather; there was a fire in her room, and one morning as she combed her hair, sitting before it, the comb dropped from her hands into the grate, where it lay on the hot cinders of the hearth. She was too weak to bend and pick it up, and waited till Martha came in, who rescued it from the singeing; then she finished her dressing and went downstairs. Almost to the end she fed the dogs Keeper and Flossie after supper; she had set her wild hawk free; there was the empty cage.

On the evening of December 18 Charlotte had been reading her an essay by Emerson; seeing she was not listening she had stopped, intending to finish it next day. In the morning Emily came downstairs as usual, and the sisters and their father breakfasted together in the dining-room, and then Mr. Brontë went to his study across the flagged passage. The meal was cleared and Emily took up her sewing.

But Charlotte, looking at her, saw that a change had come. It was no use asking her questions, for she would not answer them, and presently she went out. She walked up the lane to the moor which Emily loved: 'flowers brighter than the rose bloomed for her there,' and her errand was to search to see if even on this mid-December morning she could find just one sprig of heather-bloom, however withered, to bring back. Emily would understand what she meant. Peering short-sightedly in the more sheltered hollows she found one and plucked it, and returned to the Parsonage. She did not speak to her sister, but laid it on the table by her, as she worked at her sewing. Emily glanced at it and no more. Yet she must have known that it came from the moor; she must have guessed what Charlotte meant by going out to pick it for her. But it was too late: the withered sprig brought no message of its own, and as a token, mute and infinitely pathetic, of her sister's longing to reach her and break for a moment the ice of her reserve it was meaningless; the time for such piteous signalling was over. Perhaps she struggled with herself to give, if not a word, a look to show that she understood, or perhaps this token seemed a mere sentimentality, a cheap attempt to undo the irrevocable. She was as ruthless then to Charlotte as she was to herself, and the sprig of heather lay by her unheeded.

Useless: and Charlotte drew up to the table and wrote to Ellen. Emily, she said, was daily weaker; there was no word of hope to give. She herself had written some days before to Dr. Epps, recommended by Mr. Williams, a statement of Emily's symptoms; she had received but a vague answer with some medicine, which Emily would not take. This letter can hardly have been finished and sent to the post when the last struggle began. Emily fought for life then; she whispered that she would see a doctor now if he were sent for. But before he could come the cage was empty, and the wild hawk flown.

Those three years and a half, from that day in July 1845, when Charlotte came home and learned for what reason Branwell would go back no more to his tutorship, down to the winter day in December 1848 when Keeper followed Emily's coffin to the church and then to the grave beside her brother, comprise the most tragic act in the domestic drama of the thrice tragic family. But now those tipsy bawlings, those opium dreams, those silent animosities, those ruthlessnesses were over, and over were the agonised questions to which no answer was given, for Branwell and Emilyboth lay in the quiet earth, where she, at any rate, could not imagine for herself and him unquiet slumbers. Yet from blighted days and broken nights there had come forth the supreme felicity of the genius and of the talent of those two sisters of whom one alone remained. Never from stonier ground had there sprung so lordly a harvest, for *Wuthering Heights* was its fruit and so too was *Jane Eyre*. On that central act of this unique drama the curtain was now rung down, and there were left out of the five who had enacted it, three only. Mr. Nicholls, who was to fill so large a part in the final scene, bringing brief happiness to one who had never known it before, had as yet no share in it.

It was Charlotte who, torn with anguish for the silences of the past and the seal that was now for ever set on them, kept the domestic stability firm; without her the very pillars of the home must have crumbled. Her work on *Shirley*, discontinued when Emily fell ill, was still unhandled, for there was no energy to spare for anything but the daily duties. 'My father,' so she wrote on Christmas Day to Mr. Williams, 'says to me almost hourly, "Charlotte, you must bear up. I shall sink if you fail me."' Branwell's death was still recent, and he mourned his Absalom; the very fact that Charlotte could give him no true sympathy there made her task the heavier. But she shouldered it all, and with that stern faith which carried her through these deep waters of the soul she recorded her thankfulness that she was equal to it.

God has hitherto most graciously sustained me, [she wrote] so far I have felt adequate to bear my own burden and even to offer a little help to others. I am not ill, I can get through the daily duties and do something towards keeping hope and energy alive in our mourning household.

It was well indeed that she found in herself this power of firm constancy, for now a second tragedy (Branwell's death being confessedly nothing of the sort to her) began to threaten. Emily was scarcely in her grave when it became clear that Anne was suffering from the same dread malady as she. But here there was no such fruitless agonising as over Emily: Anne was patient and docile, and the doctors who were called in met with no contemptuous refusals of the aid they sought to bring. There was weakness, there was wasting, there were the nightly fevers and the persistent coughing which all told their tale, but Anne took her cod-liver oil and her carbonate of iron and wore the blisters which were ordered, and, according to the medical wisdom of the day, was pent in a room from which all fresh air was excluded, and hoped to wear the respirator that Ellen sent, when the weather permitted her to go out.

She sat in Emily's chair, unable to work and scarcely able to read, and when the specialist came from Leeds, his stethoscope but confirmed the worst fears. And for Charlotte below the intolerable daily burden, the heart-sickening fears, the glimpses of hope extinguished as soon as lit, the consciousness that, in spite of brief rallies and betterments, Anne was steadily losing ground, there was always the thought of Emily.

The feeling of Emily's loss [she wrote] does not diminish as time wears on; it often makes itself most acutely recognised. It brings too an inexpressible sorrow with it, and then the future is dark.

Again she wrote:

I cannot forget Emily's death-day: it becomes a more fixed, a darker, a more frequently recurring idea in my mind than ever. It was very terrible. She was torn, conscious, panting, reluctant, though resolute, out of a happy life. But *it will not do to dwell on such things*.

There spoke, with God knows what secret and incommunicable burden, that undefeated spirit as resolute as Emily's own, which refused to let itself be debilitated by despair, but turned with all its energy to the ministries which the situation demanded. She put from her all thought of her own work, her own feelings, so that the monstrous article on *Jane Eyre* which appeared in the *Quarterly* this winter, in which the author, Miss Rigby, knowing or guessing she was a woman, spoke of her as one 'who had long forfeited the society of her sex,' was read by her without a pang; ordinarily her sensitiveness would have writhed under so infamous an attack. But now she felt no personal resentment, and only regretted for Thackeray's sake that the old innuendo that in *Jane Eyre* she had reproduced the circumstances of his domestic tragedy was circulated again. Her own work on *Shirley* she abandoned altogether, sending the first volume of it to her publishers, so that, when she could tackle the story again, she might have the benefit of their views, and devoted herself entirely to Anne and her father, an unwearied nurse to her and to him an unfailing stay when he feared that his eyes were threatened again. For herself, she circumscribed the moment according to the wisdom of Marcus Aurelius; each could be borne and profitably used if she refused to contemplate anything but its immediate exigencies. 'I must not look forward,' she wrote, 'nor must I look backward. Too often I feel like one crossing an abyss on a narrow plank—a glance round might quite unnerve.' She found her solace in the sense of God's omnipotence. 'Fortitude is good,' she wrote, 'but fortitude itself must be shaken under us to teach how weak we are.' Then came the support of the everlasting arms: 'in sua Voluntade e nostra Pace.'

Throughout the spring of 1849 Anne grew steadily weaker, but the thought of her death brought no wild anguish of regret to Charlotte, nor to herself any horror.

I wish it would please God to spare me, [Anne wrote to Ellen] not only for papa's and Charlotte's sakes, but because I long to do some good in the world before I leave it. I have many schemes in my head for future practice, humble and limited indeed, but still I should not like them all to come to nothing, and myself to have lived to so little purpose. But God's will be done....

A change to some seaside place had been recommended, and in this letter Anne proposed that Ellen should accompany her. But Charlotte would not permit that: if Anne, while they were away, got suddenly worse, it would be terrible for her friend to be alone with her, and though it might be difficult for her to leave her father alone, she must certainly come too.

Finally this plan was adopted, and in the last week of May the two sisters, joined by Ellen, started for Scarborough, which Anne already knew, having stayed there with the Robinson family when she was governess to the girls. The expense would be met out of a legacy of £200 which her godmother had left her. They spent the night at York, where Anne managed to see the Minster, and on the day after their arrival at Scarborough she drove in a donkey-chair on the sands; she thought the donkey was being overtaxed and took the reins herself. Next day, being Sunday, she wanted to go to church, but was dissuaded; she had a walk in the afternoon. On Monday, like Emily on the last day of her life, she rose at seven, dressed herself and came downstairs. During the morning she felt that death was near, and wanted to leave for Haworth immediately if there was a chance that she could get home alive. A doctor was sent for, and in answer to her direct question said that her time had come. Then she wholly and serenely surrendered herself, commending Charlotte to her friend, and thanking them for their kindness to her. There was a little restlessness, and she was carried from her chair to the sofa. She said to Charlotte, 'Take courage, Charlotte, take courage,' and then, without an uneven breath, she passed away, dying at just the hour when Emily had died.

Charlotte stayed on at Scarborough with Ellen for a couple of weeks, and then went back alone to the Parsonage. Her father and Tabby and Martha were well; the dogs seemed in a strange ecstasy. 'I am certain they regarded me as the harbinger of others,' she wrote to Ellen. But the light died from their eyes, for there were none but Charlotte to return.

Having seen her father, she went alone into the dining-room and shut herself in.

I felt that the house was all silent: the rooms were all empty. I remembered where the three were laid,—in what narrow dark dwellings—never more to reappear on earth. So the sense of desolation and bitterness took possession of me. The agony *that was to be undergone*, and was *not* to be avoided came on.... The great trial is when evening closes, and night approaches. At that hour we used to assemble in the dining-room: we used to talk. Now I sit by myself: necessarily I am silent. I cannot help thinking of their last days, remembering their sufferings, and what they said and did, and how they looked in mortal affliction.

The clock ticked loud in the still house, Keeper lay outside Emily's door; her desk and Anne's must some time be gone through to find what papers they had left, and none now would resent such intrusions. The air whispered with voices of the past and trembled with memories. 'But crushed I am not yet,' she wrote, 'nor robbed of elasticity, nor of hope, nor quite of endeavour.' She took up her book again, abandoned since last October when Emily fell ill. Since then her hours had been full with other ministries, now they were empty and must be filled. Rather more than half of it had been written, now she began on the chapter called 'The Valley of the Shadow of Death.' It was finished by the end of August, and she knew that work had been her salvation, and she wrote to Mr. Williams:

The faculty of imagination lifted me when I was sinking three months ago: its active exercise has kept my head above water since: its results cheer me now, for I feel they have enabled me to give pleasure to others. I am thankful to God who gave me the faculty, and it is for me a part of my religion to defend this gift and to profit by its possession.

There was never a more magnificent fortitude in the face of so great tribulations, and she had to bear as well a load of those minor ones which can be taken lightly by an unburdened spirit, but which can so easily prove the last straw, when the weight of affliction is already accumulated to breaking point. She was in ill-health, she was sorely troubled with headaches and bilious sickness, and on the top of all these minor troubles came domestic trials. Of the two servants at the Parsonage, Martha Brown was ill and in bed, Mr. Brontë declaring that she was in imminent danger, and Tabby, now over eighty, fell as she got up from her chair with her head under the grate. Charlotte's frayed nerves for once gave way, she simply sat and cried for ten minutes; then called herself a fool and got Martha's sister in to help her with the housework. She was always at her best when things were worst: hers was one of those unflinching natures which trouble seems to anneal. Some are broken by it, but she would have scorned to be of such brittle stuff; some are softened by it, but she was not one of them. Even the death of her sisters, the loss, as she said, of the only two people in the world who understood her, had been as impotent to weaken essentially the iron confidence in which she met such bereavement, as the sufferings of her brother had been impotent, while he lived, to rouse her compassion. Life was a fight, and she was not going to be beaten.

§ 2

As was her nature, so necessarily was her religion, and they both emerged from these tragic years unshaken and unsoftened. Gone utterly, burned out of her by searing experience, were those emotional, half-hysterical aspirations of which in her adolescence Ellen had really been the source; she no longer sought that water of Life, of which once drinking she should never more thirst. She looked for no easy yoke or light burden, nor expected rest for her soul, but travail. Nor was her conception of the Omnipotence on which she leaned and to the decrees of which she gave obedience any sort of mystic ecstasy; it was the very antipodes of Emily's 'Strange Power,' that fiercely tender pagan force which set the moorland heath abloom and the lapwings mating, and so kindled the love of Catherine for the sheer beauty of the savage earth and for Heathcliff's savage adoration that, dreaming she was dead, she broke her heart with weeping to escape from the conventional tameness of heaven, 'and the angels were so angry that they flung me into the middle of the heath on the top of Wuthering Heights, where I awoke sobbing for joy.' Not less antipodal to Charlotte's God was Anne's conception of the loving and sustaining hand which led her, lacking nothing, so gently through the valley of the shadow, that far from fearing the death of the body, she rejoiced in the accomplishment of her serene journey. While here, she had her work to do for Him, and it was in His service that she had used the degradation of her brother to warn others of the disaster that attends evil courses. God was her loving Shepherd, and she, mild as Flossie, must bark at the wolves which threatened His flock.

But to Charlotte both such conceptions were incomprehensible: to her God was no pagan Pan who fluted in the 'livid hollows' of the moor, nor yet a compassionate Redeemer, but the lawgiver revealed on Sinai, who had written His commandments very distinctly on stone tables, and was powerful to save and infinite in mercy. That decalogue did not enjoin loving indulgence of the weak, nor the duty of judging not, and the charity that suffered long and was kind had no place in it. She was as unsparing in her severity to herself as she was to others; she claimed from herself, even as God claimed from her, a full account of the talents He had given her, and never did she shirk the demands of duty nor complain of the sternness of that lawgiver, but she never eased the burden with the lighter yoke of love. She suffered much, she was ready to acquiesce always in personal sacrifice, but she neither looked for nor found in self-abnegation any particle of joy. Undeviatingly through the wilderness she followed the cloud by day and the pillar of fire by night, and she never expected to find therein any oasis for her rest and refreshment. It was an arid journey, for on all sides she saw so much of what she felt herself bound to disapprove; but as long as she followed the gleam, smoky though it often was, she knew she was doing God's will, and to that she referred every decision she had to make, and every pang she had to bear. She was in constant ill-health, and it was to God's help she looked that she would not break down, and that steeled her will; the same strength enabled her firmly to face the inevitable end of Anne's illness when 'reason unsupported by religion' would have failed her.

Belief in God's guidance gave her resignation to His accomplished Will, but (not exactly in opposition to it, but trying to range herself with it) she put forth all her force in order to accomplish her own. Thus, when in the last years of her life, in consequence of Mr. Brontë's violent objections to her marriage with Mr. Nicholls, the latter left Haworth, and all seemed over, Charlotte believed that 'Providence is over all: that is the only consolation.' But she successfully set to work to get Mr. Nicholls back, and when her father's opposition was withdrawn and the marriage permitted, she equally believed that this was 'the destiny which Providence in His goodness and wisdom seems to offer me.' Again, when there was pleasure to be thankful for instead of trouble to be resigned to, she blended, with a childlike simplicity, her human satisfaction with her gratitude for the Divine favour bestowed. When, for instance, she received favourable reviews of *Villette*, she wrote: 'The import of all these notices is such as to make my heart swell with thankfulness to Him who takes note both of my suffering and work and motives. Papa is pleased too.'

§ 3

Shirley, then, was finished in August 1849, and now after ten years there came to Charlotte another offer, the third, of marriage; for the sake of continuity it will be better to dissect this odd episode out of her letters during these years, and give it for the first time a connected outline.

Mr. James Taylor was in her publisher's firm, and he had read and criticised the portion of her book which she had sent to Smith, Elder in the spring of this year; possibly Charlotte had met him when she and Anne had gone to London to disclose their identities. He was soon to pass through Leeds on his return to London from his holiday, and Mr. Williams suggested that he should come to Haworth and take the newly-finished manuscript back with him. Charlotte, as serious as a judge, wrote just the letter that Jane Austen's eyes would have twinkled over, elaborately explaining why she could not offer the 'homely hospitalities' of the Parsonage for a few days. Her father was not strong enough to take walks with a visitor on the moors, and

the peculiar retirement of papa's habits is such as to render it irksome to him to give much of his society to a stranger, even in the house. Without being in the least misanthropical, or sour-natured, papa habitually prefers solitude to society, and custom is a tyrant whose fetters it would now be impossible for him to break. Papa, I know, would receive any friend of Mr. Smith's with perfect kindness and goodwill but I likewise know that unless greatly put out of his way, he could not give a guest much of his company.

But in case Mr. Taylor cared to come for the day, she gave the most minute directions how he was to get to Haworth from Leeds, pointing out the mischances that menaced him if he forgot to change at Shipley: in fact, though rather fluttered, she did not discourage the visit at all.

Mr. Taylor came then, early in September, for the inside of a day, and they met again in London in the winter, when Charlotte went to stay with Mrs. Smith, her publisher's mother. He certainly made a strong impression on her, though, as was usual with strangers, not wholly agreeable, for he had

a determined, dreadful nose in the middle of his face (which after all was the usual place) which when poked into my countenance cuts into my soul like iron. Still he is horribly intelligent, quick, searching, sagacious, and with a memory of relentless tenacity. To turn to Williams after him or to Smith himself, is to turn from granite to easy down or warm fur.

We may infer that he proposed to her then, for two passages in a letter she wrote to Ellen in September 1850, just nine months afterwards, strongly point to this. The first is:

'Doubtless there are men whom if I chose to encourage I might marry, but no matrimonial lot is even remotely offered me which seems to me truly desirable.'

She then refers to a letter she had received from Mr. Taylor ('the little man').

I was somewhat surprised to receive his letter, having concluded nine months ago that there would be no more correspondence from that quarter.... This little Taylor is deficient neither in spirits nor sense.

Something had evidently happened nine months ago which made her think that Mr. Taylor would not write again. But he had spirit and the sense to see that there was hope for him. So little Taylor persevered in his suit, causing Charlotte to waver, for *à propos* of some abstruse badinage on Ellen's part about marriage (probably referring to George Smith), she wrote to her:

The idea of the 'little man' shocks me less—it would be a more likely match if 'matches' were at all in question, *which they are not*.... You may laugh as much and as wickedly as you please—but the fact is there is a quiet constancy about this, my diminutive and red-haired friend, which adds a foot to his stature—turns his sandy locks dark, and altogether dignifies him a good deal in my estimation.

This looked like yielding, and very likely she would have married him, had he not accepted an appointment to open a branch of Messrs. Smith, Elder in Bombay; this would take him out of England for five years. Charlotte wrote him two very proper letters, hoping that 'the change of climate would not bring a risk to health,' and referring to business as 'a Moloch which demanded personal touch in the mention of his sacrifice, which was endorsed by the moral reflections that followed: such sacrifices.' There is a faint but unmistakably personal touch in the mention of his sacrifice, which was endorsed by the moral reflections that followed:

May your decision in the crisis through which you have gone result in the best effect on your happiness and welfare: and indeed, guided as you are by the wish to do right, and a high sense of duty, I trust it cannot be otherwise. The change of climate is all I fear, but Providence will overrule this, too, for the best—in Him you can believe and in Him only. You will want therefore neither solace nor support, though your lot will be cast as a stranger in a strange land.

He had asked for a farewell interview, and in this same letter she gave him leave to come to Haworth and say good-bye. It would be a pleasure to see him, though that pleasure would be tinged with sadness. He came—and he said good-bye.

But it is evident that she had expected something different from this last interview, and her letter to Ellen recording it is puzzled and surprised. She magnified this appointment which he had 'reluctantly accepted' into something tremendous. It was a 'post of honour and danger' (though to open a branch in a publishing house in Bombay does not seem desperately perilous), and duty had compelled him to take it. Anyhow, 'he has been and is gone, things are just as they were. I feel there is a mystery about the transaction yet.' The mystery really was that she could not make up her mind whether she had done right in refusing him, and she doubted it.

And then, curiously and characteristically, in order to persuade herself of her wisdom in refusing him, she now began to see his bad points. 'He looked much older and thinner. I saw him very near and once through my glass; the resemblance to Branwell struck me forcibly, it is marked.' The lines in his face showed 'an inflexibility and, I must add, a hardness of character which do not attract. As he stood near me, as he looked at me in his keen way, it was all I could do to stand my ground tranquilly and steadily, and not to recoil as before, and his manners were jarring.' But already she found that 'his absence, and the exclusion of his idea from her mind,' left a blank she had not expected: at once she felt lonely and despondent. She determined to wean her mind from the subject, but with the very smallest measure of success, for her letters teem with speculations about the little man. Something perhaps had been said at that last interview as to whether, when he returned, she would reconsider her decision, but she doubted whether he could ever 'be acceptable as a husband,' and found yet more reasons against it. He had excellent and sterling qualities, but what discoveries of his imperfections!

I looked for something of the gentleman—something I mean of the natural gentleman ... I could not find one gleam, I could not see one passing glimpse of true good-breeding; it is hard to say, but it is true. In mind too, though clever, he is second-rate, thoroughly second-rate. One does not like to say these things, but one had better be honest. Were I to marry him my heart would bleed in pain and humiliation. I could not, *could* not look up to him. No —if Mr. Taylor be the only husband Fate offers to me, single I must always remain. But yet at times I grieve for him and perhaps it is superfluous, for I cannot think he will suffer much; a hard nature, occupation and change of scene will befriend him....

Again she found from friends in London that his temper left much to be desired; that was a point in favour of her decision, but against that must be set the fact that Mr. Brontë much liked him, and was extremely kind when he said good-bye to him,

exhorting him to be true to himself, his country and his God, and wishing him all good wishes.... Whenever he has alluded to him since it has been with significant eulogy. When I alluded that he was no gentleman he seemed out of patience with me for the objection.... I believe he thinks a prospective union deferred for five years with such a decorous reliable personage would be a very proper and advisable affair.

Perhaps Mr. Brontë even expected an immediate engagement, for he said that if she married now he would give up the Parsonage and live in lodgings. Altogether Charlotte found it a very puzzling business: she had refused Mr. Taylor and found a peck of admirable reasons for so doing, but she wondered if she had been wise, and thought it better to refer the responsibility of what she had done elsewhere. She had assured him of the protection of Providence in Bombay, and Providence had directed her also. 'Most true it is,' she wrote to Ellen after she saw him for the last time, 'that we are overruled by one above us—that in His hands our very will is as clay in the hands of the potter.'

So Mr. Taylor—'stern and abrupt little man'—went out to Bombay. He wrote to Charlotte a rather realistic description of the processes of a Turkish bath, which he had gone to see though not to indulge in. He might have omitted, she thought, some of the details, but she found his description amusing, and it tallied with what Thackeray had said about the same pleasurable institution in Grand Cairo. But she could not refrain from moral reflections in her answer:

The usage seems to me a little rough, and I cannot help thinking that equal benefit might be obtained through less violent means, but I suppose without the previous fatigue the after-sensation would not be so enjoyable and no doubt it is that indolent after-sensation which the self-indulgent Mahomedans chiefly cultivate. I think you did right to disdain it.

She lamented, for his sake, 'the deficiency in all intellectual attractions' at Bombay. She had not weaned him even yet from her mind, for she wrote to Mr. Williams asking him for an 'impartial judgment' on his character, and he spoke highly of him. But after that Mr. Taylor seems to have written no more to her, and that made her uneasy; she wondered whether the affair had come to an end. Once more, though less poignantly than when she waited to see whether the post brought her a letter from M. Héger, she was on the alert for the arrival of Indian mails, but still there was nothing for her, and she confessed she was disappointed. Several times Ellen asked if she had not heard, and eventually Charlotte begged her not to refer to the subject again: 'All is silent as the grave.' She never saw him again, for when at the end of his five years in Bombay he returned to England, she was dead.

CHAPTER XV

To return to *Shirley*. In that trying interval, before its appearance, of proof correcting and waiting for publication, Charlotte was in a high state of nervous tension. The story had been read by three members of the Smith, Elder firm (all of whom, of course, knew her identity, but were bound to secrecy), and Mr. Williams had criticised the whole presentation of the curates as being an irrelevant piece of caricature. She replied that they were positive photographs, they were as real as the Bible, they were True, and Truth was better than Art. She refused to give them up, but her real reason for retaining them (and she must have known it) was that she could not forgo the satisfaction of scarifying Messrs. Grant, Smith and Bradley under disguises that would deceive nobody, especially them. Once more she was extremely anxious that her sex as author should not be suspected by reviewers or by the public. She thought that a book by a woman was judged with 'pitiful contempt,' and hoped that *Shirley* would be considered so indubitably male in style and treatment that any doubts (of which there were already many) about the sex of the author of *Jane Eyre* would be finally set at rest.

A more forlorn hope can scarcely be imagined, for though, in *Jane Eyre*, Edward Rochester might be thought to be the creation of a man, no male character in *Shirley* could possibly be thought to be other than the creation of a woman; no sign of a 'peard' can be detected beneath their mufflers. But this longing to be considered male was indeed an obsession with her, and she thought that everyone was leagued together to unmask her. Mr. Williams, for instance, in sending her a packet of proofs for correction had not sealed the cover securely, and it had been resealed at the General Post Office in London, and then forwarded to Haworth. Charlotte suspected in that a dark design against her secret, and, forgetting that the packet had been resealed in London, was convinced that it had been opened at the Post Office in Keighley. This she was sure was the work of 'prying curiosity.... The gossiping inquisitiveness of small towns is rife at Keighley. Those packets passing backwards and forwards by the post have doubtless aggravated their curiosity.' But how she could have thought that on the publication of *Shirley* her incognito, not only of sex but of individuality, would not instantly be given away, passes understanding, for the book practically consisted of sketches, portraits and caricatures of her immediate circle. She allowed that she had seen and slightly knew the 'original' of Cyril Hall, but averred that he would no more suspect her of having 'put' him into a novel, or indeed of having written a novel at all, than he would have suspected that his dog had done so. But no sooner did the Rev. W. M. Heald read *Shirley* than he correctly recognised himself and half a dozen characters as well, and applied to Ellen, as an intimate friend of the 'unknown Currer Bell' (sending his respects also to Mr. Brontë so that there could be no mistake about his meaning), for a key to the others. Again, Charlotte had sent to one of the brothers of her friend Mary Taylor, before publication, those chapters of the book which related to the 'Yorkes,' in which every single member of his family, father, daughters (dead and alive) and sons were daguerrotyped: his comment was that she had not drawn them strong enough. Then there was Shirley herself, confessedly a portrait of Emily Brontë; there were the photographed curates; there was Mr. Nicholls in the unmistakable guise of Mr. Macarthey; Hortense Moore was equally photographic of Mlle. Haussé of the *pensionnat* at Brussels. Yet even when the book was out, Charlotte wrote, as Currer Bell, to G. H. Lewes, who was to review it in the *Edinburgh Review,* saying 'I wish you did not think I was a woman.'

But it was no use wishing anything of the sort. Charlotte, with an optimism she recognised to be ostrich-like, had fondly hoped that if she hid her head in the Parsonage she would be invisible, but her identity leaked out in London, and poured out in spate at Haworth. It could not possibly be otherwise: too many pointers were directed there; besides, she had made too many her confidants. Mr. Nicholls had his lodgings at the house of John Brown the sexton, and, when he read about himself, Mrs. Brown 'seriously thought he had gone wrong in his head, as she heard him giving vent to roars of laughter, clapping his hands and stamping on the floor ... He would read all the scenes about the curates aloud to papa, and triumphed in his own character.'

Then there were the curates themselves; they had often annoyed her, and to serve them out she had dipped in her unkindest ink, and lavished on them all her powers of contempt and ridicule. There was the master of the Haworth Grammar School, once temporary curate to Mr. Brontë, and him, under the unmistakable lineaments of Mr. Donne, she had described as of 'a coldly phlegmatic immoveably complacent densely self-satisfied nature'; he was 'a frontless, arrogant, decorous slip of the commonplace, conceited, inane, insipid.' She libellously stated that he and the others met together for drunken orgies: as a matter of fact the evenings that they spent together were passed in reading the Greek Fathers.

But her whips and her scorpions were wasted.

The very curates, poor fellows! [she dejectedly wrote to Mr. Williams] show no resentment, each characteristically finds solace for his own wounds in crowing over his brethren. Mr. Donne was at first a little disturbed; for a week or two he was in disquietude, but he is now soothed down: only yesterday I had the pleasure of making him a comfortable cup of tea and seeing him sip it with revived complacency. It is a curious fact that since he read *Shirley* he has come to the house oftener than ever, and been remarkably meek and assiduous to please. Some people's natures are veritable enigmas: I quite expected to have had one good scene with him, but as yet nothing of the sort has occurred.

The gilt was off the gingerbread. Charlotte had meant and hoped and desired that these truly Christian gentlemen should be hurt and indignant at her savage attack on them, and she was truly chagrined at their good humour; all she could make of it was that each was so delighted with the venom she expended on his friends that he forgave her for himself. They were enigmas; it was puzzling and disappointing to find them so indulgent. She wanted to hurt them. That she ever knew that her friend Mary Taylor wrote to Ellen from New Zealand saying that it was rumoured that Charlotte Brontë had been jilted by the three curates one after the other is improbable. Charlotte would not have been amused.

But though these insensitive creatures had treated her attack on them with such good humour, it was otherwise with her and the unfavourable reviews of *Shirley*, of which there were a good many that made her writhe, as she had hoped the curates would do. She was furious with their malice and their lies. She pronounced the critic of the *Daily News* to be to the last degree 'incompetent, ignorant and flippant.' His review was unutterably false: it was revolting to be judged by such a creature. The *Observer* was equally trying; such praise as it bestowed was more mortifying than its blame. The 'thundering *Times*' attacked her fiercely, and it made her cry. The notice in the *Edinburgh Review* was 'brutal and savage.' G. H. Lewes had, as she knew, written this, and he had committed the unpardonable crime of talking about her sex. So she sent him a brief note: 'I can be on my guard against my enemies, but God deliver me from my friends.' On the other hand, critical praise gave her the same quality of childish rapture as critical blame gave her of childish resentment. Just as her detractors were liars and revolting dunces, so the admirers of *Shirley* were splendid in ability and discernment. Harriet Martineau and Mrs. Gaskell, neither of whom she had at present met, were among these by reason of their appreciation, and she considered them 'far her superiors in attainment and experience.' For Miss Martineau she had 'a lively admiration, a deep esteem,' while Mrs. Gaskell's praise, conveyed in a letter 'brought tears to my eyes. She is a good, she is a great woman. Proud am I that I can touch a chord of sympathy in souls so noble.' Then there was Eugène Forçade, who had already spoken highly of *Jane Eyre*: he wrote a review of *Shirley* in the *Revue des deux Mondes*, and it was refreshing to turn from the mouthings of the entirely ignorant and incompetent to one 'whose heart feels, whose power grasps the matter he undertakes to handle.' He praised *Shirley* warmly, and therefore he was 'a subtle-thoughted, keen-eyed, quick-feeling Frenchman, who knew the true nature of things.'

He follows Currer Bell [she wrote to Ellen, to whom she sent this review] through every winding, discerns every point, discriminates every shade, proves himself master of the subject, and lord of the aim. With that man I would shake hands, if I saw him. I would say, 'You know me, Monsieur, I shall deem it an honour to know you.' I could not say so much to the mass of English critics.

Forçade, she reiterated to Mr. Williams, found no coarseness in *Shirley*; that was the discovery reserved for smaller minds. Or an anonymous correspondent wrote in a strain of wild enthusiasm about *Shirley*: 'there is power in that letter—talent, it is at times eloquently expressed.' The press she was sure, when she thought of the unfavourable reviews, was a venal concern; only praise was sincere and heartfelt. Those who saw faults in her work were not only mistaken but moral reprobates, abounding in malice and falsehood; those who appreciated it were not only discerning persons but good and great. All this enthusiasm for the enthusiastic, this spitting on the scornful is indicative of just that essentially youthful fire which Charlotte, like Swinburne, always possessed. Her intolerance, her blacks and whites, her rare but unqualified raptures, her censoriousness, were all typical of adolescence. As Sir Edmund Gosse acutely remarked (rather shocking the Brontë Society), she never grew up, nor acquired the kindly indulgence of the mature mind, off which the jagged egoistic edges have been smoothed by the wholesome wear and tear of the world.

Soon after *Shirley* appeared, Charlotte again turned her mind to *The Professor*, which had lain on her shelf since her publishers had dissuaded her from expanding it into three-volumed form. But now she contemplated bringing it out as it stood, and wrote a preface to it. Not a word of her intentions, so far as we can find in her letters, did she communicate to anyone; nor is there the slightest allusion to the subject when she discusses plans with her publishers. But after her death her husband, Mr. Nicholls, consented to the publication of *The Professor*, and it appeared in 1856 with the preface that Charlotte had written for it, and an explanatory note in which he stated these facts, adding:

'Being dissuaded from her intention, the authoress made some use of the material in a subsequent work *Villette*.' It is possible that the 'dissuasion' of which Mr. Nicholls speaks should refer to the occasion when, after the publication of *Jane Eyre*, she contemplated expanding *The Professor* into three volumes, and that now she wrote the preface and abandoned her intention again, for Mrs. Gaskell does not mention it in her *Life of Charlotte Brontë*, nor can we find any allusion to this second intention elsewhere.

With regard to the book *Shirley* itself, its faults are many and patent, and it cannot be put in the same class as *Jane Eyre* or *Villette*. *Jane Eyre* had its faults too, but in the white-hot furnace of its sincerity and passion, they were utterly consumed, appearing momentarily like specks of black in the glow of it, and then perishing. But there is no such incandescent quality in *Shirley*: *Shirley* was observed rather than felt, and Charlotte never got into the living heart of her work as she did with *Jane Eyre* and *Villette*.

She took immense trouble with it; she strained and agonised and doubted over it. But she wrote it from the outside, not the inside, and, paradoxical though it sounds, this very industry and this painstaking copying of her models are the cause of the lower level on which the book moves; study takes the place of inspiration, and observation is not fused and made molten in the furnace of imagination. Again, she wanted to inculcate certain truths, such *imprimis*, as the supreme splendour of equal love between man and woman; but whereas in *Jane Eyre* she took the live coal in the tongs from off the altar of its burning, in *Shirley*, donning the fatal vestments of the preacher, she ascended the pulpit and discoursed, with anathemas, on the world's sordid view of love. She declaimed her gospel, instead of presenting without comment, as in *Jane Eyre*, the evangelists of love. Never was there so hieratic a homily as Caroline Helstone's pronouncement and her colloquy with Shirley. Says Caroline:

'Obtrusiveness is a crime; forwardness is a crime, and both disgust: but love! —no purest angel need blush to love! And when I hear or see either man or woman couple shame with love I know their minds are coarse, their associations debased. Many who think themselves refined ladies and gentlemen, and on whose lips the word "vulgarity" is for ever hovering, cannot mention "love" without betraying their own innate and imbecile degradation: it is a low feeling in their estimation, connected only with low ideas for them.'

'You describe three-quarters of the world, Caroline.'

'They are cold,—they are cowardly—they are stupid on the subject, Shirley! They never loved—they never were loved.'

'Thou art right, Lina! And in their dense ignorance they blaspheme living fire, seraph-brought from a divine altar.'

'They confound it with sparks mounting from Tophet.'

All very true no doubt. But did two girls ever talk so unnaturally and so gratuitously, for nothing has occurred to warrant these diatribes? Charlotte was in the pulpit, preaching not creating, and, incidentally, punishing those who found coarseness in *Jane Eyre,* and putting into the mouth of her characters the precise phrases with which she had scolded them in her letters. She was lecturing on love, justifying her view of it. The same spirit of irrelevant propaganda, again in defence of *Jane Eyre,* inspires her indignation against the unfair treatment which she thought that women novelists received.

Their (men's) good woman [cries Shirley] is a queer thing, half-doll, half-angel; their bad woman almost always a fiend. Then to hear them fall into ecstasies with each other's creations, worshipping the heroine of such a poem-novel-drama, thinking it fine—divine! If I spoke all I think on this point; if I gave my real opinion of some first-rate female character, in first-rate works, where should I be? Dead, under a cairn of avenging stones in half an hour. Women read men more truly than men read women. I'll prove that in a magazine paper some day when I have time....

Charlotte, through the mouthpiece of *Shirley,* is merely venting her views on the literary arena.

It is this same personal motive which, with similar punishment in view, turns her presentation of the curates into sheer caricature. They had annoyed her, and her intention was to give them 'what for,' taking in her hand not the rapier of satire but the bludgeon of abuse. These were grotesque puppets which she set up, in order to knock them down, and her observation of them was falsified by personal antipathy. These outbursts of propaganda and vituperation are pieces of rubbish which might have perished in the consuming heat of *Jane Eyre,* but in *Shirley* there is no such reverberating furnace. Louis Moore, Shirley's preordained mate, personifying man's ideal love for woman, is so falsetto a troubadour that, frankly, romance withers. The love-scenes are largely conveyed by means of his highly rhetorical diary instead of by direct narrative; Charlotte invites the reader to stoop over her shoulder and read what he scribbles: 'Since Shirley has appealed to my strength,' he writes, 'I abhor solitude. Cold abstraction—fleshless skeleton—daughter—mother and mate of Death!...' Shirley was shy, 'but to my perception a delicate splendour robed her.... I looked like a stupid block, I dare say: I was alive with a life of Paradise, as she turned *her* glance from *my* glance, and softly averted her head to hide the suffusion of her cheek.' Louis Moore retails page after page of dialogue between his mistress and himself, and it is all tinsel and froth compared with the gleams of those deep waters of passion that move us so profoundly when Jane Eyre and Rochester are together. For their simplicity we get eloquence: Louis calls her 'Sister of the spotted, bright, quick-fiery leopard,' and after great fireworks, with the sun 'a dizzying scarlet blaze' and the sky 'a violet vortex,' there is a dismal descent of the rocket stick, and Shirley having accepted him, says (quite in the Jane Austen style):

Mr. Moore, your judgment is well balanced; your heart is kind; your principles are sound. I know you are wise; I feel you are benevolent; I believe you are conscientious. Be my companion through life; be my guide where I am ignorant, be my master where I am faulty; be my friend always.

The same fault, that of mere external observation, marks and mars Charlotte's presentation of Shirley herself. She confessedly meant Shirley in this volume of 'sketches from the life' to be the full-length portrait of her sister Emily. She noted and reproduced traits that were characteristic of Emily, such as her long abstracted musings on the moor as she gazed into some pool. She gave Shirley the fierce and devoted Tartar who would not stand a blow, in reproduction of Emily's Keeper; Shirley's refusals to admit she was ill were a trait of Emily's, as Charlotte was bitterly aware ('*She* say she is ill! I believe, sir, if she were dying, she would smile and aver "Nothing ails me"'); the story of Shirley being bitten by a dog, and cauterising the wound with a hot iron is also traditionally ascribed to Emily, but all these traits and incidents are observed only, and when it comes to that fusion of observation and penetration through which is produced a portrait not a photograph, we find that Charlotte has not penetrated; she has never got to the heart of Emily, to the genius that made her what she was, and not one glimpse of that mysterious soul is really revealed to us. In nothing is this more plain than in Charlotte's attempt to render, through Shirley's mouth, Emily's attitude towards Nature, that pagan pan-theistic mysticism, that sense of the immanent and unifying Divinity in man and beast and moor, which glows and throbs in her poems. Charlotte could discover the poems themselves, but secret for ever from her was the inspiration of them, and her attempt to reproduce it was less photograph than parody. In Shirley's famous rhapsody Charlotte definitely set herself to unveil Emily's soul.

Nature is now at her evening prayers: she is kneeling before those red hills. I see her prostrate on the great steps of her altar, praying for a fair night for mariners at sea, for travellers in deserts, for lambs on moors, and unfledged birds in woods. Caroline, I see her! and I will tell you what she is like: she is like what Eve was when she and Adam stood alone on earth.... I saw—I now see—a woman Titan: her robe of blue air spreads to the outskirts of the heath, where yonder flock is grazing: a veil white as an avalanche sweeps from her head to her feet, and arabesques of lightning flame in its borders. Under her breast I see her zone, purple like that horizon; through its blush shines the star of evening. Her steady eyes I cannot picture: they are clear, they are deep as lakes—they are lifted and full of worship—they tremble with the softness of love and the lustre of prayer. Her forehead has the expanse of a cloud and is paler than the early moon, risen long before dark gathers; she reclines her bosom on the ridge of Stilbro' Moor; her mighty hands are joined beneath it. So kneeling, face to face she speaks with God. That Eve is Jehovah's daughter, as Adam was his son.

Now we may differ about the beauty and the force of this passage; some may find it a piece of exquisite English, others a patch of rather shrill purple, but all must agree that, as a rendering of Emily's mysticism, it is a failure. Nor could it have been otherwise, for Charlotte had no touch of the mystic in her religious perceptions; and the very strength and sincerity of them made it impossible for her to comprehend a rapture to which her soul was alien. When she attempted to express it, her speech betrayed her.

But hear Emily:

He comes with western winds, with evening's wandering airs,

With that clear dusk of heaven that brings the thickest stars,

Winds take a pensive tone and stars a tender fire,

And visions rise and change, that kill me with desire.

But first a hush of peace—a soundless calm descends,

The struggle of distress and fierce impatience ends:

Mute music soothes my breast—unuttered harmony,

That I could never dream till Faith was lost to me.

Then dawns the Invisible: the Unseen its truth reveals,

My outward sense is gone, my inward essence feels.

Its wings are almost free—its home, its harbour found,

Nearing the gulf it stops—and dares the final bound.

Oh! dreadful is the check—intense the agony—

When the ear begins to hear, and the eye begins to see,

When the pulse begins to throb, the brain to think again:

The soul to feel the flesh, and the flesh to feel the chain.

There is the true voice; the expression may fail because the singer tells of things ineffable, but behind is the experience of the mystic's sacramental communings, of his almost losing his identity because he is so nearly made one with God immanent, of his racked return to himself as to a prison, when the splendour fades. None but a mystic could have written that, and all Charlotte's talent could not enable her to reproduce, with any wealth of poetical imagery, the faintest semblance of it. In this attempt to reveal Emily she only reveals her own incomprehension of her.

Shirley is often spoken of as Charlotte's memorial to Emily. That is not quite the case, for nearly two-thirds of the book, down to the chapter entitled 'The Valley of the Shadow of Death,' were written before her death. She began it after hesitations as to whether to recast *The Professor* in three-volume form, as soon as *Jane Eyre* was off her hands; thus, while Anne was using Branwell as a model in *The Tenant of Wildfell Hall*, Charlotte was using Emily in *Shirley*. Then her work was interrupted by Emily's rapid decline in the autumn of 1848 and not taken up again till after Anne's death in May 1849. Charlotte found this break exceedingly difficult to bridge over, and it is permissible to wonder whether there was not a change of plan at this point in the book. Louis Moore, though the story was two-thirds done, had only made his first appearance a couple of pages before; it looks as if his wooing and winning of Shirley was possibly an afterthought. Already the book had faltered; for several chapters before the break no development takes place at all; Caroline Helstone's love story hung fire, a school-feast, a guying of the curates were obvious padding; it is as if Charlotte was feeling her way, uncertain of her direction. Then after the break she made up her mind, and the book moves swiftly to its appointed end.

CHAPTER XVI

Charlotte went up to London in December of the year 1849 to stay with her young publisher George Smith and his widowed mother. Mrs. Smith, she tells Ellen, appeared to have received strict orders to pay her the greatest attention; morning and evening there was a fire in her bedroom and wax candles, and she felt she inspired respect and alarm in her hosts. It was not till this wore off that she perceived that real friendliness was at the bottom of these sybaritic arrangements, and she 'began to like' Mrs. Smith; her son also impressed her more favourably than he had done at first sight, and she acknowledged that she saw no reason to regret her decision to make her principal stay with them instead of going, after a day or two, to the house of Laetitia Wheelwright, who had been a school friend at Brussels. By now she was known to be Currer Bell and no more concealment or vain hopes that her books would be taken as products of a male brain were possible.

From this time onwards she ceased to be a hermit at Haworth, for in the few years that were to elapse before her marriage, she paid four visits to London, she went twice to Scotland, though once only for a single night, and she stayed with new-found friends in the Lakes, Sir James Kay-Shuttleworth and Miss Harriet Martineau (to whom she formed a violent attachment, and as violently brought it to a sudden close). She also formed a warm and cordial though never an intimate friendship with Mrs. Gaskell, and stayed with her at Plymouth Grove, Manchester.

Moreover, high fame was personally hers; pilgrims came to Haworth to follow the topography of her books and get a word from the author. More especially in London the literary world was intensely curious about her, eager to be friendly with her and to make her the lioness at home in circles whose appreciation she most coveted. But fame had come too late for her enjoyment; she had been through bitter waters and the salt still clung to her, or perhaps she had always lacked the ease which springs from geniality. She could not let herself go; her shyness and her self-consciousness were by now an inveterate disease. To be brought up against an unfamiliar face, even if it shone with kindliness, was always discomforting; she distrusted strangers and was always apt to notice their defects before their qualities, and a further misery-making quality in her temperament lay in the habit of thought which suggested that others saw the worst in her. She noticed, for instance (or thought she noticed), that if any man got a good look at her, he would take pains, after that, to avert his eyes from the quarter of the room in which she sat. The natural reaction followed those uncomfortable fancies; she never credited the casually encountered stranger with goodwill towards her. Nowadays we should call this instinct an inferiority complex dating from her schooldays, when it had been impressed on her that she was ugly and insignificant. Indeed, she designedly and auto-biographically made these physical disabilities a feature in *Jane Eyre*. This morbid self-consciousness, this lack of geniality, and a complete absence of any social effervescence made for her one of the most unfortunate equipments for general intercourse, in the rôle of lioness, that it is possible to conceive.

There was a certain underlying ungraciousness also that unfitted her for the part; at times she was silent and miserable, at times she roared in a manner socially devastating. Twice during this visit she was taken to see Macready act and subsequently wrote:

I astonished a dinner-party by honestly saying I did not like him. It is the fashion to rave about his splendid acting—anything more false and artificial, less genuinely impressive than his whole style I could scarcely have imagined; the fact is, the stage system altogether is hollow nonsense, they act farce well enough, the actors comprehend their parts and do them justice. They comprehend nothing about tragedy or Shakespeare, and it is a failure. I said so, and by so saying produced a blank silence, a mute consternation. I was, indeed, obliged to dissent on many occasions, and to offend by dissenting. It seems now very much the custom to admire a certain wordy, intricate, obscure style of poetry, such as Elizabeth Barrett Browning writes. Some pieces were referred to about which Currer Bell was expected to be very rapturous, and failing in this he disappointed.... I think I should scarcely like to live in London, and were I obliged to live there, I should certainly go little into company, especially I should eschew the literary coteries.

Again, Mr. Smith brought together a dinner-party of critics, five of them, representing leading papers, in her honour. She 'enjoyed the spectacle of them greatly,' but fixed a deadly eye on Mr. Chorley.

He is a peculiar specimen—one whom you could set yourself to examine, uncertain whether, when you had probed all the small reserves of his character the result would be utter contempt and aversion, or whether for the sake of latent good you would forgive obvious evil. One could well pardon his unpleasant features, his strange voice, even his very foppery and grimace, if one found these disadvantages connected with living talent and any spark of genuine goodness. If there is nothing more than acquirement, smartness, and the affectation of philanthropy, Chorley is a fine creature.

One wonders what the fine creature thought of the silent little lady who drew such deadly conclusions from his small-talk.

But, it must be again repeated, it was chiefly her shyness that, by making her miserable in the presence of strangers, rendered her ill-disposed to them; it was like some acute physical pain which renders abominable all that is experienced while it is in possession. Not being herself at ease, her own discomfort led her to lay the blame of it on them, even though the meeting had been desired and looked forward to on both sides. This was very markedly so in the case of Thackeray, for whom, before she met him, she had a wild hero-worship comparable with that which, in the days of her childhood, she had cherished for the Duke of Wellington. He was unique, he was a Titan, he was the legitimate high priest of Truth, and 'a hundred years hence the thoughtful critic, looking down on the deep waters, will see his work shining through them, the pearl of great price. He is alone in his power, alone in his simplicity, alone in his self-control.' He was a great knight-errant gloriously tilting against and triumphantly overthrowing the pomps and empty pretensions of the world, with his burnished spear of noble-hearted satire.

Reality based on such glowing expectations was almost bound to prove a disappointment, and the first meeting seems to have been a dreadful fiasco. Thackeray was invited to dine at Mrs. Smith's to meet her, but Charlotte had been out all morning, she had missed her lunch, and by seven o'clock exhaustion and the excitement of meeting him had made 'savage work' of her. It must have been by her own wish that he was not introduced to her before dinner, but he came up and shook hands. Afterwards he talked to her a little, but she could hardly reply to him at all; everything was 'dreamlike.' 'Had I not been obliged to speak,' she wrote to Mr. Williams, 'I could have managed well, but it behoved me to answer when addressed and the effort was torture—I spoke stupidly.' Unfortunately this meeting had been arranged in order that, at her wish, she might get to know Thackeray, so speech could hardly be avoided. But speech being torture, she chiefly listened, and, alas, she found his talk 'very peculiar, too perverse to be pleasant'; he was 'cynical, harsh and contradictory.' The torture of her own shyness, coupled with the self-conscious sense that something 'brilliant, eccentric and provocative was expected of the author of *Jane Eyre*' made her critical of him. Though still an intellectual Titan, he lost something of his moral stature, and the glamour began to fade from his work as well.

I have come to the conclusion [she wrote to Mr. Williams] that whenever he (Thackeray) writes, Mephistopheles stands on his right hand and Raphael on his left: the great doubter and sneerer usually guides the pen; the Angel noble and gentle, interlines letters of light here and there. Alas, Thackeray, I wish your strong wings would lift you oftener above the smoke of cities into the pure region nearer heaven.

The preacher, we fear, who was never very far from Charlotte's right hand, held the pen for her there, and when she next saw Thackeray in London in June 1850, he inspired her tongue. Her shyness had worn off, and, no doubt to his extreme astonishment, she went for the Titan.

He made a morning call, [she wrote to Ellen] and sat about two hours. Mr. Smith only was in the room, the whole time. He described it afterwards as a 'queer scene,' and I suppose it was. The giant sat before me: I was moved to speak to him of some of his shortcomings (literary, of course); one by one the faults came into my mind, and one by one I brought them out, and sought some explanation or defence. He did defend himself like a great Turk and heathen; that is to say the excuses were often worse than the crime itself. The matter ended in decent amity; if all be well I am to dine at his house this evening.

A queer scene indeed! Only once before had he met her, and then she was too awe-struck with him to utter more than a syllable; now for two hours he was in the dock before this ferocious little lady, who cross-examined him on his literary misdeeds and poured scorn on the pleading which only aggravated his offence. It must have been in some trepidation that he looked forward to that evening, for who could tell whether she might not again arraign him before the distinguished company whom he had honoured with an invitation to come in after dinner and see the great authoress? But there was no real fear of that; the presence of strangers exercised the usual paralysing effect on her. She was more tongue-tied than she had been on the first occasion of their meeting, and there ensued the most ghastly party ever recorded in the melancholy history of social pleasure.

Lady Ritchie, Thackeray's daughter (whose admirable account of it I follow), was present throughout the evening. To her and her sister, then young girls, the occasion was of the most thrilling, for they had surreptitiously dipped into *Jane Eyre*, which, though chiefly unintelligible, was highly stimulating. Her father went down to the front door to receive his guest, and in she came, escorted by him and Mr. Smith, 'in mittens, in silence, in seriousness,' tiny and hardly reaching up to Thackeray's elbow. She was somewhat grave and stern, thought Lady Ritchie, especially 'to forward little girls who wished to chatter'; evidently Charlotte remembered, from the governess days, the necessity and the difficulty of repelling the rude familiarities of children. Then, after this family dinner, the brilliant company began to assemble. Mrs. Crowe who wrote *The Nightside of Nature* was there, and Thomas Carlyle and his wife, Mrs. Proctor and her husband, Barry Cornwall (who, so rumour had once said, were the joint authors of *Jane Eyre*) and their daughter, Adelaide Anne Proctor, who wrote *The Lost Chord* and other poems.

Everyone waited (says Lady Ritchie) for the brilliant conversation which never began at all. Miss Brontë retired to the sofa in the study and murmured a low word now and then to our kind governess, Miss Truelock. The room looked very dark, the lamp began to smoke a little, the conversation grew dimmer and more dim, the ladies sat round still expectant, my father was too much perturbed by the gloom and the silence to be able to cope with it at all. Mrs. Brookfield who was in the doorway by the study near the corner in which Miss Brontë was sitting, leant forward with a little commonplace, since brilliance was not to be the order of the evening. 'Do you like London, Miss Brontë?' she said; another silence, a pause, then Miss Brontë answered 'Yes and no,' very gravely....

It is indeed little wonder that, after the lioness had gone, Thackeray quietly let himself out of his house and spent the rest of the evening at his club, quite unable to face his other guests. One is sorry for them for having had so poor an entertainment, one is especially sorry for the host, but most of all for Charlotte. Further acquaintance with Thackeray in later visits to London, even now that she was no longer shy of him, was productive only of ironical comments on his faults. She went to a lecture of his at which the audience was 'the cream of London society,' and she was surprised that he noticed her at all, when so many 'admiring duchesses and countesses were seated in rows before him.' When he asked her afterwards if she had enjoyed it, she found this harmless inquiry over-eager and naïve. And what a snob!

He postponed his next lecture at the earnest petition of the duchesses and marchionesses who, on the day on which it should have been delivered, were necessitated to go down with the Queen and Court to Ascot races. I told him I thought he did wrong to put it off an their account—and I think so still....

Then there was a fancy dress ball given by the Queen, and the

great lords and ladies have been quite wrapt up in preparation for this momentous event. Their pet and darling, Mr. Thackeray, of course, sympathizes with them. He was here yesterday to dinner and left very early in the evening in order that he might visit respectively the Duchess of Norfolk, the Marchioness of Londonderry, Ladies Chesterfield and Clanricarde, and see them all in their fancy costumes of the reign of Charles II before they set out for the Palace.... Amongst others the Lord Chancellor attended his last lecture, and Mr. Thackeray says he expects a place from him: but in this I think he was joking. Of course Mr. T. is a good deal spoiled by all this, and indeed it cannot be otherwise.

It was a sad disenchantment, but indeed she was on the alert for disenchantment, and there underlies her criticism of him an uneasy jealousy of one who could enjoy his success while she could not enjoy her own. Thackeray offered to introduce her to galaxies of great folk who would receive her with open arms, but she thought '"society" produced so ill an effect on him that she had better avoid it.' She can no longer find an agreeable trait in him, and when Mr. Smith sent her an engraving of his portrait by Lawrence, she noticed that 'the expression of *spite*, most vividly marked in the original, is here softened.' And his work also did follow him into the darkness of her disapproval. She went to his lecture on Fielding: it was 'a painful hour,' and she had nothing but horror for his lightness over evil and drunken ways. Branwell, of course, was still bitterly and hardly in her mind, but there was more cavilling than criticism in her indignation with the lecturer: anyone would think that Thackeray had made an impassioned address exhorting every young man to take to drink without further delay.

If only once [she wrote] the prospect of a promising life blasted at the outset by wild ways had passed close under his eyes, he *never* could have spoken with such levity of what led to its piteous destruction. Had I a brother yet living, I should tremble to let him read Thackeray's lecture on Fielding. I should hide it away from him. If in spite of precautions it fell into his hands, I should earnestly pray him not to be misled by the voice of the charmer, charm he never so wisely.

Then Mr. Smith sent her an early copy of the first volume of *Esmond*, and though, when she had finished the whole, she was generous in praise, her first instinct was to find fault with Thackeray's motives.

But what bitter satire, [she writes] what relentless dissection of diseased subjects! Well, and this too is right, or would be right, if the savage surgeon did not seem so fiercely pleased with his work. Thackeray likes to dissect an ulcer or an aneurism, he has pleasure in putting his cruel knife or probe into quivering, living flesh. Thackeray would not like all the world to be good; no great satirist would like society to be perfect.

It was indeed seldom in this new world of London, which so cordially opened its arms to her in welcome and admiration, that she registered agreeable first impressions of anybody: she was unchanged in that respect from the days when she had first seen in M. Héger an insane tom-cat and a delirious hyena. But Miss Harriet Martineau was an exception. Charlotte was predisposed in her favour, for she had enjoyed *Deerbrook* and, writing to her before her first visit to London in the name of Currer Bell, expressed the 'pleasure and profit he has derived from her works,' and sent her a copy of *Shirley*. This erasure of the pronoun of sex was evidently intentional, for Charlotte meant to disclose herself, and Miss Martineau, firmly grasping the idea, wittily addressed her envelope of reply to 'Currer Bell, Esq.,' but began her letter 'Dear Madam.' Then the spirit of social comedy took this promising situation in hand. Currer Bell, on going up to London for that first visit in which Thackeray stocks went down, wrote to Miss Martineau that 'he' was in town and would like to see her. There was a small party, all eager to see Currer Bell, but, before he-she arrived, a male guest six feet high was announced, and the party thought this was Currer Bell. Then Currer Bell arrived, and, disclosing herself indistinctly to the footman, she was announced not as 'Miss Brontë,' but as 'Miss Brogden,' and there entered, so Miss Martineau wrote, 'the smallest creature I had ever seen except at a fair.' There for the present the budding friendship stayed, to burst out into amazing bloom a year afterwards.

Meantime, before Charlotte met Miss Martineau again, other friendships had been forming; that with Sir James Kay-Shuttleworth, an eminent doctor now retired and rewarded with a baronetcy, had features peculiarly characteristic of Charlotte's almost comical inability to let herself go, easily and naturally. He was certainly a lion-hunter, and his persistent stalking must have been tiresome, but his amiability was undefeated. He and his wife appear first on the stage among those who 'came boring to Haworth on the wise errand of seeing the scenery described in *Jane Eyre* and *Shirley*' They insisted that she should spend a few days with them at Gawthorpe, their place on the borders of East Lancashire, and, since Mr. Brontë would not hear of her refusing, she was left 'without plea or defence.' The baronet was a fine-looking man and quite 'unpretending,' but, with her habitual prejudice against strangers which, in spite of her resolutions, remained as robust as ever, Charlotte had fears that he might not be what he seemed. 'I wish he may be as sincere as he is polished,' she wrote. 'He shows his white teeth with too frequent a smile, but I will not prejudge him.' So to Gawthorpe with some misgiving she went. The embarrassment of being obliged to talk, which wrecked her first meeting with Thackeray, was spared her, since 'the dialogues (perhaps I should say monologues, for I listened far more than I talked) by the fireside in his antique oak-panelled drawing-room, while they suited him, did not too much oppress and exhaust me.' He was not at all well, his nerves were very sensitive and the state of his health 'exaggerated sensitiveness into irritability.' Still he was gracious and dignified, and his 'tastes and feelings were capable of elevation.' Then there was Lady Shuttleworth, rather handsome, without any pretensions to 'aristocratic airs,' frank, good-humoured and active, but 'truth obliges me to say that, as it seems to me, grace, dignity, fine feeling were not in the inventory of her qualities.' Charlotte liked the German governess better than anyone in the house, and had heart-to-heart talks with her. She was well treated 'for a governess,' but said she was homesick, 'and wore the usual pale, despondent look of her class.'

So the visit passed off not amiss, but, writes Charlotte,

the worst of it is, that there is now some menace hanging over my head of an invitation to go to them in London during the season.... This was his (Sir James's) theme when I was at Gawthorpe. I then gave notice that I would not be lionised.... I shall probably go. I know what the effect and what the pain will be, how wretched I shall often feel, how thin and haggard I shall get, but he who shuns suffering will never win victory. If I mean to improve, I must strive and endure. The visit will, however, be short, as short as I can possibly make it; would to God it was well over! I have one safeguard. Sir James has been a physician, and looks at me with a physician's eye: he saw at once that I could not stand much fatigue nor bear the presence of many strangers. Papa is restless and eager for me to go, the idea of a refusal quite hurts him.

There is something truly pathetic about this letter. It shows us what real torture she suffered from her morbid shyness and self-consciousness, and how she strove to get the better of them. But if there had been a serious operation hanging over her head, instead of a short visit to London, and it was doubtful if she could stand the shock, she could not have spoken more apprehensively of it. It becomes easy to understand how her first impressions of strangers were always disagreeable, for they were, so to speak, the surgeons and nurses who conducted the operation; only the anæsthetist was lacking. But, in spite of the prospective pain, she meant to face it, and there was true courage, for that which to others would be a pleasant experience was to her a real agony. At other times the flesh was weak, and in order to justify on moral grounds her profound hatred of sojourning among strangers, she says that 'indiscriminate visiting leads only to a waste of time and a vulgarising of character ... besides' (as an afterthought) 'it would be wrong to leave papa often.' But papa on this occasion was 'quite hurt' at the thought of her refusing.

Further menaces were brewing. The persevering baronet now proposed that she should go up with him and his wife to London by road, and stay at several of his relations' houses on the way. Providence thwarted that more formidable plan; Mr. Brontë was ill, Charlotte did not like to leave him, and with solemn thankfulness she records her relief. 'I cannot say that I regret having missed this ordeal: I would as lief have walked among red-hot ploughshares.' Eventually she got out of staying with them at all, and when she went to London in June 1850, she stopped at the more familiar house of her publisher instead. But Sir James called with agonising proposals. 'To my great horror he talks of my going with them to Hampton Court, Windsor, etc. God knows how I shall get on, I perfectly dread it.' But she escaped from that snare of the fowler.

It was on this visit to London that Charlotte, as we have seen, arraigned and dined with Thackeray; she also saw the idol of her childhood, the Duke of Wellington; she sat to George Richmond the artist for the crayon portrait of her which Mr. George Smith commissioned and gave to her father, and which was bequeathed to the nation by her husband and now hangs in the National Portrait Gallery. She also met G. H. Lewes for the first time, whom she had taken to task for his review of *Shirley*. She confessed that she felt 'half sadly, half tenderly' towards him, his face almost moved her to tears, so wonderfully it resembled Emily's; 'in consequence, whatever Lewes does or says, I believe I cannot hate him.' There was less of social entertainment on this visit, and less lionising, and in consequence she enjoyed it more than her first. But what she called 'a trying termination' of it remained, which she looked forward to with apprehension, but enjoyed enormously. This was an expedition to Edinburgh with her young publisher, George Smith, who was six or seven years younger than she, and it showed a daring disregard of the Victorian conventions of 1850, for she went there alone with him and his sister without any middle-aged chaperon at all, feeling that 'my seniority and lack of all pretensions to beauty, etc., are a perfect safeguard.' The expedition was a glorious success; she found music and magic at Melrose and Abbotsford, and London 'compared to Dun-Edin, "mine own romantic town," is prose compared to poetry or as a great rumbling, rambling heavy epic compared to a lyric, brief, bright, clear, and vital as a flash of lightning.' The Scotch, too, had grand characters and that gave Scotland its charm and greatness.

She went back from Scotland to Haworth, where she stayed a month; it was like the return home after Anne's death. 'There was a reaction,' she wrote, 'that sunk me to the earth: the deadly silence, solitude, desolation, were awful; the craving for companionship, the hopelessness of relief, were what I should dread to feel again.' She was morbidly oppressed with the sense of the shortness of life, and of 'the sickness, decay, the struggle of spirit and flesh' that must come before the end of it. Her father was anxious about her health; this caused, she thought, the gloomy thoughts that assailed her, and made a canker in her mind, and she entreated him not to worry about her.

In turn she was anxious about him, and two people worrying about each other, with little or no external diversion, brews a deadly atmosphere. Charlotte's nerves were frayed, she had no literary project on hand and she dwelt morbidly on the past, and thus grew apprehensive about the future. 'I think grief,' she writes, 'is a two-edged sword, it cuts both ways: the memory of one loss is the anticipation of another.'

Sir James Kay-Shuttleworth, robbed of Charlotte's visit to him in London, now urged her to come and stay with him at a house he had taken near Bowness on Lake Windermere, and again Mr. Brontë, who by no means wanted her always to be with him at Haworth, said that her refusal to go would much annoy him. Her dutifulness was rewarded, for it was now she met Mrs. Gaskell for the first time and a friendship and a correspondence began which, though never intimate, lasted to the end of Charlotte's life. There was already a mutual predisposition, for Mrs. Gaskell had written to Charlotte in praise of *Shirley*, and Charlotte had therefore settled she was a great and a good woman. Now these pleasant expectations were realised: Charlotte found her a kind and cheerful companion of high talent. Mrs. Gaskell also was attracted and interested: Charlotte's shyness and silence struck her first, and the absence of 'any spark of merriment.' But her well-meaning host still could not do right, for he took Charlotte for a drive in a carriage to see the beauties of the Lake country. That sounds harmless, but no—she writes to Miss Wooler: 'Decidedly it does not agree with me to prosecute the search of the picturesque in a carriage; a waggon, a spring-cart, even a post-chaise might do, but the carriage upsets everything.' But could poor Sir James have foreseen this fatal flaw? Even if he had, and if he had sent Charlotte out in a waggon, she would surely have founded an even graver complaint at being supplied with so unusual a conveyance. It was not really the carriage that worried her; it was the presence of other people and her own self-consciousness. She was afraid of growing in any degree enthusiastic, and thus drawing attention to the 'lioness, the authoress, the artist.' Not till her next visit to the Lakes, in the winter, when she stayed with Miss Martineau and fell victim to her robust charm, did she realise Sir James's kindly intentions. 'I begin to admit in my own mind,' she wrote, 'that he is sincerely benignant to me.'

She went back home at the end of August, and was, as usual, much cheered by an article in the *Palladium,* by Sidney Dobell, entitled 'Currer Bell,' which expressed the warmest admiration not only for *Jane Eyre* and *Shirley,* but for *Wuthering Heights.* It revived, however, the suggestion that*Wuthering Heights* and *The Tenant of Wildfell Hall* were also of Currer Bell's authorship. Mr. Williams had seen this article, and he now wrote to Charlotte proposing to reissue *Wuthering Heights* and *Agnes Grey* in one volume, with a biographical notice by her which should make known the history of the three pseudonyms. Emily and Anne were dead, and there was no longer any reason why the mystery should not be authoritatively dispelled. He also made some suggestion about reissuing *The Tenant of Wildfell Hall.* Charlotte was opposed to that: she did not think the book should be preserved. Anne had written it under a strange, conscientious, half-ascetic notion of accomplishing a painful penance and a severe duty: it had better drop out of existence. But she warmly favoured the other suggestion, only the book must be republished by Smith, Elder and not by its original publisher, Newby. She also decided to make a selection from her sisters' manuscript poems, not hitherto published, and issue them in the form of an appendix.

She set to work at once, and before the end of September a rough copy of the 'Biographical Notice' was in the hands of her publisher. She described, with a simplicity she rarely attained, Emily's last illness; none can read that page unmoved, so sincere and heart-broken is the regret and the anguish for those estranged days that inspired it.

Never in all her life had she lingered over any task that lay before her, and she did not linger now. She sank rapidly, she made haste to leave us. Yet while physically she perished, mentally she grew stronger than we had yet known her. Day by day, when I saw with what a front she met suffering, I looked on her with an anguish of love and wonder. The awful point was that while full of ruth for others, on herself she had no pity: the spirit was inexorable to the flesh: from the trembling hand, the unnerved limbs, the faded eye, the same service was exacted as in health. To stand by and witness this and not dare to remonstrate was a pain no words can render....

Truly, if Charlotte was reaping the hardness she had sown, she made expiation in that bitter harvesting.

Then, when the 'Biographical Notice' was finished, Charlotte read *Wuthering Heights* over again, and wrote a Preface regarding it to this new edition. She tells us that she has now got a clear glimpse of its faults, and craves indulgence for them:

Had she (Emily) but lived, her mind would have grown like a strong tree, loftier, straighter, wider-spreading, and its matured fruits would have attained a mellower ripeness and sunnier bloom, but on that mind time and experience alone could work.

But we stare incredulous at such a conclusion. What does it mean? It is as if Charlotte predicted that some dryad of the moor, in whose eyes shone the knowledge of things veiled and primeval, would be tamed by time and experience into losing her elemental quality, and be thereby ripened and mellowed. Surely, had Emily lived, exactly the opposite must have happened. What more would have been revealed to her by the 'Strange Power' that inspired her we cannot tell, for the ways of genius are past finding out, and its paths in the dark waters through which it alone can lead us, but any such development as Charlotte predicted must have been to the detriment of that supreme quality. She missed all that *Wuthering Heights* stands for: she shuddered at its 'horror of great darkness,' she wished to cease 'to breathe lightning,' not knowing that the darkness and the lightning are It; and, apologising for them, she pointed out 'those spots where clouded daylight and eclipsed sun still attest their existence.' Eagerly, defending the book, she calls our attention to 'the homely benevolence of Nelly Dean,' to the 'constancy and tenderness of Edgar Linton': Emily *could* render such, and had she lived she would have developed her power further in that regard. But when it came to the true genius of the book, namely the loves of Heathcliff and Catherine, that soaring of fierce eagles out of sight, or to the passionate mystical yearning for the unsheathed beauty of the world, for the wakening and being satisfied with it, she was blind: Emily's 'descriptions of natural scenery are what they should be, and all they should be.' As for the eagles, Heathcliff 'stands unredeemed ... except for his faint regard for Hareton,' and his 'half implied esteem for Nelly Dean'; his love for Catherine 'is a passion such as might boil and glow in the bad essence of some evil genius!' All she can say for Catherine is that 'she is not destitute of a certain strange beauty in her fierceness, or of honesty in the midst of her perverted passion and passionate perversity.' Such was her estimate of the book when loyally and lovingly she tried to appreciate and understand it.

There is scarcely in the whole history of the family a more heart-rending picture than that which Charlotte paints of herself sitting in the dining-room of the Parsonage, in a loneliness which her occupation accentuated and rendered the more intolerable, and going through her sisters' papers. She spent hours peering into the minutely written manuscripts, selecting the poems to be published, and writing little lost explanatory notes: in one she said, 'the Genius of a solitary region seems to address his wandering and wayward votary'; in another, 'the same mind is in converse with a like abstraction'; in another, 'the wakened soul struggles to blend with the storm by which it is swayed....' As in her portrait of her sister in *Shirley*, as in her Preface, these notes are mere external observations; Emily is beyond her. She had thought, she wrote to Mr. Williams, that this intellectual exertion would rouse her mind from the sense of despairing loneliness, but it was not so. All turned to memory; memory was 'both sad and relentless.'

The reading over of papers, the renewal of remembrance brought back the pang of bereavement, and occasioned a depression of spirits well-nigh intolerable. For one or two nights I scarcely knew how to get on till morning; and when morning came I was still haunted with a sense of sickening distress.

She breakfasted with her father, she worked alone, and alone she walked on the moors on days of autumn sunshine 'with solitude and memory for companions, and Heathcliff haunted every glen and hollow.' She sat down to her solitary dinner, for Mr. Brontë dined by himself, and soon after the early closing in of the shortening days began to darken. Now she must put her work aside, for her eyes would not stand the strain of deciphering these scripts by candle-light; also she dared not work in the evening for fear of the sleepless nights that followed. Rainstorms swept over the garden and glimmering tombstones of the graveyard, and she drew the curtains across the panes, but still the voice of the wind called from without, as of Cathy wailing 'Let me in!' and fingers tapped at the pane.

Memory; everything was memory, and all memories were bitter. The silent house was astir with ghosts, and these lonely evening hours were the worst of all, for they were those in which once there had been excitement and eager talk over plans, over literary ambitions, over projects for keeping a school. The horror grew, and perhaps she would take her knitting into the kitchen and talk with Tabby for an hour; then, still alone, she supped and fed Anne's or Emily's dogs, whose mistresses had not yet returned, unless it was their voices in the wind from the moors. Mr. Brontë went early to bed, winding, as he passed, the clock on the stairs, whose ticking could be heard throughout the house; but Charlotte sat up till midnight, for where was the use of lying lonely in the dark? As one of those rare visitors to Haworth wrote to Mrs. Gaskell, it seemed 'that joy can never have entered that house since it was first built.'

Such was the autumn of 1850.

CHAPTER XVII

As soon as this new edition of *Wuthering Heights* and *Agnes Grey* was out of her hands, Charlotte went to pay a long-promised visit to Miss Martineau. She lived at Ambleside, but had been away when Charlotte was staying with Sir

James Kay-Shuttleworth in the summer, and they had not met since she had been introduced a year ago as 'Miss Brogden.' Instantly she succumbed to the breezy, efficient, rather masculine charm of her new friend, who had the most vivifying effect on her after the desolate, memory-haunted autumn. 'She is a great and a good woman,' she wrote to Ellen, 'of course not without peculiarities, but I have seen none as yet that annoy me.... Miss Martineau I relish inexpressibly.' It was her tremendous vitality that was so bracing and admirable, and not less her mental vigour. She was up at five in the morning, and after a cold bath took a walk by starlight, and had finished breakfast and got to work by seven. The morning was spent in solitude; they walked and talked till dinner; and after Miss Martineau conversed 'fluently and abundantly,' and sat up for a couple of hours after Charlotte had gone to bed at ten, writing letters. Charlotte wrote to her father with the same rare unqualified enthusiasm:

As to Miss Martineau I admire her and wonder at her more than I can say. Her powers of labour, of exercise, and social cheerfulness are beyond my comprehension. In spite of the unceasing activity of her colossal intellect, she enjoys robust health. She is very kind to me, though she must think I am a very insignificant person compared to herself.

To Mr. Williams she wrote:

Her animal spirits are as unflagging as her mental powers. It gave me no pain to feel insignificant, mentally and corporeally, in comparison with her.

To another friend she wrote:

She is certainly a woman of wonderful endowments, both intellectual and physical, and though I share few of her opinions, and regard her as fallible on certain points of judgment, I must still accord her my highest esteem. The manner in which she combines the highest mental culture with the nicest discharge of feminine duties filled me with admiration, while her affectionate kindness earned my gratitude.

To Mr. Taylor she wrote:

I find a worth and greatness in herself, and a constancy, benevolence, perseverance in her practices, such as wins the sincerest esteem and affection. She is not a person to be judged by her writings alone, but rather by her own deeds and life, than which nothing can be more exemplary and nobler. Faults she has, but to me they appear very trivial weighed in the balance against her excellences.

There is scarcely a qualifying phrase in these enthusiasms: Charlotte let herself go in almost undiluted appreciation. She had never admired any woman so unreservedly since the days of her adolescent passion for Ellen, and it was almost as if the sunshine of the morning, long obscured and eclipsed, had returned to her and warmed her into uncritical enjoyment. Moreover, Charlotte could render her an intellectual homage such as she had never been able to accord to Ellen, and this homage was at present reciprocated, for Miss Martineau greatly admired *Jane Eyre* and *Shirley*, 'and,' wrote Charlotte, 'while she testifies affectionate approbation, I feel the sting taken away from another class of critics.'

Miss Martineau told Mrs. Gaskell two little anecdotes about this visit which, though she relates them as independent, may have had a connection. She had mesmeric powers (or as we should say now, hypnotic powers), and Charlotte constantly urged her to mesmerise her. This she refused to do, thinking that Charlotte was in a low nervous condition and that harm might come. She made excuse, saying again and again that she was tired. But there came a day when she could not plead fatigue, and Charlotte 'fell under the influence.' In other words, she began to go into a light trance, and Miss Martineau stopped. Soon after Miss Martineau had to give a lecture: Charlotte sitting sideways to her never took her eyes off her, and when the lecture was over came and stood by her, and in Miss Martineau's 'very voice' repeated the words from Shakespeare which she had quoted, 'Is my son dead?' They went home in silence, and again Charlotte staring at her said, 'Is my son dead?' The two stories seem connected; it looks as if some hypnotic influence had been established which renewed itself when Charlotte fixed her eyes on Miss Martineau.

She returned to Haworth, having spent Christmas with this tonic and marvellous friend, vastly restored, rather severe on herself for having been so feeble as to need a change, and full of critical impressions. She had been to see Mrs. Arnold, widow of Dr. Arnold, and her family at Fox How, and had surveyed them with a magisterial eye. Mrs. Arnold was good and amiable, but intellect was not her strong point, and her manner at first lacked genuineness and simplicity. The daughters were like her both in their qualities and their defects; 'their opinions on literary subjects were rather imitative than original, rather sentimental than sound.' Matthew Arnold's manner was 'displeasing from its seeming foppery,' and Charlotte regarded him at first with 'regretful surprise: the shade of Dr. Arnold seemed to me to frown on his young representative.' Also his theological opinions were very vague and unsettled, but he like the rest of the family improved upon acquaintance: the unfavourable first impression had only been the effect which strangers always had on her. Then Amelia Wooler came in for some rough handling. She had written Charlotte a letter full of 'claptrap sentiment and humbugging attempts at fine writing.' Also she had asked for Wordsworth's, Southey's, Miss Martineau's, and Charlotte's autographs: this showed that the 'old trading spirit' was still alive.

Then there were matrimonial subjects to be discussed with Ellen: Mr. James Taylor at this time, in spite of discouragement, was prosecuting his suit, and Charlotte at present felt well-disposed to him. There are also allusions to a younger man, not named, but certainly to be identified with her young publisher, George Smith, with whom she had made that daring expedition to Scotland. Ellen's badinage (there is no other word for it) on this subject was frightfully arch, for she alluded to him and Charlotte as Jupiter and Venus, and Charlotte, evidently highly delighted, bade her have done with this 'heathen trash.' Towards him she was more than well-disposed, perhaps she was a little in love with him, for Jupiter, encouraged by the success of the Scottish visit, had proposed to Venus that she should make a trip up the Rhine with him, and she wrote to Ellen: 'I am not made of stone, and what is mere excitement to him is fever to me.... I cannot conceive either his mother or his sisters relishing it, and all London would gabble like a countless host of geese.' Her common sense told her that it would never do to marry him, even if he proposed to her. There was a great difference of fortune between them, and it was part of her creed that there should be approximate equality of means between husband and wife; also he was considerably younger than she, and 'personal regard and natural liking do not compensate for that.' She writes with admirable wisdom: 'I am content to have him as a friend, and pray God to continue to me the common sense to look on one so young, so rising, so hopeful in no other light.' But there the matter stayed, and there is no kind of reason to suppose that George Smith ever did propose to her.

Very soon a trial tested that high adoration for Miss Martineau, but it stood firm. She, in collaboration with Mr. Atkinson, published early in February 1851 a book called *Letters on the Nature and Development of Man*. Though it is impossible to suppose that Charlotte, after all those long intimate talks with her, had no inkling of what Miss Martineau's theological opinions were, the publication of them shocked her a good deal. Making allowance for the fact that she often worked herself up, when pen in hand, to exaggerated statements of her feelings, it is evident that she was much upset.

It is the first exposition of avowed Atheism and Materialism [she wrote] that I have ever read: the first unequivocal declaration of disbelief in the existence of a God or a Future Life I have ever seen.... Sincerely—for my own part—do I wish to find and know the truth, but if this be truth, well may she guard herself with mysteries and cover herself with a veil. If this be Truth, Man or Woman who beholds her can but curse the day he or she was born....

Again she wrote: 'I deeply regret its publication for the lady's sake: it gives a death blow to her future usefulness. Who can trust the word or rely on the judgment of an avowed atheist?' But shocked though she was, she did not let this crucial division on religious questions put an end to the friendship, and she continued to correspond with her. She got into her head, though quite mistakenly, that Miss Martineau's friends were as shocked as herself and that they had, one and all, refused to have anything more to do with her. So she determined to stick to her and, when questioned by Miss Wooler as to the wisdom of friendship with an atheist, wrote a characteristic homily in reply:

I do not feel it would be right to give Miss Martineau up entirely. There is in her nature much that is very noble. Hundreds have forsaken her, more I fear in the apprehension that their fair name may suffer if seen in connection with hers than for any pure conviction, such as you suggest, of harm consequent on her fatal tenets. With these fair weather friends I cannot bear to rank. And for her sin, is it not one of those which God and not man must judge?... If you had seen how she secretly suffers from abandonment, you would be the last to give her up: you would separate the sinner from the sin, and feel as if the right lay rather in quietly adhering to her in her strait, while that adherence is unfashionable and unpopular, than in turning your back when the world sets the example.

These are certainly very creditable sentiments, and evince a much larger charity than Charlotte sometimes showed; but we wonder whether she really meant that nobody 'could trust the word of an avowed atheist.' Anyhow, the friendship continued, and she sent Miss Martineau favourable comments which she had received on her book, with the intention of cheering her Coventry. But Miss Martineau, rather disconcertingly, was not in the least in need of being cheered. She referred to Charlotte's notion that her friends had forsaken her as 'an unaccountable delusion': the book which Charlotte had averred had given the 'death blow to her usefulness' had only earned for her a new world of sympathy.

The depression of solitude and silence at Haworth returned. Mr. James Taylor had his final interview, which left the situation as it was, and Charlotte began to reckon up what had happened. He would be absent for five years; 'a dividing expanse of three oceans' would come between them; and though it was entirely of her own choice that anything divided them any more at all, she regretted what she had done, in spite of the excellent reasons for refusing him, of which she found more, and Ellen's 'soft consolatory accents' did not console her. Her father was not well, and she felt that having him to think about 'took her thoughts off other matters, which have become complete bitterness and ashes.' The 'seeming foundation of support and prospect of hope' had completely crumbled away with James Taylor's departure to India, and there was nothing again to look forward to.

And then, amazingly and uniquely (though only briefly), a new interest enlivened her: dress. She was soon to pay a month's visit to Jupiter and Jupiter's family in London, and she wanted all sorts of things: chemisettes of small size, and a new bonnet, and in particular a lace mantle to 'go with' a black satin dress. She had bought a black lace mantle, but it looked 'brown and rusty' over the satin, and she exchanged it for a white one, which looked better and was also cheaper, for it cost only £1 14s. She went to Leeds to buy a new bonnet to wear with the black satin, but when she tried it on 'its pink lining looked infinitely too gay.' Then she wanted a new dress: there were 'beautiful silks of pale sweet colours, but they were five shillings a yard,' so she chose black silk at three shillings. For the moment Charlotte was violently concerned with her frocks.

These vanities being duly provided, Charlotte went up to London again, at the end of May 1851, to stay with her publisher and his mother and sisters for a solid month. Everyone was disposed to make much of her: she breakfasted at the house of Mr. Rogers the 'patriarch poet'; she was asked to a big party at Grosvenor House but declined; she attended Thackeray's lectures, and, though Thackeray did not repeat the experiment of getting together a party to meet her, he pointed her out to 'his grand friends,' and Lord Carlisle and Monckton Milnes introduced themselves. When one of these lectures was over, so Mrs. Gaskell tells us, the audience formed up in two lines and she had to pass down an aisle between rows of eager and interested faces. She retailed these social triumphs to her father and Ellen with considerable gusto: one cannot but think that in her heart, especially when they were over, they gave her a good deal of satisfaction, but at the time her shyness and self-consciousness discounted them. She was not well, she suffered from headache and sickness, and she felt inclined to murmur at Fate, 'which compels me to comparative silence and solitude for eleven months in the year, and in the twelfth, while offering social enjoyment, takes away the vigour and cheerfulness which should turn it to account.' Her malaise caused her to make some severe remarks about certain of these entertainments. She went to a meeting of a Roman Catholic Society, at which Cardinal Wiseman presided. He had a quadruple chin, a large mouth with oily lips betokening greed. 'He came swimming into the room, smiling, simpering and bowing like a fat old lady, and sat down very demure in his chair, the picture of a sleek hypocrite.' Dark-looking, sinister priests surrounded him; he spoke in a smooth, whining voice like a canting Methodist preacher. A horrid spectacle, but she certainly enjoyed telling Ellen about him. She went to see Rachel act:

a wonderful sight, terrible as if the earth has cracked deep at your feet, and revealed a glimpse of hell. She made me shudder to the marrow of my bones: in her some fiend has certainly taken up its incarnate home. She is not a woman, she is a snake, she is the ——.

Rachel made a deep and horrible impression on her; months afterwards, writing to Mr. Taylor in Bombay, she compared her acting to 'the poisoned stimulants to popular ferocity' of gladiatorial shows. 'It is scarcely human nature that she shows you: it is something wilder and worse: the feelings and fury of a fiend. The great gift of genius she undoubtedly has: but, I fear she rather abuses it than turns it to good account.'

Then there were visits to the Crystal Palace, no less than five of them. It impressed her immensely; it was like a bazaar created by Eastern genii, and arranged by supernatural hands. But it palled: it soon became a bustling and fatiguing place, and she did not want to go so often but was forced to. Her last days in London were spoiled because Sir James Kay-Shuttleworth, from whom she had hitherto concealed her presence, discovered her, and it was hard to ward off his eager hospitalities.

The chronicle of these pleasures reads but drearily. She had made valiant efforts to overcome that deplorable killjoy shyness which turned normal social intercourse into torture, but they seemed unavailing, and her health could not stand the cheerful stir and bustle which is in itself so enjoyable to others, but which, getting on her nerves, caused her to look with a jaundiced eye on what others found entertaining. We must not therefore imagine, as certain of her biographers state, that except for the sense of duty and filial piety which kept her at Haworth she would have led a brilliant life in London, the centre of some high literary circle. She disliked London, and she affirmed that if she had to live there she would studiously avoid literary circles. London life was impossible for her; a few weeks of it was as much as she could stand, and after that, according to her own rueful picture of herself, she returned home meagre and old and hollow-eyed. Besides, it was at Haworth only she was able to write, and writing was to her the sole panacea for the weary fret of life, and for the morbid melancholy that so often beset her. Once only again did she spend a holiday in London, and then she avoided what she had learned, by repeated experience, gave her more discomfort than pleasure.

On her way home she spent two days at Plymouth Grove, Manchester, the house of Mr. and Mrs. Gaskell, and there suddenly a new trait of tenderness towards children manifested itself. In her governess days, perhaps because she could not manage them, perhaps because they formed part of a *milieu* she detested, she had certainly not cared for them, and shrank from their tokens of affection. But now, as if surprised at and distrustful of her own unwonted feelings, she wrote to Mrs. Gaskell after her visit, asking her to manage 'to convey a small kiss to that dear but dangerous little person Julia. She surreptitiously possessed herself of a minute fraction of my heart, which has been missing ever since I saw her.' It was a diffident, humble access; she 'felt like a fond but bashful suitor who views at a distance the fair personage to whom in his slavish awe he dare not risk a near approach.' She felt a stranger to children.

Charlotte got home by the beginning of July, and set to work on her new book. As may be remembered, she had thought of following up *Jane Eyre* with an expanded version of *The Professor*, and had also thought, after the publication of *Shirley*, of bringing it out as it stood, and even wrote a preface for it, but nothing came of it. But she had never personally abandoned the idea of using much of the material in a future book, and she now did so in the writing of *Villette*. Instantly, as always before, she found healing for her despondence and depression in the exercise of her imagination; her letters to her friends much diminish in volume and in vividness, for all her energy was being poured into her work. It went well, for she was handling the molten stuff of her experiences in Brussels which was still live fire; she got on quickly, and hoped to have the book ready for publication in the spring of the next year, 1852. She refused to leave Haworth in spite of invitations from Miss Martineau, Mrs. Gaskell and Ellen Nussey, for while the wind of imagination blew she must sail before it. None of the usual causes for dissatisfaction prevailed against her. Tabby got influenza and Martha quinsy, and she nursed them both; her father got a cold; Keeper, Emily's dog, died; but all burdens were light when her work prospered.

Then in the winter her health broke down, and she had many weeks of illness and enforced idleness; headaches and bilious attacks continually prostrated her; her letters are a catalogue of miserable symptoms and ineffectual remedies. The spring brought improvement, but when she tried to get to work again, the happy inspiration of the autumn would not return, and, as she wrote to Mr. Williams, 'When the mood leaves me (it has left me now, without vouchsafing so much as a word of a message when it will return) I put by the MS. and wait till it comes back again.' For more than four months this barrenness persisted; she slept ill at night, and sat idle all day, longing to work but unable, and afraid sometimes that the pain she suffered was a symptom of the disease of which her four sisters and her brother had died. Then at last the blessed mood returned, and before the end of March she was at work again.

There was no visit to London this summer; in June she went to Filey, close to Scarborough, partly for the sake of sea-air, partly in order to see to the relettering of the stone over Anne's grave. She must have heard that there were some errors on it (and indeed found five), for she referred to this as a duty that had long lain heavy. For some reason she felt that she had to be alone for this task of piety; why, it is impossible to say. Ellen had been with her at Scarborough when Anne died, and she doubtless would have accompanied her now, but Charlotte did not even let her know that she contemplated going, writing her when she had got there a mysterious and rather melodramatic letter, beginning:

I am at Filey utterly alone. Do not be angry, the step is right. I considered it and resolved on it with due deliberation. I walk on the sands a good deal, and try not to feel desolate and melancholy. How sorely my heart longs for you, I need not say.

But she only had to tell Ellen she wanted her, and Ellen would have come; clearly she just did not want anybody's company, and having discharged her duty to the tombstone stayed there for three weeks in great tranquillity and content. She bathed and it seemed to brace her; she walked along the sands for three or four hours every day, as she had been told that this was good for a torpid liver, and became as sunburnt as a bathing-woman. She watched a rough sea with awe and admiration, she saw a dog battling with the waves, she set out to go to Filey Bridge but was frightened back by two cows, she went to church at some small and shabby tabernacle, and could hardly help laughing at the ludicrous seating arrangements, for the singers in the gallery turned their backs on the congregation, and the congregation on the parson. She wished Mr. Nicholls had been there to see it; he would certainly have laughed out, and she sent him her kind regards. Her letters in her utter loneliness were full of good spirits and cheerfulness, and this first kindly mention of Mr. Nicholls is significant.

She was back at Haworth in July, and had a serious fright about her father, who was threatened with a stroke of apoplexy. He was dangerously ill for a while, but made a steady though slow recovery, and once more Charlotte got to work on *Villette*, resolved not to quit her labours, but not to hurry them, till the book was finished. There were fits of depression when her work went ill, in which she confessed that she was lonely and likely to remain lonely, but denied, still wondering whether she had been right to refuse Mr. Taylor, that the thought of continuing 'single' was the cause of them. She felt she would neither 'know nor taste pleasure' until the book was finished, and worked steadily on, refusing for some weeks to let Ellen come to Haworth or to interrupt herself by going to her. Before the end of October she had sent two of the three volumes to her publishers, asking for criticisms. She admitted, when she received them, that there was something in them, and then refused to alter a single word. She could not write otherwise, as she had told Mr. Williams before, and she must write in her own way or not at all. But she was in an agony of nervous apprehension about the whole; she even wanted the book to be published anonymously. Then by the end of November the long task was finished, and she said her prayers.

She was still all to bits with the strain of her accomplished work and, not less, with the reaction that followed, for receiving from her publishers her cheque of £500 payable on delivery of the complete manuscript without a line of comment on the third volume, she instantly made up her mind to rush up to London and see whether this silence betokened disapproval. The letter came next morning, and Charlotte scolded George Smith soundly for not having sent it with the cheque, reminding him that 'Inexplicable delays should be avoided when possible, for they are apt to urge those subjected to their harassment to sudden and impulsive steps.' As for his criticisms on the third volume, she pronounced them just, and took no further notice of them.

Charlotte was right in not attempting to alter the book; she could no more have done that than she could have added a cubit to her stature, for *Villette*, to a far higher degree than anything she had ever written, was herself, and it was composed of her own experience, her character and her soul. The book, once written, was as real and as inevitable as the past on which it was founded. Technically, *Villette* has grave faults; it lacks unity; the interest is shifted from one set of characters to another, Lucy Snowe falls in love with Dr. John, and when she discovers that he regards her with absolute indifference, she falls in love with Paul Emmanuel, who, though this affair is the *clou* of the book, hardly appears till we are half-way through. All this had been pointed out to Charlotte, but the book was written indelibly with her heart's blood and it could not be otherwise. For into it she had put, and now was done with, the bitterness of that second year at Brussels, which had robbed her of all peace of mind for two years. Now she externalised these miseries, and by the alchemy of her art transmuted her pangs into pictures, and even as once she in her own person had sought relief from them in the chapel of St. Gudule's under the seal of confession, so now under the seal of fiction she told the world what she had told a priest, and was rid of the perilous stuff. With minute detail and with photographic fidelity she reproduced the *pensionnat* in the Rue d'Isabelle, and made eternally substantial the phantoms which for her haunted its corridors. Her imagination fused and made molten the actual, and the third volume of *Villette*, enacted by Lucy Snowe, Paul Emmanuel, and Madame Beck, could never have been written had it not been for the adventure of Charlotte Brontë, Constantin Héger, and Madame. Whether or no she actually muttered *Je me vengerai* to that lady when she left Brussels for the last time, she had kept these things in her heart, even as she had nursed there the miseries of Cowan Bridge, speaking of them to no living soul; and now releasing them she took her revenge, and wrote immortally of them. Long as she had waited, Madame Héger had to wait longer yet for the justification of her spyings and suspicions as set forth in *Villette*; and it was not till sixty years later, when all those immediately concerned had long been dead, that there were published the four letters of Charlotte's to Madame Héger's husband, which she had picked out of the waste-paper basket and pieced together. They were quits.

CHAPTER XVIII

It was in December 1852, when *Villette* was going through the press, that the final act in the drama of Charlotte's life began. It started in storm and trouble, it ended with a spell of such tranquil happiness as she had never known.

Mr. Nicholls had now been curate at Haworth for over eight years, and Charlotte had often alluded to him with disparagement and dislike. His narrowness of mind was what chiefly struck her; he was just a 'highly uninteresting narrow and unattractive specimen of the coarser sex,' she could not see the germs of goodness which Ellen perceived in him. The parishioners generally shared her view, and they hoped that when he went for his holiday to Ireland he would not trouble to return. But by the time she was writing *Shirley* she regarded him with a kindlier eye, and in her presentation of him as Mr. Macarthey, which amused him so enormously, she allowed that he was 'decent, decorous and conscientious.' Now for some months she had suspected that 'he cared something for me and wanted me to care for him.' Her father, she thought, had suspected the same, and alluded to his low spirits and ill-health with 'much indirect sarcasm.' Charlotte wondered if Ellen, who was sometimes too quick to observe the earliest symptom of the love-lorn, had noticed this too. Ellen had: she had already been scolded by Charlotte for her prospective match-making.

One evening in December Mr. Nicholls came to tea with her and her father in Mr. Brontë's study.

After tea, [she wrote to Ellen] I withdrew to the dining-room as usual. As usual, Mr. Nicholls sat with papa till between eight and nine o'clock. I then heard him open the parlour door, as if going. I expected the clash of the front door. He stopped in the passage: he tapped: like lightning it flashed on me what was coming. He entered, he stood before me. What his words were you can guess: his manner you can hardly realize, nor can I forget it. Shaking from head to foot, looking deadly pale, speaking low, vehemently yet with difficulty, he made me for the first time feel what it costs a man to declare affection when he doubts response.

Charlotte promised him a reply next day, and when he had gone, she went to her father and told him what had happened. A Bedlamite scene followed.

If I had *loved* Mr. Nicholls, [she wrote] and had heard such epithets applied to him as were used, it would have transported me past my patience; as it was, my blood boiled with a sense of injustice. But papa worked himself up into a state not to be trifled with: the veins on his temples started up like whipcord and his eyes became suddenly bloodshot. I made haste to promise him that Mr. Nicholls should on the morrow have a distinct refusal.... Attachment to Mr. Nicholls, you are aware, I never entertained, but the poignant pity inspired by his state on Monday evening by the hurried revelation of his sufferings for many months, is something galling and irksome.

This was not a promising beginning of a love affair, for the lady, so she protested, had not the slightest feeling of affection towards her suitor, and her father got blood to the head at the notion of her marrying him. Normally, therefore, one would have thought that, when Mr. Nicholls thereupon resigned his curacy, the affair was finished; as a matter of fact, it had barely begun. Unsoftened by Charlotte's promise that she would not marry Mr. Nicholls, Mr. Brontë wrote him what Charlotte called a 'pitiless despatch.' The poor man was already 'entirely rejecting his meals,' and so Charlotte accompanied the pitiless despatch with a note dissociating herself from these violent expressions, and she exhorted him to maintain his courage and spirits. She had already taken sides against her father (whose violence certainly suggests that there was some truth in the stories about him which Mrs. Gaskell had to suppress), for she wished that Ellen could be at Haworth now 'to see papa in his present mood: you would know something of him.' She was afraid also that 'papa thinks a little too much about his want of money: he says that the match would be a degradation, that I should be throwing myself away, that he expects me, if I marry at all, to do very differently.' Charlotte did not share these worldly views against her marrying Mr. Nicholls, but she had some even more valid ones of her own. 'My own objections,' she writes, 'arise from a sense of incongruity and uncongeniality in feelings, tastes, principles.' Her 'dearest wish' for the immediate future was that 'papa would resume his tranquillity, and Mr. N. his beef and pudding.' The writing of the pitiless despatch, however, seemed to have been a safety-valve to Mr. Brontë's indignation, for Charlotte adds a postscript to this remarkable letter, saying that 'the incipient inflammation in Papa's eye is disappearing.'

Elements of comedy began to enter into this extremely serious situation. Mr. Nicholls, having received Charlotte's letter of exhortation, quitted Haworth, leaving Mr. Brontë to look after the parish alone. A week afterwards he was back again, and wrote to Mr. Brontë withdrawing his resignation, clearly because of the contents of Charlotte's letter. Mr. Brontë allowed him to stop on, but only on condition of his giving a promise in writing that he would never mention the word marriage again either to him or Charlotte. Mr. Nicholls took no notice of that, but remained. Ever since the first frightful disclosure which caused Mr. Brontë a return of his apoplectic symptoms, parson and curate had not spoken to each other at all, nor met even in church, for Mr. Nicholls got somebody to take his duty for him, and Charlotte wrote to Ellen that 'she feels persuaded the termination will be his departure for Australia.' Meantime feeling at Haworth ran high against him. 'Martha,' Charlotte gravely records, 'is bitter against him; John Brown (the sexton) says "he should like to shoot him."' Her own state of mind indeed defies unravelment, and she certainly could not unravel it herself. She assembles public opinion about his presumption in proposing to her, and yet writes to assure him of her sympathy in such terms that he recanted his resignation.

The tenseness of the situation was temporarily relieved by Charlotte's departure on the last visit she ever made to London, in order to see *Villette* through the press. She told her father that he must not write her abusive letters about Mr. Nicholls, and he promised not to. But he could not always cork up his virulence, and so he wrote her one letter as from Flossie, Anne's dog; and Flossie, of course, could say what she liked. This instance of humour at Haworth must be cherished: it was not common in that tense atmosphere. On this visit, which Charlotte spent as usual with Mr. George Smith and his mother and sisters, and which lasted nearly a month, there was no lionising now nor any attempt to make her mix with what she called 'the decorative side of life.' Social gaieties were agony to her: it was no use trying to enjoy them. London, again, on its side, had learned that she was not a satisfactory lioness, and made no effort to induce her to roar. She had promised to let the importunate baronet Sir James Kay-Shuttleworth know when she was in town, but she evaded his hospitalities by not telling him till towards the end of her stay, and thus was not vexed with 'his excited fuss.' She was allowed her own choice in the way of engagements and sight-seeings, and selected 'the real side of life,' visiting two prisons, Newgate and Pentonville, the Bank, the Exchange, the Foundling Hospital, and the lunatic asylum at Bethlehem Hospital. Then there was work to be done on the proof sheets of *Villette*: it must have been odd to correct them in the house of George Smith, for he and his mother confessedly appeared in the book as Dr. John and his mother. They were both perfectly aware of this, and though the presentation of them was wholly appreciative they did not entirely relish it. His comment on Lucy Snowe had been that she was 'an odd fascinating little puss,' and that he was not in love with her.

Charlotte most considerately postponed the appearance of *Villette* till the end of January 1853, in order that it should not clash with the publication of Mrs. Gaskell's *Ruth*. A week before it was issued she wrote to Miss Martineau, her friendship with whom had survived the shock of the latter's atheistical views, asking her for her frank criticism on the forthcoming novel.

I know [she said] that you will give me your thoughts upon my book as frankly as if you spoke to some near relative whose good you preferred to her gratification. I wince under the pain of condemnation like any other weak structure of flesh and blood; but I love, I honour, I kneel to truth. Let her smite me on the one cheek—good! the tears may spring to the eyes; but courage! there is the other side, hit again, right sharply.

No more forcible though rather rhetorical request for candour can be imagined. Charlotte had also previously begged Miss Martineau to tell her if she detected anything coarse in her work, as certain reviewers of *Jane Eyre* had done. It is, then, little wonder that Miss Martineau, thus solemnly adjured, dealt frankly with her friend about *Villette*. She wrote:

As for the other side of the question, which you desire to know, I have but one thing to say, but it is not a small one. I do not like the love, either the kind or the degree of it; and its prevalence in the book, and effect on the action of it, help to explain the passages in the reviews which you consulted me about, and seem to afford some foundation for the criticisms they offered.

The rest of the letter was suppressed by Mrs. Gaskell, but it must have been laudatory, for Charlotte answered that it was fair, right, and worthy of her, but against this passage she violently protested; it struck her dumb. She did not turn the other cheek at all, but the tears sprang to her eyes and an undying resentment to her heart. She replied:

I know what *love* is as I understand it; and if man or woman should be ashamed of feeling such love, then there is nothing right, noble, faithful, truthful, unselfish on this earth, as I comprehend rectitude, nobleness, fidelity, truth and disinterestedness.... To differ from you gives me keen pain.

Then Miss Martineau wrote an anonymous review of *Villette* in the *Daily News*, in which she made public the same sort of criticism as had privately given Charlotte such deep offence, pointing out, as is indeed true, that Lucy Snowe's love for Dr. John is superseded without recorded transition by her love for Paul Emmanuel; she also accused her of attacking Popery with virulence. That was enough, and more than enough. Charlotte ascertained that the review was by her, and instantly determined to have nothing more to do with her.

She has shown with reference to the work [she wrote to Miss Wooler] a spirit so strangely and unexpectedly acrimonious, that I have gathered courage to tell her that the gulf of mutual difference between her and me is so wide and deep, the bridge of union so slight and uncertain that I have come to the conclusion that frequent intercourse would be most perilous and unadvisable and have begged to adjourn *sine die* my long projected visit to her. Of course she is now very angry, and I know her bitterness will not be short-lived—but it cannot be helped.

That was the end: Charlotte never saw Miss Martineau again, nor sent her a notification of her marriage.

The reception of *Villette* in spite of some severe reviews was sufficiently favourable to please the author, and she returned to Haworth to take up again the situation concerning Mr. Nicholls, which had been left suspended in her absence. A great social event was impending, namely, the visit of Dr. Longley, Bishop of Ripon, and subsequently Archbishop of Canterbury, who spent a night at the Parsonage. He was 'a charming little bishop, the most benignant little gentleman that ever put on lawn sleeves,' and all passed off very well except for Mr. Nicholls's conduct. He came to tea and supper, but made no effort to be cheerful, rather he called attention to his dejection, and showed temper in speaking to Mr. Brontë. He dogged Charlotte up the path to the vicarage after evening service, and when Charlotte went upstairs, he cast after her some 'flaysome looks,' which 'filled Martha's soul with horror,' for Martha, standing by the kitchen door, had her eye on him, and reported these sinister glances. He got up a 'pertinacious dispute' with the Inspector of Schools, which revived all Charlotte's unfavourable impressions of him; 'if he was a good man at bottom, it is a sad thing that nature has not given him the faculty to put goodness into a more attractive form.' He grew so gloomy and reserved that the rest of his clerical brethren shunned his company. 'Papa has a perfect antipathy to him, and he, I fear, to papa. Martha' (we are reminded for the third time) 'hates him. I think he might almost be dying and they would not speak a friendly word to or of him.' Charlotte even managed to doubt the genuineness of his love towards her.

He was never agreeable or amiable, [she wrote] and is less so now than ever, and, alas! I do not know him well enough to be sure there is truth and true affection, or only rancour and corroding disappointment at the bottom of the chagrin. In this state of things I must be, and I am, *entirely* passive.

In fact, in this letter to Ellen in the spring of 1853 Charlotte collects, as for a criminal trial, every atom of evidence she could find, including her cook's opinion of him, to demonstrate what a thoroughly undesirable fellow Mr. Nicholls was.

But she was not trying to convince Ellen of that; she was trying to convince herself, and without full success. She began to doubt her own conclusions, and in the very letter in which she set forth this formidable *dossier* against him she completely betrayed herself. 'I may be losing the purest gem, and to me far the most precious life can give—genuine attachment—or I may be escaping the yoke of a morose temper.' So, pending her own decision on the matter, she laid the responsibility on her father. 'In this doubt,' she wrote, 'conscience will not suffer me to take one step in opposition to papa's will, blended as that will is with the most bitter and unreasonable prejudice.' But all the time she knew that papa's will was not a determining factor at all; she would see about papa's will when she had made up her mind about her own, and she was looking out for some convincing opportunity to tear up her *dossier* altogether.

Was ever woman in this humour wooed?

Was ever woman in this humour won?

Her opportunity came. Mr. Nicholls found the situation intolerable; he again resigned his curacy and was to leave Haworth at the end of May. Whit-Sunday came, and next day Charlotte wrote to Ellen an account of what had happened the day before at church:

It seems as if I were to be punished for my doubts about the nature and truth of poor Mr. Nicholls's regard. Having ventured on Whit Sunday to stop to the sacrament, I got a lesson not to be repeated. He struggled, faltered, then lost command over himself, stood before my eyes and in the sight of all the communicants, white, shaking, voiceless. He made a great effort, but could only with difficulty whisper and falter through the service. I suppose he thought this would be the last time, he goes either this week or the next. I heard the women sobbing round, and I could not quite check my own tears. What had happened was reported to Papa either by Joseph Redman or John Brown; it excited only anger, and such expressions as 'unmanly driveller.' Compassion or relenting is no more to be looked for than sap from firewood.

It may be taken that from this moment Charlotte made up her mind to marry him. She had surrendered, and, though his departure was imminent and there were many difficulties in the way yet, she was convinced of the sincerity of his devotion, and knew in her heart that he was her man. There was a school feast at which Mr. Brontë spoke to him 'with constrained civility but still with *civility*.' He did not reply civilly, he cut short further words. Considering that his vicar had not spoken to him for months, this was hardly to be wondered at, and Charlotte was justly afraid that they were both unchristian in their mutual feelings. Then, in spite of Mr. Nicholls's apparently extreme unpopularity in the parish, his flock got up a handsome testimonial for him in the shape of a gold watch. Mr. Brontë, not being very well, absented himself from the presentation.

Mr. Nicholls came to the Parsonage to deliver up deeds and account-books and to say good-bye to his future father-in-law. Charlotte would not see him in her father's presence, and he left the house. But now she had really chosen him as he had chosen her, and she could not let him go like that.

Perceiving that he stayed long before going out at the gate, and remembering his long grief, I took courage and went out trembling and miserable. I found him leaning against the garden door in a paroxysm of anguish, sobbing as women never sob. Of course I went straight to him. Very few words were interchanged, those few barely articulate. But he wanted such hope and encouragement as I could not give him.

He went, and Charlotte instantly perceived that it was not he only, but she personally who was suffering. 'In all this,' she complains to Ellen, 'it is not I who am to be pitied at all, and, of course, nobody pities me. They all think in Haworth that I have disdainfully refused him.' That she had certainly done, assigning any amount of excellent reasons for her decision, and endorsing it with the approval of Martha and John Brown. But now she intended to marry him, and, though she could not at parting give him any promise until her father's objections were overcome, she set to work quietly and secretly, making no mention of what she was doing in her letters at the time, and embarked on an amazing and entrancing intrigue.

She had for secret ally and fellow-conspirator the Rev. Joseph Brett Grant, master of Haworth Grammar School. She had pilloried him in *Shirley* as Mr. Donne, but he had borne her no grudge (rather disconcertingly) for that, and now he proved his active good-will. For in July, only two months after Mr. Nicholls had left Haworth, apparently for good, he was staying *perdu* with this admirable Mr. Grant at the Grammar School, and there were meetings between Charlotte and him. He had not therefore to wait long for the encouragement she had been unable to give him when they parted at the gate of the Parsonage, and instead of being 'entirely passive' she was taking some very romantic measures 'in opposition to papa's will.' This manœuvre, as yet unnoticed by the devout biographer but proved by the indisputable evidence of her own letters, when the course of love ran smooth, is almost too 'wildly dear,' and we figure her, as demure and mouse-like and determined as Jane Eyre herself, stealing from the Parsonage, when Mr. Brontë was safely occupied over his sermon, to keep her assignation with her lover at the house of one of the *Shirley* curates. Did Martha know, we wonder? Did John Brown know? Then she kept in touch with him as well by correspondence; but the correspondence weighed on her mind, and she told her father that she was writing to him. That probably was a well-calculated confession, for the new curate, Mr. de Renzi, Charlotte perceived, did not suit her father nearly as well as Mr. Nicholls had done, and the hint that Mr. Nicholls was not yet entirely severed from Haworth would not be amiss. But Mr. Brontë was told nothing about his clandestine visit to the Grammar School, and his daughter's meetings with him.

While these hidden intrigues were in progress, life at the Parsonage went on with its unswerving monotony. Charlotte paid visits to Ellen and Mrs. Gaskell in the spring, and in company with Mr. and Mrs. Joe Taylor, *née* Amelia Ringrose, and their baby went to Scotland in August; but was in that country for one night only, since the baby had some slight ailment, and the parents felt sure that the air of Scotland did not agree with it. They retraced their steps at once to Ilkley, but Charlotte lost her box, which was labelled to Kirkcudbright, and lack of clothes compelled her to return after three days to Haworth. Literally nothing else happened that summer except what was hidden from all eyes until Mrs. Gaskell came to stay with Charlotte towards the end of September.

In her charmingly written account of her visit she dwells much on minutiæ, describing the exquisite cleanness of the house, the clockwork regularity of the routine, the silence, the undisturbed tranquillity, the appearance of the parlour, the hours for meals, the walks on the moor, the long talks they had over the fire; but this wealth of detail over trivialities rather suggests that no very intimate intercourse in conversation passed between them. But Charlotte must have given her then her version of Branwell's affair with Mrs. Robinson, and she also spoke a good deal of Emily, 'about whom,' says Mrs. Gaskell, 'she is never tired of talking, nor I of listening. Emily must have been a remnant of the Titans....' It is curious, however, to notice that Mrs. Gaskell, speaking elsewhere of Emily, says: 'All that I, a stranger, have been able to learn about her has not tended to give either me or my readers a pleasant impression of her.' These constant talks with Charlotte about Emily must have been in her mind when she wrote that, and it is impossible not to wonder what these communications were which produced the disagreeable impression. Some reflection, maybe, of estrangements and of bitter days, when Emily befriended Branwell and scolded Anne for using him as a model in *The Tenant of Wildfell Hall*: or the rather horrible story of Emily thrashing her dog? It is impossible to tell, but it was thus that Charlotte's talk of Emily struck the mild, kindly woman who listened to it.

Of Mr. Brontë himself, Mrs. Gaskell shows high appreciation. 'He was a most courteous host, and when he was with us—at breakfast in his study, or at tea in Charlotte's parlour,—he had a sort of grand and stately way of describing past times, which tallied well with his striking appearance.' This favourable impression did not last, for when she saw him again in 1860, she wrote of him to Mr. Williams: 'He still talks in his pompous way, and mingles moral remarks and somewhat stale sentiment with his conversation on ordinary subjects.' But it must be remembered that she had in the interval brought out her *Life* of Charlotte, and his indignation at what she had said about him had put another complexion on his admirable stateliness. Mrs. Gaskell, finally, knew that Mr. Brontë was violently opposed to the idea of Charlotte's marriage with Mr. Nicholls, and 'deeply admired the patient docility which she displayed in her conduct towards her father.' But the docility was not quite so patient as she imagined, for Charlotte was in correspondence with her lover, and Mr. Nicholls was in Haworth, for the second time since his departure, staying secretly once more with Mr. Grant. Charlotte did not see so much of him as she had done in July, for she had her duties to perform to her guest. But the household in the Parsonage went early to bed, and Mrs. Gaskell records how she always heard Charlotte come downstairs again when she was in her room. Is it too much to hope that Mr. Nicholls was waiting in the churchyard?

Throughout the autumn and winter Charlotte's correspondence with the friends to whom for years she had written so regularly and voluminously practically ceased. Five letters in four months was the meagre sum of them. The correspondence with Mr. Nicholls may have occupied her, but of the volume of it or of its contents we have no idea, for after her death he seems to have destroyed every letter she had ever written to him. Then in January 1854 she judged that the time was ripe for another move. She arranged for him to come to Haworth once more and stay with Mr. and Mrs. Grant, and now she told her father that he was here, and 'stipulated with papa for opportunity to become better acquainted. I had it and all I learned inclined me to esteem and affection.' This reads strangely, for Mr. Nicholls had been her father's curate for over eight years, and one would have thought there must have been ample opportunity for forming an acquaintance with him. Though Mr. Brontë was still 'very hostile, and bitterly unjust,' he was evidently getting used to the idea; he consented to Charlotte's seeing her lover, and she saw much of him during this ten days' stay. Off he went again without meeting his late vicar, to resume his duty at Kirk Smeaton, where he had taken a curacy, and again the process of detrition of Mr. Brontë's hostility went quietly on throughout the spring, and the plans of those who were now lovers were complete before Mr. Nicholls paid his next visit to the Grants at Easter. As Easter approached, Charlotte got into a slight flutter about it, for she expected that her engagement would then be formally settled, and she first wrote to Ellen asking her to come to Haworth because Mr. Nicholls would be there ('perhaps too he might take a walk with us occasionally'), and then revoked her invitation for exactly the same reason, namely, that he *was* going to be there.

He came, they were engaged, and their plans, which did equal credit to their heads and their hearts, were disclosed in schedule to Mr. Brontë. The curate, Mr. de Renzi, who had always been unsatisfactory, would be dismissed, and Mr. Nicholls would resume his duties at Haworth. Charlotte would not leave her father, but Mr. Nicholls, when the marriage took place in the summer, would come to live at the Parsonage. Mr. Brontë's 'seclusion and convenience' would be left uninvaded, and Mr. Nicholls would subscribe to household expenses in so liberal a manner that 'in a pecuniary sense the marriage would bring Mr. Brontë gain instead of loss.' These plans for his comfort caused him to give his consent, 'and papa began really to take a pleasure in the prospect.'

Considering that little more than a year ago he had nearly had an apoplectic fit at the presumption of the now accepted suitor, Charlotte's management of the affair, and her quiet vanquishing of difficulties that seemed insurmountable, must have been a work of consummate strategy. She gave credit to Mr. Nicholls for his perseverance, but granted that he wanted to marry her, all he had to do was to carry out her orders: she was alone at Haworth with a singularly obstinate father, and success in bringing him round was entirely due to her. Ambition for her, paternal pride, 'ever a restless feeling,' as she wrote to Ellen, she considered had been at the bottom of his opposition, and 'now that this unquiet spirit is exorcised, justice, which was once quite forgotten, is once more listened to, and affection, I hope, resumes some power.'

Then having herself worked for and triumphantly carried her scheme to a successful issue, she attributed it all to Providence. 'Providence,' she wrote, 'offers me this destiny. Doubtless then it is the best for me.' But, without questioning the supremacy of the Divine decrees, we must observe that Providence had offered her that destiny a year and a half ago, and she had rejected it because she had no affection for her lover. Afterwards, coming round to the belief that it was best for her, and that she really wanted it, she had by the exercise of tact, intrigue, and will power secured it. Providence, in fact, would not have had much chance without her firm co-operation.

She was certainly happy in the prospect of her marriage, but there was no sort of ecstasy; she wrote that her happiness was 'of the soberest order,' and she could analyse it exactly. She trusted that she would love her husband, and she was grateful for his love. She believed him, without glamour, to be an 'affectionate, a conscientious and high-principled man,' and 'if with all this I should yield to regret, that fine talents, congenial tastes and thoughts are not added, I should be most presumptuous and thankless.' She was aware that this destiny which, she repeats, Providence has offered her 'will not be generally regarded as brilliant, but I trust I see in it some germs of happiness.' There was nothing resembling any personal sense or anticipation of the great thing that at last was coming to her: she hoped that 'this arrangement will turn out more truly to papa's satisfaction than any other it was in my power to achieve.' She looked into the future tranquilly and serenely, but never for a moment did she foresee that her marriage would bring her such happiness and forgetfulness of self as she had missed all her life. One thing alone troubled her at all, and that was Mr. Nicholls's rheumatism, and over this she grew very solemn. It had been, she told Ellen, 'one of the strong arguments against her marriage,' and there was fear that it was chronic, but Charlotte 'resolved to stand by him now whether in weal or woe.... And yet the ultimate possibilities of such a case are appalling. You remember your aunt?' But Mr. Nicholls had to do his part, too, in averting such a fate, and his neglect of it brought on him a good wigging. He had evidently had a strict dietetic supervision on the last of his visits to Haworth, and had got much better, but on his return there he was worse, and Charlotte was frightened till she found out that he had been careless about himself at Kirk Smeaton, and his aches were entirely his own fault; so what he needed was not sympathy but a sound rating. The nature of it may be gathered from the remarks she made to Ellen on the subject:

Man is indeed an amazing piece of mechanism when you see, so to speak, the full weakness of what he calls his strength. There is not a female child above the age of eight but might rebuke him for spoilt petulance of his wilful nonsense. I bought a border for the table-cloth and have put it on....

Mr. Nicholls, we feel, would think twice before he was careless about his rheumatism again. She took him in hand, too, in other ways. Ellen had asked him to go to Brookroyd, but Charlotte did not give him the message—'for it would be like tempting him to forget duty.'

There was sewing to be done, there was a modest *trousseau* to be bought of such new garments for the wedding-day as would come into use afterwards. The storeroom by the kitchen in the Parsonage had to be converted into a study for her husband; paper and curtains of green and white matched each other well. Then there were the arrangements to be made about the wedding itself. About that the utmost secrecy was observed: only Ellen and Miss Wooler were to be bidden to it, and though the parishioners at Haworth knew now that the marriage was to take place, Mr. Nicholls, at Charlotte's wish, so managed it that not a soul in the place should know the date except the officiating clergyman, and as a further precaution the service was fixed for eight o'clock in the morning, when there would be but few people about. To other friends of the bride and bridegroom there would be sent out, when the ceremony was over, a printed card making the announcement; Charlotte wished the envelope to be plain with a silver initial on it. More of these had to be ordered, 'for there was no end to Mr. Nicholls's string of parson friends,' and he thought sixty would be required. Charlotte's own list was much less numerous than his and consisted of only eighteen names. The hermit-like seclusion in which she must have lived all her life is witnessed to by the fact that only five of these were inhabitants of Haworth and its neighbourhood. Among the rest were Mrs. Gaskell, George Smith, his mother and his sisters, Mr. Williams and Mr. Monckton Milnes. Neither Thackeray, Lewes, nor Sir James Kay-Shuttleworth received the notification, nor, we regret to say, Miss Martineau.

Mr. Nicholls had wanted to be married in July, and though Charlotte, in the early days of her engagement, thought that this was too soon, and that some date of the later summer was time enough, it took place on June 29. The officiating clergyman, the Rev. Sutcliffe Sowden, and the bridegroom arrived the evening before, and stayed with Mr. Grant, whose house had been so hospitable to the intrigue, and Ellen Nussey, the solitary bridesmaid, and Miss Wooler were guests at the Parsonage: Mr. Brontë was to give Charlotte away. As the party at the Parsonage was going to bed that night, this disconcerting parent suddenly announced that he would take no part in the ceremony, and indeed not attend it at all. What his reason was is quite unknown; but it seems likely that this inconvenient gesture was intended to be a final protest against the marriage, of which really he now entirely approved. The form for the Solemnization of Matrimony in the Prayer Book was hurriedly examined, and the happy discovery was made that Miss Wooler, as a friend of the bride, might legitimately take his place. So Mr. Brontë stayed in bed.

CHAPTER XIX

The wedding tour was made in Ireland: they did not visit the ancestral home of the Bruntys in County Down, but after a tour to Killarney went to Banagher, where relations of the bridegroom lived. They told Charlotte that she was a very fortunate person in having got so good a husband, and already she agreed with them. Indeed she had got more than they knew, for now she had what her nature had long subconsciously longed for as the medicament for her bitterness and her morbidity, and it was a perfectly new kind of woman who came back to Haworth with her husband in August. Henceforth, instead of her letters being full of sharp criticism of others they abound in praises of Arthur: instead of being so often concerned with the symptoms of her own ill-health, she is jubilant about the improvement in his, for he had gone up twelve pounds in weight in the month succeeding their marriage, and the sinister anticipations of what might have been the issue of marrying a man with rheumatic tendencies (remember your aunt) were thrust into limbo. Years ago she had told Ellen, with the pontifical certainty of the spinster, that after marriage a woman might allow herself prudently and cautiously to fall in love with her husband, but now she did not stay to consider the wisdom of such slow going. Like an echo from her own distant voice, she could repeat that her marriage would secure papa comfort and aid in his old age, but the newer voice was stronger.

She fell in love with her husband recklessly, as a good Victorian wife should: his judgment was infallible, and she submitted everything to it. When she asked Ellen to come and stay at Haworth it was no longer her invitation but his: Arthur would be pleased to see her, and 'one friendly word from him means as much as twenty from most people.' If she wanted to pay a visit to a house where there had been a case of fever, though she had no fear of infection on her own account, 'there are cases where wives have to put their own judgments on the shelf, and do as they are bid.' They entertained to tea and supper the Sunday and day-school pupils and teachers, the choir and the bell-ringers, and Charlotte, who in her maiden days would have been altogether unable to face such a function, was thrilled with pride and with love, for Arthur's health was proposed, and when the speaker alluded to him as a 'consistent Christian and a kind gentleman' Charlotte, deeply touched, 'thought that to merit and win such a character was better than to earn either wealth or fame or power. I am disposed to echo that high and simple eulogium.'

The whole colour and temper of her life was changed. It is with glee that she warns Ellen that 'a married woman can call but a very small portion of her time her own'; the large stock of it which she was wont to have on hand had been grabbed by her husband, but she grudged him not a minute of it. She had regretted before her marriage that there were no congenial tastes or thoughts common to him and herself, but now she thinks it 'not bad for her that he should be so little inclined to the literary and the contemplative.' She marvels how some wives grow selfish: matrimony, in her experience, 'tends to draw you out of and away from yourself.' Even in her most private and personal affairs she now defers to the wishes of her 'dear boy,' who 'grows daily dearer,' and she transmits a message to Ellen from him that he wished her to burn all the letters that Charlotte now writes her. Ellen declined to promise any such thing, and again Charlotte pressed the point.

Arthur complains you do not promise to burn my letters as you receive them. He says you must give him a plain pledge to that effect, or he will read every line I write and elect himself censor of our correspondence.... Write him out the promise on a separate slip of paper in a legible hand, and send it in your next.

Whether Ellen gave this promise on the repetition of Arthur's wish we do not know; if she did, she certainly broke it, for she continued to preserve Charlotte's letters to her exactly as before, and he had to content himself with reading them before they were sent.

A spirit of fun, of lightness, enters into them now, which had been absent from them since the days when Celia Amelia had sent valentines and passionate verse to all the young ladies of Haworth. Charlotte describes, for instance, how that flighty Amelia Taylor, who had made such a goose of herself over her baby when she went with them to Scotland, paid them a visit. Amelia was a simpleton: no doubt she was right not to be jealous about her husband's 'former flames,' but why cultivate their society in that unnatural way? Arthur read that letter before it was posted and was quite serious about it: he thought his wife had 'written too freely about Amelia,' and Charlotte couldn't help laughing at him. Such a precaution as burning these letters seemed to her truly ridiculous, but Ellen must promise; otherwise she would receive just such letters as he wrote to his clerical brethren, unspiced by affection or critical comments on friends. Certainly if joy had never come to the grim Parsonage since it was built, as one of Mrs. Gaskell's friends felt, it had come now at long last.

But the days were full and Charlotte had little time for correspondence, and though she wrote with regularity to Ellen, she addressed few letters to anyone else, and her once voluminous correspondence with Mr. Williams ceased altogether. Nor did she want visitors: Ellen came to Haworth once, and once the steadfast Sir James Kay-Shuttleworth and a friend for the Sunday. For this visit there was a particular and kindly reason: he wanted to see Mr. Nicholls, and, liking him, he offered him the living of Padiham, near his place at Gawthorpe. No thought of that could be entertained, for he and Charlotte were both bound to remain at Haworth while Mr. Brontë lived, and though the offer was again pressed when they went to stay for a few days at Gawthorpe in the winter, it was again declined, evidently without any sort of regret that they were not free to take it, for the contract to look after Mr. Brontë was thankfully, not grudgingly, performed.

May God preserve him to us yet for some years [she wrote to Ellen]. The wish for his continued life, together with a certain solicitude for his happiness and health seems, I scarcely know why, even stronger in me now than it was before I was married. Papa has taken no duty since we returned, and each time I see Mr. Nicholls put on gown or surplice I feel comforted to think that this marriage has secured papa good aid in his old age.

But though, whenever her husband was at leisure, Charlotte 'must have occupations in which he can share,' he had practically the whole of the work of the parish on his hands, for Mr. Brontë took little or no duty, and while Mr. Nicholls was busy she took up her writing again. Just as she had done before getting embarked on *Shirley*, she made several beginnings of a new novel; one of these got as far as its fiftieth page. This renewed industry disposes of the supposition that her husband discouraged her literary work, and he himself emphatically denied that he had ever done so. She only wrote when the mood was on her, and in the year and a half that had elapsed between the publication of *Villette* and her marriage she had only written a fragment of eighteen pages called *Willie Ellin*. It was not till after she was married that, as a matter of fact, she set to work again.

The autumn passed into winter. Snow had fallen early, then melted again, and one morning she and her husband walked out a distance of over three miles to see the waterfall on the moor. Rain came on, and she returned drenched, and never quite recovered the excellent health that she had enjoyed ever since her marriage. She was well enough to go to Gawthorpe for a day or two, early in January, and she had planned a visit to Ellen for the end of the month. But before that could be paid, she became really unwell and took to her bed.

She knew now that she was with child, and the doctor was reassuring: these fits of sickness were normal symptoms. But she grew worse and weaker, prostrated with the continued sickness and fever, though there was as yet no acuteness of anxiety. From bed, in pencil, she wrote just three more notes, and in them all, clear and unwavering, shone the lamp of love which had illuminated these last months for her, with a light serene and tranquil, such as she had never known before. To one friend of the far-off Brussels days she wrote: 'No kinder, better husband than mine, it seems to me, there can be in the world. I do not want now for kind companionship in health and the tenderest nursing in sickness.' And then to Ellen: 'I want to give you an assurance that will comfort you—and that is that I find in my husband the tenderest nurse, the kindest support—the best earthly comfort that ever woman had.'

Then came the third and last note: 'I cannot talk—even to my dear, patient, constant Arthur I can say but few words at once.'

Then there seemed to be an improvement, and it was not till within a few days of her death that her recovery was despaired of. She was conscious till the end, speaking but seldom, and at the very last she turned her dimmed eyes to her 'dear boy,' clinging to the life which his love had made sweet for her. She whispered: 'Oh, I am not going to die, am I? He will not separate us—we have been so happy.'

She died in the night of March 30, 1855.